Equity and Excellence
in Higher Education

American University Studies

Series XIV
Education
Vol. 35

PETER LANG
New York • Washington, D.C./Baltimore • San Francisco
Bern • Frankfurt am Main • Berlin • Vienna • Paris

Alan R. Sadovnik

Equity and Excellence in Higher Education

The Decline of a Liberal Educational Reform

PETER LANG
New York • Washington, D.C./Baltimore • San Francisco
Bern • Frankfurt am Main • Berlin • Vienna • Paris

Library of Congress Cataloging-in-Publication Data

Sadovnik, Alan R.
   Equity and excellence in higher education: the decline of a liberal
educational reform / Alan R. Sadovnik.
      p.   cm. — (American university studies. Series XIV, Education;
vol. 35)
   Includes bibliographical references.
   1. Education, Higher—United States. 2. Compensatory education—
United States. 3. Educational equalization—United States. 4. Educational
change—United States. I. Title. II. Series.
LA227.4.S23   1994   92-25798
 ISBN 0-8204-1593-6   CIP
 ISSN 0740-4565

Die Deutsche Bibliothek-CIP-Einheitsaufnahme

Sadovnik, Alan R.:
Equity and excellence in higher education: the decline of a liberal educational
reform / Alan R. Sadovnik. - New York; Bern; Frankfurt/M.; Paris; Wien:
Lang, 1994
   (American university studies: Ser. 14, Education; Vol. 35)
   ISBN 0-8204-1593-6
NE: American university studies / 14

Cover design by George Lallas.
Front cover and author photograph by Douglass Ridgeway.

∞

© Peter Lang Publishing, Inc., New York 1994

To my parents, Ruth and Morris Sadovnik

whose lives and struggles
have been an inspiration

ACKNOWLEDGMENTS

This book would not have been completed without the help of a number of caring colleagues and friends. It began over a decade ago as my doctoral dissertation at New York University. My dissertation committee in the Sociology Department at New York University, Caroline Hodges Persell, Floyd Hammack, and Edward Lehman provided important intellectual guidance. Little did I imagine that when, during my dissertation defense, Ed Lehman commented that his comments were for the book, not the dissertation, would it be over ten years to its publication. The reasons for this are discussed in the Preface.

At State College (a pseudonym), a number of faculty and administrators were extremely helpful. These include Naomi Block, Mary Edwards, Ina Schlesinger, Renneth Sorhando, and Major Thomas.

A number of colleagues read all or parts of the manuscript in its various forms. These include Peter Agree, Peter W. Cookson, Jr., Juan Corradi, Kevin Dougherty, Barbara Falsey, Claudia Grinberg, Edward Lehman, David Levinson, Caroline Hodges Persell, Susan F. Semel, and Patricia Sexton. Claudia Grinberg and Susan F. Semel both copyedited the manuscript at different stages and made valuable editorial and substantive suggestions. Heidi Burns, my editor at Peter Lang, copyedited the final draft and provided support from acquisitions through final production. Additionally, Kathy Iwasaki, Christine Marra, and Michael Flamini at Peter Lang all provided assistance during final production.

This book would not have been completed without the help of a number of people at Adelphi University. My secretary, Janet Murphy, typed the original manuscript into the computer. My graduate assistants over the past two years, Claudia Grinberg and Theresa Bellisio, provided outstanding editing, research, and computer support. Danielle Daum and Brian Helman of the Adelphi Computer Center provided essential computer advice. Additionally, my colleagues and friends in the School of Education at Adelphi University, Peter W. Cookson, Jr., Susan F. Semel, Dale Snauwaert, and Pierre Woog have made Adelphi an intellectually stimulating and caring place to spend one's academic life.

Dr. Arthur Weider has been a constant source of support and assistance from the dissertation through the completion of this book and I thank him.

Students in the EOD program struggled to make up for their past educational weaknesses within an often difficult educational setting. As this book chronicles, many of them graduated from State College; more of them did not. I thank all of them for their contributions to this book and for their impact on my own intellectual and educational development.

This book would not have been possible without the love and support of my family: my parents, Ruth and Morris Sadovnik, my aunt and uncle, Jeannette and Gabriel Herczeg, and my cousins, Emily and Leonard Herczeg. I have dedicated this book to my parents who came to the United States from Europe. My father from Poland, in 1937, two years before the Nazi invasion and the beginning of the horrors of the Warsaw ghetto. My mother left Germany in 1939, at the age of 12, as part of the Kinder Transport of Jewish children to England. She lived in Hull, in Yorkshire, with a foster family until 1945. She was reunited with her parents and sister, who left Nazi Germany for the United States on one of the last trains permitted to leave in 1941. Others from my parents' families were not so lucky and died, either in the Warsaw ghetto or in concentration camp. I grew up understanding the worst of what human beings are capable, but also with an understanding of how individuals can and must make a difference in creating a more just world. My parents, grandparents (my mother's parents), and aunt and uncle taught me by example and by pushing me, of the value of learning and education. It was clear to me early in my adolescence that I would follow in my grandfather's footsteps and receive a Ph.D., as he had. My parents' lives, both in Europe and the United States, make my life seem easy and privileged, by comparison. From my parents, I have learned to persevere and to do good works. This book is dedicated to their lives and accomplishments; without them, my own accomplishments would not have been possible.

TABLE OF CONTENTS

PREFACE

This book began as my doctoral dissertation, which was completed at New York University in 1983. It has taken over ten years for it to be published, in different form, as a book. There are a number of reasons for this. First, the dissertation was much too long to publish as a book. Second, in 1983, case studies were not being published in great numbers and prospective editors kept asking if the study was generalizeable. By 1990, however, methodological orthodoxy in educational and social science research had changed sufficiently to the point that case studies were not only acceptable, but in demand. At that point, given my continued desire to publish the study, I began the task of researching, updating, editing, and rewriting the text.

This study is based on participant observation, interviews, and archival research. My participant observation was observation as a participant, as I taught in the Educational Opportunity Division at State College (a pseudonym), from 1978–1983. Thus, I was a participant during the key years that this study covers. Douglas (1972) and Semel (1992) discuss the problems associated with participant observation as a participant and both conclude that, although difficult, it is an acceptable form of historical and sociological investigation.

Although I was not nearly as involved in the history of the EOD as Semel was in the history of the Dalton School, her discussion of distancing and objectivity in her study of that school, are applicable to this study. I had to treat my own subjective experiences as one piece of evidence and had to be careful to weigh my own subjective perceptions in light of the other historical and sociological data. Since I was one of the junior faculty members to lose his job indirectly through the elimination of the EOD, I had to carefully analyze my own feelings about the events. In some respect, putting this project away for seven years until 1990, gave me the time and distance to reexamine the events that resulted in the demise of the EOD. Additionally, by 1990 I had served as an Assistant Dean, and was a Department Chair and tenured faculty member. My experiences as a faculty member and administrator have given me important insights into the complexities of higher education and have made me skeptical of simplistic, one dimensional analyses of educational change. The completion of this book, in some respects, has been a psychoanalytic journey. Looking back in 1994, the events that I was so much a part of, now seem distant. At times, as I read the book, it is as if I was never there. At other times, I have vivid memories of the events. I am convinced, however, that I have provided a sound historical and sociological analysis of the history of the EOD.

In revising and rewriting the dissertation into this book I had a number of editorial decisions to make. The dissertation was too long (653 pages) and included historical, sociological, and empirical sections. The second part of the dissertation included a detailed empirical analysis of the academic achievement and attainment of EOD students. Given problems with available data and the uniqueness of both State College and its EOD, it was impossible to generalize to other campuses or opportunity programs. Therefore, I decided that the history of the EOD provided an important case study in the study of higher education reform. This book, then, is a historical and sociological case study. It does not include any detailed empirical analysis of student achievement and attainment. Readers interested in these analyses should consult my dissertation, available through Dissertations Abstracts International.

In 1992 and 1993, I returned to State College to interview the Director of its EOP program (the same individual who was the Director of EOD in 1983) and selected faculty who were still at the college. Based upon these interviews, as well as data from the New York State Office of Special Programs (for EOP students at State College for the 1982–1987 Admissions classes), I decided that little would be accomplished from an in-depth history of the years following the elimination of the EOD. This study examines the rise and fall of an educational opportunity program and therefore the story ends in 1983. The concluding chapter, however, relies on data for the 1982–1987 Admissions classes, as well as interviews with the director and faculty, to reach some general conclusions about the decision to eliminate the EOD.

After I left State College, I went to Adelphi University. During my years at Adelphi, I have continuously had to come to grips with the problems of underprepared students. First, as an Assistant Dean I was one of the founders of Adelphi's General Studies Program, a program for underprepared college students. Although different in the racial composition of its student population, I tried to apply the difficult pedagogical lessons of the EOD, especially with regard to negative labeling and stigmatization. I also was determined to develop a program that helped underprepared students succeed without lowering academic standards. I spent two years building the General Studies Program, before I returned to being a faculty member in the School of Education. Today, the General Studies Program is very successful, with approximately 40% of its students graduating from Adelphi (a high graduation rate for a compensatory higher education program). Hopefully, the lessons learned from the EOD have paid off. Second, as a faculty member helping to prepare teachers, the question of underpreparation and the lowering of standards continues to be a difficult one. Some of our students come to us underprepared and desparately wish to be teachers. To pass them along if they do not make up for their past deficiencies only helps to reproduce the cycle of underpreparation, as teachers without the necessary skills and knowledge may contribute to the creation of future underprepared students. When these students are black and Latino, as they sometimes are, the pressure to pass them along, given the need for black and Latino role models as teachers, is sometimes increased. I have learned from years of experience that passing students along is both patronizing and often an insidious form of racism. We need to provide the resources needed to ensure that underprepared students succeed by making up for past weaknesses. If we cannot provide the necessary services, colleges and universities should not admit these students to only set them up for failure.

Under continuing economic constraints, colleges and universities often need to admit underprepared students, but often cannot afford the services needed to educate them properly. This causes considerable difficulty for faculty and administrators who have to live with the contradictions. Although I do not pretend to have simple solutions for complex problems, I hope this book sheds some light on the complexities of teaching underprepared students and how the politics of higher education may often negatively affect them.

1

INTRODUCTION

Compensatory higher education programs developed as part of the liberal educational reforms of the 1960s and 1970s. Their goal was to provide equal educational opportunity for "educationally and economically" disadvantaged students who previously would not have had the opportunity to attend college. Their mission, therefore, was to compensate for unequal precollege education through remediation, providing a foundation for the successful completion of a college education.

This study is concerned with the organizational and educational processes within educational programs that define their attempts to solve educational and social problems. In order to analyze these issues, the study examines the evolution and demise of an educational opportunity program on a state college campus, in the suburbs of a large northeastern city. The program, initiated as an off-campus opportunity center in 1969, moved to the main campus in 1978, and as a separate academic division provided a two-year curriculum for educationally and economically disadvantaged students (almost 90% minority) deemed inadmissable by the college's regular admissions procedures. In 1983, it was eliminated as a separate academic division, but maintained as a tutorial and counseling program. The Educational Opportunity Division (EOD) at State College was an example of a special placement compensatory program, with students taking a majority of their coursework for the first two years within the program, before being mainstreamed for the junior and senior years. The division offered both remedial and regular college courses in mathematics, English, the social sciences, natural sciences, and humanities and was a unique program in its integration of both skills and content in all courses.[1] Unlike most compensatory programs where students take only remedial courses in the program, the EOD provided a separate and complete curriculum for its educational opportunity students.

In the Spring 1983, the State College administration, after years of college debates over the merits of the separate placement of the disadvantaged college student, announced the elimination of the EOD as a separate division and the integration of its students and faculty into the college mainstream. From 1983, State College has had the traditional integrative educational opportunity program offering only remedial courses, tutoring, and counseling services, with educational opportunity students integrated into all other regular college level discipline courses.

The mission of the educational opportunity division (EOD) was to provide a quality liberal arts education to its students in order to provide the academic and intellectual foundation for the successful completion of the college degree. Emphasis was placed on rigorous and demanding course-work based on the belief that compensatory programs need not dilute the quality of higher education. This point was eloquently revealed in the division's accreditation report:

> The philosophy of the educational Opportunity Division rests on the idea that a society is diminished if its members are not encouraged to realize their full potential. The natural corollary of that idea is the contention that a democratic society suffers if even a few of its intellectually capable members are denied processes for reasons of poor academic preparation or economic disadvantage or both. The philosophy of the division rests on the principle that its population can compensate for past academic inadequacies if sufficient effort is rendered on its part and in its behalf. The liberal education is an essential emancipating experi-ence.... Integral to the faculty's and staff's position on industry and access is their conviction that without quality a liberal education is one in name only.[2]

The formal organization of this program was substantially different from that of other compensatory models. Traditional compensatory programs provided remedial and developmental courses to underprepared students throughout the campus, while providing counseling, tutorial and student support services for designated educational opportunity students. These students, while taking basic reading, writing and mathematics (skills courses) within the programs, registered for regular discipline courses (sociology, biology, literature, etc.). The important characteristic of these programs was that educational opportunity students were integrated into the regular college community through attendance in regular course offerings, with the compensatory program providing support services to enhance academic achievement. Examples of these programs today are the SEEK program at CUNY and the EOP programs at most public and private colleges and universities throughout New York State.

The educational opportunity program under examination was unique in the state system as the only separate compensatory division with its own faculty in both skills and discipline areas. The purpose of the organizational framework, according to its advocates, was to avoid placing underprepared students in regular courses before they have had the opportunity to develop the requisite skills for success. Moreover, based on the belief that regular college discipline courses can combine content and skills development, the division offered its own content courses, for college credit, in addition to its remedial and developmental offerings.[3] During its years on the main State College campus (1978-1983), although the division gradually loosened its separate walls and allowed its students to cross register into mainstream courses, for the most part, educational opportunity students took a majority of their first 56 credits within the EOD.

The unique organizational framework coincided with the educational mission of academic success for minority college students. Hoping to avoid the revolving door attrition rates of many compensatory programs (McMannus Report, 1979) the division stressed the concern for quality education and academic achievement. Hoping to eliminate the possibility that lowering admissions criteria necessitated the lowering of academic standards, the division attempted to deliver a rigorous educational program that compensated for past shortcomings while ensuring competent academic preparation by the junior year.

Although the analysis of this separate organizational structure is central to the study, the division's relationship with other sectors of the college community was another factor affecting its evolution. The divisional student population recruited from the public high schools of the college's metropolitan area was 95% black and Latino, from lower socioeconomic backgrounds. The regularly admitted population of the rest of the College was about 90% white and middle class. The presence of a separate division of minority students (composing almost the entire minority population on the campus) officially designated as "disadvantaged" on a campus of white middle class students posed some interesting and perplexing sociological problems concerning its effect on the academic performance of minority students. The sociological research on ability grouping, tracking and school integration (Hurn, 1993:Chapter 6; Sadovnik, Cookson, Jr. and Semel, 1994:Chapter 9) is a central aspect of the literature on the effect of precollege educational processes on the ability of minority children. However little is known about similar organizational and interactive processes at the postsecondary level. The existence of "separate but equal" programs for the express purpose of ensuring academic equality provides a valuable opportunity to gain insight into the social and educational effects[4] of this organizational framework on minority group achievement. Furthermore, this institutional arrangement allows for the analysis of the latent functions of a homogenous educational organization, such as tracking and labeling. As Rist (1977) pointed out, the consequences of educational processes such as labeling are directly related to the educational outcomes of minority students. Accordingly, the organizational structure of the Division of Educational Opportunity combined with the institutional label placed upon its members presents a valuable opportunity to analyze the effects of these interactive phenomena.

Finally, the organization and mission of the overall college is important in understanding the processes that affected the educational opportunity division and its students. State College, a branch of a large northeastern state university system, was founded in 1969 and originated with a number of educational innovations including a pass-no credit grading system (the college adopted a letter grading system in 1981), junior field examinations, and a senior thesis requirement. In many respects its curriculum resembled graduate study at the undergraduate level and the faculty stressed an elite conception of higher education where a commitment to the training of "junior academics" was a primary goal.

The relationship between a division of educational opportunity consisting of underprepared minority students and the other divisions of a college committed to elite goals provides an opportunity to analyze the tensions between the goals of educational quality and equality. This study concentrates on the various tensions relating to academic quality and standards. In addition, the processes of interorganizational interactions comprise a central concern of this book.

The Analysis of the Educational Opportunity Division

During the past two decades, compensatory higher education programs have been subjected to critical examination. First, conservatives have argued that the goals of equality of opportunity have been superseded by the attention to equality of outcomes resulting in the decline of academic standards and the threat to meritocracy (Heller, 1973; Marshak, 1981, 1982; Mayer, 1973; Wagner, 1976). From a very different perspective, radical critics suggested that these programs, despite their often good intentions, perpetuate the systems of educational inequality initiated at the primary and secondary schools through tracking systems at the college level (Gorelick, 1978; Karabel, 1972a, 1972b; Trimberger, 1973). On the other hand, a comprehensive evaluation of the CUNY Open Admissions experiment (Lavin, Alba, and Silberstein, 1981), although finding evidence to support the perpetuation of educational inequality, also pointed to the opening of opportunities for various ethnic and minority groups.

Previous discussions and evaluations of liberal educational reform at the postsecondary level have provided little understanding of the organizational and educational processes within compensatory programs. Relying on theoretical or ideological perspectives or basing their analyses solely on the use of educational achievement and attainment data compiled from individual programs, very little has been revealed about the process by which the colleges attempted to educate an academically underprepared population. The analysis of compensatory higher education must include a discussion of the formal and informal processes that affect the academic performance, and educational careers of minority and working class students before a comprehensive assessment of their educational and social value can be made. Moreover, the various intraprogram and intercollege conflicts over the aims, methods, and outcomes of these programs, often alluded to, but rarely documented in the literature, need to be explored.

Using a multidimensional approach to the study of educational inequality that stresses the relationship between the societal, institutional, interactional, and intrapsychic levels (Persell, 1977:1-33), this study examines the history of one compensatory higher education program in order to illuminate the ways in which colleges attempted to ameliorate the problems of educational underpreparation and inequality. Through a historical and ethnographic analysis of the emergence, development, and subsequent decline of the program the possible role of liberal educational reform as a solution to the problems of social and educational inequality is examined.

This study focuses on a series of specific questions:

1. In terms of educational and organizational processes: What are the factors related to the emergence, development and decline of the Educational Opportunity Division? This study attempts to understand the rise and eventual demise of the EOD as a separate division of the college and focuses on the organizational, educational, political, and economic factors that are associated with the historical events. Additionally, it frames the division's development within the larger context of social, political, and educational reform.

2. The analysis of the separate placement model of the EOD. A focus of this study concerns the relationship between organizational structures and educational processes and outcomes. As the EOD's separate model placed a large percentage of the college's minority population in a separate division, and by virtue of this placement publicly labeled them as underprepared, this study focuses on the questions of labeling and stigmatization. Although this book does

not provide an empirical evaluation of the efficacy of separate versus regular placement of the underprepared college student, the debates concerning divisional separation, its effects on students, and student reactions to this separation are discussed.

In order to understand these issues, this analysis relies on Persell's (1977:1–33) discussion of the levels of sociological analysis. By concentrating on the relationship between societal, institutional, interactional and intrapsychic factors the complexities of educational organization and processes are discerned. Using this approach the study explores a number of interrelated themes:

At the societal-institutional levels: the research briefly examines the systemic relationships between institutions of postsecondary education and the economic, social, political, and cultural forces that shape them.

At the institutional-interactional levels: the research examines the formal and informal processes of the educational opportunity division and the intraorganizational (within the EOD) and the interorganizational (between the EOD and other segments of the campus community) interactions and conflicts that defined the history of the EOD.

At the institutional-interactional-intrapsychic levels: the research examines the effects of these processes and relationships on students and faculty. Specifically, the study explores the interactions between EOD students and regular admissions students, between EOD and non-EOD faculty and the debates concerning the separate divisional structure.

Working from these general themes, the following specific questions are explored (some of these are explicitly discussed, others are implicitly included in the discussions):

In terms of *organizational structure and processes*:

1. What factors explain the elimination of the EOD as a separate division of the college?

2. What was the relationship between the educational opportunity program and the external political and educational forces? How was the division's program shaped by the educational requirements of the state and federal government regarding higher educational opportunity programs?

3. What was the mission of the educational opportunity program and how and by whom was it defined?

4.   What was the educational philosophy of the division, and how did it relate to its educational structure and processes? For example, how did the divisional curriculum and its teaching methodologies reflect the goals of the program? What specific programs and policies were instituted to maximize student performance? What factors contributed to the decision-making process concerning educational policy? How was the educational philosophy interpreted in concrete academic programs? How did the division institute educational change to meet the needs of its population? What were the intraorganizational interactions that defined the EOD?

5.   What were the functions and consequences of divisional separation? Did the educational philosophy emphasizing the need for an autonomous divisional organization in reality lead to a successful compensatory effort? Or did the organizational structure produce the latent functions outlined by the radical critics of these programs, such as tracking, negative teacher expectations, labeling, stigmatization and cooling out?

6.   How did students in the program perceive and react to the separate divisional structure? Did the homogeneous structure result in the development of a cohesive student culture and if so, what was its role on the campus? Within the division?

7.   What were the consequences of the "separate but equal" racial composition of the campus? How did the divisional separation affect race relations? How did the differing cultural backgrounds of white middle class and minority students influence the social and educational environment? Was there evidence of cultural and racial conflict and if so, what was its effect on the educational policies of the division of educational opportunity?

In terms of interorganizational relationships the following questions are addressed:

1.   What was the relationship between the division and the other divisions of the college; with the college administration? How did the interactions between the various components affect the division's educational mission? What was the relationship between divisional faculty and other faculty members on issues concerning the role of the educational opportunity program?

2.   What was the effect of teaching in the educational opportunity program on the careers and status of faculty members? Did EOD faculty receive less status (for example, in terms of promotions, collegial recognition, etc.) in the college and if so, how did this affect the perception and action of the faculty? What were the organizational ideologies that emerged in this context and what forms of political labor (Collins, 1979) were used to negotiate for status? How did status conflicts contribute to the institutional culture of the division and consequently affect its educational mission?

3.   How did the division deal with the problems associated with the tensions between quality education and educational equity? Did these conflicts between quality and equality lead to the lowering of academic standards, as posited by the conservative critics? Were students pushed along for political purposes (for example, to ensure a low attrition rate)? How did the college's elite perception of itself affect these issues?

Research Methodology: Data Collection and Analysis

The purpose of this study is to increase our understanding of the organizational and educational processes contributing to equality or inequality of educational opportunity at the postsecondary level. The most effective method for this task is the intensive case study utilizing a variety of methodological tools. As Denzin (1970) pointed out, triangulation, or the combination of several research strategies, is essential to understanding the complexities of social reality. As social life is the product of ongoing social interaction, and organizational structures are formed by negotiation, the social researcher must understand how members interpret and construct their institutional arrangements. Therefore, the intensive longitudinal case study relying on both quantitative and qualitative methodologies was the appropriate design for this study.[5]

This study is based on four years of participant observation within the Educational Opportunity Division at State College and follow-up interviews with members of the community. It includes both ethnographic and historical sections which are based upon these observations, interviews with students and faculty and in-depth analyses of years of the minutes of faculty meetings.

Problems in the Research: The Limitation of the Case Study Method

The purpose of sociological research is to understand and explain social phenomena. Moreover, the systematic study of a sample (in survey research) and a particular case (in field research) should enhance our ability to explain the larger social issues of which they are a part. Therefore, we study particular cases in order to construct general propositions about a population. In this case, the study of one compensatory higher education program should reveal important educational processes related to the problems associated with similar attempts at liberal educational reform. However, as Denzin (1970), Bogdan and Bicklin (1992) and Williamson, Karp and Dalphine (1977) have pointed out, the weakness of the intensive case study method concerns the validity of such generalizations. In order to construct a general explanatory theory the case study must be representative of the larger population. In this case a number of problems limit our ability to make conclusive generalizations:

1. Since the EOD represented a unique model of compensatory higher education (separate placement, homogeneous grouping) the ability to generalize to other models (integrative and regular placement) is limited. Nonetheless, the importance of this particular research is not diminished. Although a comparative study would strengthen the conclusions and the ability to generalize, the validity of studying a particular organization is methodologically sound (Denzin, 1970). As Williamson et al. (1977) have pointed out, the case study reveals significant knowledge of organizational processes providing the basis for future explanatory research. More importantly, this study highlights important trends and problems in compensatory higher education. Combined with on-going research on such programs, it enhances our ability to formulate general conclusions. Finally, since the Educational Opportunity Division was unique in the state system, this study provides significant knowledge about the separate placement of the underprepared college student; this is information that need not be generalized to other opportunity programs to be relevant for educational policy.

2. A second problem concerns the effects of the overall college on the compensatory program and its students. Since State College was also a unique institution, significantly different from other four-year institutions in curriculum, politics, and student population,[6] generalizations to other four year colleges are impossible. Nonetheless, given the exceptional tensions between the elite model of higher education at State College and the egalitarian model of

higher education of the EOD, this study provides an important illumination of this central conflict.

Significance of the Research

Although the uniqueness of both the Educational Opportunity Division and State College provides methodological concerns, the value of this case outweighs its limitations. The concern for equality of educational opportunity remains a central issue. In the face of government cutbacks and the conservative assault on liberal educational reforms, the delineation of processes contributing to the successful education of minority and working class populations has never been as necessary. During a period when the prevailing political wisdom supports traditional ideologies of meritocracy and individual failure, with little or no concrete evidence, sociologists must continue to probe the institutional factors affecting educational success and failure. Furthermore, during periods of extreme budgetary constraints, knowledge contributing to the efficient and effective use of limited resources is crucial.

On a more general level, the study contributes to a growing literature on the dynamics of liberal educational reform. During a period of ongoing assault upon social reforms, the study's contributions to the understanding of such a reform program is needed to clarify problems and to work toward solutions. On a practical basis, these findings have applications in the realm of social policy. On a theoretical level, they may illuminate the limitations and possibilities of these reforms in ameliorating educational, social, and economic problems. Finally, as this study examines the organizational and educational processes that contributed to the elimination of the EOD as a separate program, it provides important insight into the politics and sociology of higher education.

The following chapters examine the evolution of the Educational Opportunity Division. Chapter 2 provides a general discussion of compensatory higher education and relates the major theoretical issues and perspectives to the specific aspects of the case study. The development, criticisms and decline of compensatory programs are discussed and the major theoretical perspectives are introduced and related to the Educational Opportunity Division. Chapter 3 presents a detailed description of the EOD and State College, and provides a discussion of organizational structure, educational philosophy and methods, the differences between the Educational Opportunity Program and other programs in the college, its students, and its faculty. Chapter 4 traces the emergence of the EOD as an off-campus program (1969–1978), its decline and reemergence on the main campus in

1978, and the transitional years at State College (1978–1981). The major focus of this chapter was the movement from the defense of divisional separation to the loosening of separate boundaries and the factors leading to this process. Chapter 5 discusses the movement toward complete integration with the State College mainstream programs and the politics of negotiation that resulted in the end of separation (1981–1982). Chapter 6 examines the politics of the division's decline and its final demise of the EOD as a separate academic division. Chapter 7 provides a sociological analysis of the division's history and discusses why the division was eliminated. It examines the organizational, political, educational, and economic factors related to its demise and relates them to the larger issues of organizational and educational change. Chapter 8, the conclusion, briefly examines what has happened to EOD type students at State College since 1983 and raises some policy questions concerning the role of higher education in ameliorating problems of social and educational inequality.

A Cautionary Note

It is important to note at the outset that the fact that State College eliminated the EOD as a separate academic division should not necessarily be taken as evidence of racism or the failure to support a program for minority students. Empirical data (see Sadovnik, 1983) were inconclusive as to the necessity for a separate placement model. Furthermore, comparisons to integrative type EOP (educational opportunity programs) programs in the state system suggested that there were not significant positive differences between the State College program and other EOP programs. In fact, most of these programs had higher retention and graduation rates. The fact that State College retention and graduation rates were often lower than other EOP programs before the program was eliminated and continued to be under the new integrative program may suggest more about State College than its Educational Opportunity Division.[7] The point is that the program was eliminated independent of such empirical evidence, and the decision was the result of political and educational conflicts. This study does not attempt to answer the question as to whether or not the program should have been eliminated as there is insufficient evidence to reach such a conclusion. Rather, it is concerned with the conflicts over different definitions of higher education, and how one compensatory higher education program and its students were affected by these conflicts.

NOTES

1. This skills-content synthesis was a major aspect of the division's educational philosophy. Put simply, the EOD believed that remedial and college-level discipline courses should not be separate (as in most colleges), but that all college discipline courses for disadvantaged students should have integrated basic skills instruction into the content of the course.

2. This accreditation report was part of a larger State College Self-Study Report. It was originally prepared by an EOD faculty committee and subsequently edited as part of the final State College document.

3. The remedial offerings included reading, writing, and mathematics. The granting of credits for these courses was a continual dilemma for the division, as critics often opposed the granting of college credits for what they considered pre-college work.

4. This book will not examine empirically the effects of this program. Rather this study, as a qualitative and historical case study is concerned with the educational and organizational dynamics of the program's separate divisional structure and the perceptions of students and faculty about this structure. For a detailed empirical analysis of the academic effects of this program and how its retention, attrition, and graduation rates compared to other, integrative EOP programs in New York State see Sadovnik (1983). Thus, my use of the term *effects* throughout the book is not meant empirically and should not be confused with educational outcomes.

5. Although the larger study upon which this book is based relied on extensive empirical methods, including questionnaires and data analysis, the research discussed here is almost exclusively qualitative, including participant observation, historical analysis (including document analysis), and intensive interviews with students, faculty, and administration.

6. From its inception State College was viewed as an alternative college and attracted a unique student population, many of whom in the 1970s reflected many of the countercultural attitudes of the 1960s. In addition, the presence of its School of the Arts made for a highly creative and artistic student body. Although by the 1980s the college began to lose its alternative label, and more traditional students attended, it remained a somewhat unique setting.

7. This is based on official statistics of the State University of New York Office of Special Programs.

2

COMPENSATORY HIGHER EDUCATION: LIBERAL EDUCATIONAL REFORM AND THE REDUCTION OF EDUCATIONAL INEQUALITY

The reduction of social, economic, and racial inequalities has been a central concern of liberal social policy in the United States since the New Deal. The view that schools could ameliorate problems of inequality has been a significant aspect of these reform efforts. The persistent belief that the educational system could act, in Horace Mann's words, as a balance wheel of the social machinery resulted in a pattern of educational reform aimed at the equalization of access, opportunity and results.[1] From the 1950s to the 1970s, in response to a national commitment to equal educational opportunity and social justice, American higher education opened its doors to a new population of students, many of whom were unprepared for the academic demands of postsecondary education.

The expansion of American higher education involved the rejection of previous ideologies that justified university attendance based upon privilege and meritocracy and the development of an egalitarian ideology legitimating college attendance as a right. Based upon democratic-liberal assumptions concerning the relationship between schooling and inequality, the democratization of higher education was a vital aspect of a social policy aimed at providing social mobility for minority and working class students.

The opening of access to higher education required programmatic adaptations within postsecondary institutions. The shift from meritocratic selection processes[2] to more open admissions standards contributed to changes in the social and economic characteristics of the student population.[3] The admittance of a higher proportion of working class and minority students presented educational challenges to the open door colleges, as this population's unequal precollege education often left it at a disadvantage in its ability to handle the traditional college curriculum.

The relationship between socioeconomic status, race and educational performance is thoroughly documented in the sociology of education literature.[4] Although the epidemiology of unequal minority achievement is less certain, it is clear that as the products of a declining and often failing public educational system, many of the new students were academically unprepared for a college education (Cross, 1971; Lavin et al., 1981). Therefore, the development of open access to postsecondary educational opportunities resulted in the creation of special college programs to compensate for past academic deficiencies, while simultaneously developing the conditions for the successful achievement of the new population.

The goals of these compensatory higher education programs were both educational and social. Educationally, the programs were designed to close the gap in majority-minority school performance in order to equalize educational attainment. Based upon democratic-liberal assumptions concerning the relationship between education and social mobility, the educational success of the mission was seen as the first step in ensuring social equality for minority groups. At the most general level, this study is concerned with the limitations and possibilities of this type of liberal educational reform and the ability of educational programs to ameliorate educational and perhaps social problems. With this in mind, let us begin with a survey of various sociological perspectives on the role of education in solving social and economic problems and the consequent rise of liberal educational reform.

Theoretical Perspectives and Issues

For the past twenty years considerable theoretical debate over the role of education in reducing social and economic inequality has provided the impetus for empirical investigations in the sociology of education. Two major perspectives, the democratic liberal and the radical (critical) model have emerged as competing theoretical frameworks. As their general principles have been summarized at length elsewhere (Hurn, 1993:42–70), this section will explore each perspective's treatment of liberal educational reform. Since this study focuses on reform in higher education, the treatment of the expansion and democratization of American higher education in the 1960s is an appropriate starting point.

The democratic-liberal perspective viewed education as a vital institution in a modern capitalist society defined by its technocratic, meritocratic and democratic characteristics (Hurn, 1993:44–47). Although considerable inequality remains, this society is characterized by the revolutionary movement from ascription to achievement with equal educational opportunity, the crucial component of a fair and meritocratic order. According to this perspective, the historical pattern of academic failure by minority and working class students was a blemish on the principles of justice and equality of opportunity expounded by a democracy. This educational pattern necessitated the formulation of reform programs to ensure equality of opportunity. Whereas democratic-liberal theorists disagreed on the causes of academic failure, they vigorously believed that the solutions to both educational and social problems were possible within the capitalist social structure. As Diane Ravitch argued:

> It is indisputable that full equality has not been achieved, but equally indisputable in the light of the evidence is the conclusion that a democratic society can bring about effective social change, if there is both the leadership and the political commitment to do so. To argue, against the evidence, that meaningful change is not possible is to sap the political will that is necessary to effect changes (1978:114-115).

The central distinction made by the democratic-liberal perspective was between equality of opportunity and equality of results. A democratic society is a just society, according to this tradition, if it generates the former. Therefore, democratic-liberal theory rested on a positive view of meritocracy as a laudable goal, with education viewed as the necessary institutional component in guaranteeing a fair competition for unequal rewards. The just society, then, is one where each member has an equal opportunity for social and economic advantages and where individual merit and talent replace ascriptive and class variables as the most essential determinants of status. Education is thus the vehicle in ensuring the continual movement toward this meritocratic system. Democratic-liberal theory also rested on a functional theory of stratification[5] that argued that social inequality is a necessary component of all societies and, as long as unequal distribution is based on achievement, the society remains committed to social justice. Therefore, the democratic-liberal tradition rejected equality of results as neither possible nor laudable.

Since educational achievement and attainment were viewed as part of the solution to social and economic inequality, or at the least, the elimination of class and racial barriers to equality of opportunity, the academic performance of minority and working class students became a central concern of liberal social policy. Moreover, as the cornerstone of the democratic-liberal perspective was the belief in an instrumental meritocratic hypothesis (that successful life outcomes are in large measure based on earned educational attainment), higher education was viewed as a necessary component of social mobility and its absence a cause of continued economic inequality. Therefore, the expansion of higher education to minority and working class students was viewed as a logical extension of egalitarian social policy. Likewise, the democratic-liberal perspective viewed liberal educational reforms as consistent with the goals of a democratic society and the development of compensatory higher education programs as necessary components to ensure that minority and working class students obtain the educational tools vital to economic success.

Beginning in the early 1970s, some sociologists of education began to question the positive portrait painted by the democratic-liberal perspective by examining the instrumental-meritocratic hypothesis. The role of education as a great equalizer was viewed with increasing skepticism by emerging critical theories of education. The critical perspective viewed schools as playing a crucial role in reproducing existing social and economic inequalities rather than eliminating them. Two complementary theoretical perspectives, neo-Marxism and conflict theory offered critical insight into the role of education in the American stratification system.[6]

The neo-Marxist perspective argued that education serves the interests of the ruling capitalist elites in the domination of the working class. Based upon a correspondence theory concerning the relationship between schooling and society (Bowles and Gintis, 1976:130–141), neo-Marxists suggested that the schools mirror the needs of the capitalist division of labor and produce the vital ingredients of a capitalist economy, a trained and obedient labor force, through a class stratified educational system. Moreover, this perspective rejected the view that schools have historically worked to the advantage of the working class in terms of mobility, but rather have maintained unequal class relations. Most importantly, neo-Marxists viewed educational reforms, despite their often noble intentions, as limited by the realities of the capitalist relations of production. Bowles and Gintis summarized this viewpoint:

> The history of U.S. education provides little support for the view that schools have been vehicles for the equalization of economic status or opportunity. Nor are they today. The proliferation of special programs for the equalization of educational opportunity had precious little impact on the structure of U.S. education, and even less on the structure of income and opportunity in the U.S. economy. It is clear that education in the United States is simply too weak an influence on the distribution of status and opportunity in the U.S. economy to fulfill its mission as the Great Equalizer....In the history of U.S. education it is the integrative function (author's note, the role of education in reproducing a class stratified labor force) which has dominated the

purpose of schooling, to the detriment of the other liberal objectives (1976:48).

Conflict theory, although positing a more multidimensional view of conflict involving various status groups, also supported the thesis that schools reinforce rather than reduce inequality (Collins, 1971; Hurn, 1978). Conflict theorists, most notably Randall Collins (1971, 1979) dismissed the meritocratic thesis that because schools provide the cognitive skills necessary in a modern technocratic society, their successful graduates are highly rewarded. Contrary to this popular view, Collins argued that the schools are credentialing institutions that favor dominant cultural elites in their struggles to maintain social and economic advantages. Moreover, Collins suggested that there is little evidence to support the view that schools successfully train workers and therefore he rejected what he termed the technocratic myth of the role of education (Collins, 1979:1–22). The common thesis then, derived from both neo-Marxist and conflict theory, was that the educational problems experienced by minority and working class students were actually a consequence of society's structures of domination (Persell, 1977:5–53) rather than a commitment to equality.

The critical perspectives of education developed an alternative explanation for the expansion of higher education and the development of liberal educational reforms. The American belief in the value of education and the validity of the instrumental-meritocratic hypothesis resulted in successive generations seeking and obtaining higher education as a vehicle for upward mobility. According to Collins (1979), as various ethnic and minority groups increased their levels of educational attainment, the culturally dominant middle and upper-middle classes continued to increase their own levels, resulting in a continual progression of educational require-ments. The opening of higher education and the reforms relating to this expansion is viewed less as the outcome of democratization and more as the product of status competition. Christopher Hurn summarized this point:

> Because education is closely linked to power and status, Collins argues different groups will attempt to improve their position by obtaining more education for their children than they themselves had in the past. Disadvan-taged groups, for example, will try to improve their positions by seeking more education for their children. Ironically, however, the success of disadvantaged groups in this respect will stimulate middle and upper-class groups to maintain their relative position in the hierarchy by increasing their own levels of education as well (1993:87).

Whereas conflict theory stressed the issue of status conflict as central to educational expansion, neo-Marxists such as Bowles and Gintis (1976:-151–241) offered a more dialectical and economic analysis[7] of the dynamics of educational change and the development of liberal educational reforms. The expansion of American higher education was viewed as the result of the dual processes of legitimation and accumulation. From the correspondence principle, they argued that changes in the requirements of capitalist production necessitated the development of an educated white collar proletariat. Secondly, and perhaps more importantly, the contradiction between the American creed of equality and the reality of inequality was central to the development of liberal educational reforms. Since the belief in education as a means for mobility was strong, and as the educational system reinforced this belief as a means of legitimating social inequality, the schools became a primary target for the amelioration of disparities.[8] For example, as part of the broader demands of the civil rights movement, minority groups sought access to higher education as a means for mobility. As the inherent conflicts between the ideology of a democratic society (equality of opportunity) and the structural tendencies of capitalism (large social and economic inequalities) resulted in prolonged legitimation crises,[9] the state diffused the problems through the institution of liberal educational reforms, such as open admissions and compensatory higher education programs. In Wolfe's words, "the legitimacy crisis is produced by the inability of the late capitalist state to maintain its democratic rhetoric if it is to preserve its accumulation functions, or the inability to spur further accumulation if it is to be true to its democratic ideology" (1977:329). Part of the solution to the legitimation crisis was the initiation of liberal educational reform. The next section explores the process by which public demands resulted in the development of particular types of reforms in education.

An Application of Social Problems Theory
to Liberal Educational Reform

Despite the differences in the three perspectives, they converge on one important point. They all suggested that public belief in the value of higher education contributed to the expansion of access. The fact that some theorists believed this support was warranted and others did not, that some believed educational reform was the work of democratic interests in action and others suggested it represented the response to tensions and demands, that some believed that such reforms can and do work and others were less optimistic about their ability to eliminate substantial sources of inequality is less important to our understanding of the development of these reforms than the fact that, to some extent, people brought about these changes through action and demands. Whatever their underlying reasons, and however we view the decision of the state to respond, the fact remains that the educational reforms of the 1960s were in part a response to the demands of significant numbers of people. At this point, the use of social problems theory becomes extremely useful in understanding the development of educational reform.

Spector and Kitsuse (1977) proposed a natural history approach to the study of social problems that stressed the definitional process by which members label conditions as significant problems. Within their model, the implementation of specific solutions was viewed as the institutional response to the claims making activities of members for the amelioration of these situations. Drawing upon the earlier works of Fuller and Myers (1941) and Lemert (1951) and combining these with a labeling approach to deviance, they viewed social problems as defined by the political activities of members and their solutions as the response to these conflictual interactions. For the purpose of addressing the development of liberal educational reforms, specifically those leading to the expansion of access to higher education, the first two stages in their natural history model are appropriate.

According to Spector and Kitsuse (1977:142), in stage one "groups attempt to assert the existence of some condition, define it as offensive, harmful, or otherwise undesirable, publicize these assertions, stimulate controversy and create a public or political issue over the matter." This first stage involves what Spector and Kitsuse called *claims making activities.* According to the authors:

> Social problems activity commences with collective attempts to remedy a condition that some group perceives and judges offensive and undesirable. The complaining group may or may not be the victim of the imputed condition; for example, the complaint that the welfare system demoralizes its clients may be made by an organization of social workers, clergymen, or another humanitarian group not directly subject to the condition. However, groups directly affected by the condition may act in their own interests (1977:143).

Through various claims making strategies, the claims making groups attempt to influence those in power to recognize the validity of their complaints. During this initial stage the development of group conflict often occurs, with counter-claims making groups publicly rejecting the claims introduced by the first group and offering substantially different views of the nature or existence of the problem. At some point, one group's claims may prove to be more successful than the other's. It is at this point that the definition of the alleged conditions as a social problem is ensured through an official response by those in power as to the legitimacy of the claims.

Stage two, according to the authors, is "the recognition of the legitimacy of these groups by some official organization, agency, or institution. This may lead to an official investigation, proposals for reform, and the establishment of an agency to respond to these claims and demands" (Spector and Kitsuse, 1977:142). The second stage, then, represents the acknowledgement that a social problem does exist and is the first step in the implementation of particular solutions. Although Spector and Kitsuse's model spent little if any time on actual solutions, it suggested that this stage was the appropriate place for the investigation of the problem and the preliminary recommendation for its solution. While the rest of their model discussed group reactions, support and rejection of proposed solutions, it is clear that at some point particular solutions are implemented and then become the subject of renewed claims and counterclaims, not only about the original condition, but also the success of the solutions. It is within this context of claims making, official recognition and legitimation, and the implementation of solutions and subsequent debates over their efficacy, that the development of liberal educational reforms makes the most sense.

Since this study is concerned with compensatory higher education as an example of such a liberal reform, the application of social problems theory will be concentrated on the more general issue of open access, of which compensatory higher education is a central part. It is appropriate to begin with the decisions to expand access.

Because Americans in large numbers believed in the liberal view of higher education as the best means to mobility and the elimination of gross inequalities, the schools became the central feature in the claims against continued minority inequality. Therefore, in stage one, members defined the problem of minority group inequality as the general problem and access to higher education as a necessary step in its solution. The universities, they argued, were still the bastions of the privileged and the prepared, and because most minorities were the victims of unequal precollege education, the traditional admissions standards became the institutional barrier to the advancement of minority group members. Their central claim, then, was that minority groups had to have access to higher educational opportunities in order to advance, but this access would be impossible without a radical transformation of admissions criteria. Lavin et al. (1981:1-20) documented the claims making activities and confrontation that resulted in the implementation of the open admissions experiment at the City University of New

York. Arguing that the initial claims were brought by minority students and the larger minority community and supported by a significant segment of the CUNY leadership, the final impetus was the confrontation at City College, where these groups demanded a policy of expanded access.

That claims making groups chose to direct their anger at the City College of New York was both appropriate and ironic. As a tuition free public institution, its historical mission had been to provide quality higher education to the qualified urban poor. However, as the admissions requirements grew more stringent, the opening of access to minorities remained a difficult problem. At the heart of these confrontations was the insistence that City College expand its mission to the urban minorities and, if necessary, eliminate those admission standards that had become, in the eyes of the proponents of open admissions, the structural barriers to minority advancement.

The first stage witnessed the emergence of counter claims against the demands for open access. To many members of the academic community higher education represented the foundation of the meritocratic society, and the loosening or elimination of admission standards would surely mean the inevitable decline in standards and the resultant demise of the quality of culture.[10] Martin Mayer presented a critique of the egalitarian visions underlying the demands for open access:

> Though I know many brilliant people I would not care to have as my doctor or my lawyer or my children's teacher, it is undoubtedly true that a unidimensional measure of academic excellence can be used to set a special, higher floor for many occupations and professions. The ardently egalitarian...are fundamentally unconvincing: one can dismiss them with the curse that they should cross the river on a bridge designed by an engineer from an engineering school where students were admitted by lottery; and that their injuries should be treated by a doctor from a medical school where students were admitted by lottery, and that their heirs' malpractice suit be tried by a lawyer from a law school where students were admitted by lottery (1973:47).

The controversy over an open admissions policy at CUNY was indicative of a national debate over the loosening of admissions standards and the expansion of access. On the one hand, supporters of open admissions rejected traditional views of the university's autonomous function as a disseminator of knowledge (Trow, 1970:1–42) and argued that higher education was a central tool in the reproduction of social inequality. They rejected the existence of any objective meritocratic selection process and demanded the elimination of restrictive barriers to educational mobility. On the other hand, critics of this liberal reform policy defended the selective admissions process and argued that the elimination of these meritocratic criteria would inevitably lead to the decline of academic standards and the eventual demise of the university system.

Karabel (1972b) suggested that open admissions questioned some fundamental assumptions about the purpose of higher education. He pointed to the distinction between the "value added" concept of higher education at the heart of liberal educational reforms. Stating that "the philosophy underlying open admissions emphasizes not picking winners, but maximizing the educational growth of students" (1972b:270), Karabel defended open admissions as presenting the opportunity to significantly change and improve both the cognitive and noncognitive abilities of students who, without this reform, would never have this opportunity for intellectual and personal growth. The "value added" approach to open admissions, then, suggested that the amount of growth is more important than the level at which it occurs. To the critics of open access, although the amount of growth was indeed an important component of education, it was not the role of colleges to make up for precollege weaknesses. To suggest that a college should be defined as successful if it moves a student from a third to an eighth grade reading level (while certainly an example of added value) would be to debase the very concept of higher education.

In the final analysis, the defense of open admissions rested on the allocative functions of higher education. Since college had become a primary method for attaining adult occupational status, and the lack of credentials was a major factor in minority and working class inequality, the expansion of access to postsecondary education became the primary remedy in liberal policy solutions. Reformers demanded fundamental changes in the selection process in order to guarantee an equal opportunity for those historically cut off from the reward system. As Karabel noted:

> The advent of open admissions raises some fundamental questions about the nature and the purpose of the university. Conceiving of itself as most essentially devoted to the discovery and transmission of knowledge, the university has, in reality, become a principal mechanism for distributing privilege in American society. Avenues previously open to those who did not attend college are now closed, most middle level jobs and all elite positions now require a college degree. The pressure for open admissions arose, in good part, as a response to this trend (1972b:285).

Furthermore, in commenting on the overall meaning of open admissions, Karabel added:

> The controversy over open admissions has been impassioned. Opponents have waged battle primarily on the grounds that universal access will lower academic standards, but the evidence indicates that such an outcome is by no means inevitable. Advocates have described open admissions as a poverty interrupter and as a powerful egalitarian force, but it is quite possible that the degree of inequality of educational opportunity in American society will remain constant, especially if the institutional pecking order within higher education is maintained. Clearly both the promise and mission of open admissions have been exaggerated....Yet, as indicated by the proliferation of state master plans for universal access and by the vast growth of free-access institutions, it is fast becoming a national reality. The question now is not whether there will be open admissions, but rather what form it will take and how it can be best made to work (1972b:285–86).

Therefore, the outcome of the emotional conflicts over universal access resulted in the adoption of less restrictive admissions policies on a national level. Using Spector and Kitsuse's model, we can say that the claims making activities defined unequal educational opportunity as a social problem and offered open admissions as a potential reformist solution. After a series of debates and struggles, the proponents of expanded access emerged victorious, and with this victory began a shift away from highly selective admissions processes. However, as Lavin et al. pointed out, the adoption of liberalized selection criteria was only the first step in what promised to be a protracted controversy. They stated:

> The focus of these reactions (to open admissions at CUNY) has been the issue of academic standards. This issue has probably generated more heat than any other surrounding the policy. Before open admission began, there were gloomy prophesies about the plan's prospects for success. Some feared that open admissions students, with their weaker high school records, would stand little chance of performing satisfactorily. Others felt that despite the University's commitment to large scale programs of remediation, the political pressures stemming from the open

admissions effort would lead to a dilution of academic
standards with the veneer of academic success concealing
an underlying deterioration of rigor. The University thus
found itself in a no win situation. If students succeeded
beyond expectations, it would be on account of lowering
standards. If they failed, the gloomy prophets would,
happily or not, see their fears confirmed (1981:37–38).

At the heart of this dilemma was the tension between educational quality and
equality. Would it be possible to increase educational equality of opportunity
without a decline in academic quality? Or would the admission of a large
population of students without the traditional predictors for academic success
either result in their large scale failure or their survival at the expense of
educational standards? In order to avoid the problems inherent in these
dilemmas, the colleges and universities had to develop special programs for
their new population of students. The expansion of access was only the first
step: now, the postsecondary institutions had to attempt to prove the
prophets of gloom incorrect by avoiding the transformation of this equality
of opportunity into mass failure.

Liberal Educational Reform Programs at the College Level: The Attempt to Turn Opportunity into Successful Results

The opening of access to postsecondary institutions resulted in the influx of
large numbers of students without the prerequisite skills for traditional
college work. As these students rushed through the floodgates, the need for
remediation at the college level became apparent (Cross, 1971; 1976). While
many academics reacted with dismay at the decline in student skills and
what they considered the inevitable decline in standards, and major conflicts
emerged over the necessity for reaching these students at their level or
making them adapt to traditional standards (Cross, 1976), the colleges
launched a comprehensive effort to raise the educational levels of the new
population. It became clear to a growing number of educational reformers
that the tensions between quality and equality need not result in the sacrifice
of one at the expense of the other if the colleges made an extraordinary
effort to compensate for past skills deficiency. To merely place the
underprepared in traditional college classrooms without additional programmatic services would indeed guarantee failure or the necessary decline in
standards to ensure passing. However, if the colleges instituted special
programs to help the new population overcome its educational deficiencies,
the reformers believed that equality and quality could coexist. Based upon

the writings of John Roueche (1972) and K. Patricia Cross (1971; 1976), educational reformers instituted special college programs to compensate for precollege deficits and prepare students for success in college. While the critics of open admission continued their assault, the developers of new compensatory higher educational programs were experimenting with methodologies in remedial and developmental education.[11]

To a large degree, the new population inhabiting the compensatory programs consisted of minority students. As products of a declining and often failing public educational system, they brought with them a legacy of academic underachievement. Since the traditional admissions criteria had been altered or discarded to provide access, the programs faced the difficult task of making up for the failures of primary and secondary education. Considerable sociological research had been centered on the etiology of minority group underachievement. Most of it, however, had been concentrated exclusively on the precollege level. Although the causes are complex and multidimensional,[12] what is clear is that the colleges inherited these problems and had to develop effective strategies for their amelioration.

The causes of unequal minority academic achievement have been the topic of heated debate and research for the past thirty years. Explanations centering on the schools,[13] the family,[14] the cultural differences in minority students,[15] sociolinguistic differences,[16] societal structures of domination,[17] and the castelike nature of American society[18] have all received considerable support. Persell (1977) summarized and synthesized the evidence and concluded that the interplay between societal level structures of domination and the institutional and interpersonal aspects of schooling were at the root of the problem. The evidence on inequality of educational performance pointed to a variety of related factors explaining minority group underachievement, and indicated that a large proportion of this new population entered college with serious skills deficiencies. The task of compensatory higher education, then, was to provide educational intervention at the postsecondary level so that these students could successfully make use of their newly acquired opportunities. Therefore, in order to avoid the likelihood of a revolving door, compensatory programs searched for appropriate methods to ensure the success of this population.

The basic assumption behind the compensatory higher education programs was that colleges could compensate for past deficiencies and thus make a difference. As Grant and Riesman (1978) pointed out, colleges are highly adaptable in their methods and curriculum, as proven by a multitude of innovations and changes at the postsecondary level. Furthermore, as Cross (1971) and Roueche and Snow (1977) suggested in their studies of remediation, the college was a valid setting for compensation of past deficiencies, as college age students are capable of making rapid gains in learning and skills development. Therefore, the programs charged with educating the underprepared population, although faced with a difficult task, could conceivably make a difference.

Compensatory Higher Education: Solutions and Criticisms

Roueche and Snow (1977:20) stated that the underpreparation of college students may be the most significant problem facing higher education. They argued:

> Everyone agrees that there is a problem in American education. More and more students are graduating from high school each year without the basic skills necessary to survive, let alone succeed, in a rapidly developing technological society.... Students spend more time and effort in English courses than in any other subject required in public education; yet all indications are that verbal skills, so necessary in our culture are deteriorating at an alarming rate. Students spend years in mathematics; yet deficiencies in basic quantitative and problem solving skills have also been noted and well documented.

During the 1960s and 1970s, a growing literature on the problem of the underprepared student emerged as significant numbers of this population entered the open access institutions. Moreover, as it became clear that underpreparation was not a small problem localized to the new minorities in the system, but was instead endemic to significant numbers of majority students as well, colleges began to direct serious efforts at the amelioration of these deficits. Furthermore, as Roueche and Snow (1977:20) pointed out, although the open door policies initially affected primarily community colleges, the decline of the college age population, the continued decline in educational preparation of all students, and the expansion of the egalitarian philosophy of education to four-year institutions contributed to the recognition of this educational problem at a significant proportion of postsecondary institutions. While many critics bemoaned the failings of American public education, the task of the colleges in this respect became clear: to institute successful compensatory programs for these students.

Throughout the 1960s and 1970s, educational reformers struggled to understand the keys to the successful remediation of what Roueche and Snow labeled these "high risk" students (1977:2). In their study of remedial college education, they concluded that the period witnessed a multitude of experiments and a great deal of failure. At many institutions, the revolving door pattern defined the educational experiences of the underprepared student. The authors stated:

> In 1969, the senior author was invited to visit an "exemplary" program in a southeastern college. Upon arrival he discovered that the program had been in existence for three years and that 400 students took part in the program every year. According to the dean, this stable enrollment was proof positive that the program was meeting the needs of students. The dean even brought out students who had succeeded in the developmental program and had gone on to complete degrees and certificates in the college to testify to the effectiveness of the program.... By the end of the afternoon we had discovered that 80 to 90 percent of all who began the program never completed it. Most either dropped out or were flunked out. The enrollment figures indicated only the tremendous demand for the program; that is, new students continued to enroll, thus maintaining the illusion of a successful program (1977:24).

Throughout the 1970s, compensatory educators attempted to construct programs to alleviate this revolving door pattern. If open access was to become more than the opportunity to fail, then remedial strategies needed to be implemented and the epidemiology of underprepared student failure systematically addressed. An experimental and pedagogical literature grew,[19] and numerous organizational and instructional strategies emerged at the college level.

Two major organizational models of compensatory higher education, the integrative and the holistic, were constructed to meet the needs of the underprepared population. In the first model, educational opportunity students (as they often were labeled), took basic skills courses in reading, writing and mathematics within the compensatory program, and registered for regular college level discipline courses (literature, biology, sociology, etc.) with the rest of the college population. The important characteristic of this model was that the underprepared students were integrated (mainstreamed) into the overall college community through attendance in regular course offerings, with the compensatory program providing support services to enhance academic achievement.

The second model was the holistic or separate placement model, which developed in response to a number of shortcomings in the integrative programs. Based upon the educational philosophy that the underprepared student needed a specially trained faculty and separate courses, the holistic programs offered a complete and independent curriculum, including both remedial and discipline courses. Such an organizational framework provided a setting in which the student could have both time and instruction to overcome educational deficits before moving into the demanding academic mainstream. At four-year colleges, students usually completed the equivalent of two years of college within the program before being mainstreamed into the regular college curriculum. Intensive remediation was provided to make up for past deficiencies and to ensure a successful transition to the upper level. In some respects, the holistic model represented an institutional tracking system whose goal was to track for success.

The central question underlying these organizational models is what constituted the appropriate educational setting and placement of the underprepared student? As in precollege special education, the question of mainstreaming or regular versus special placement of students with special needs became a burning issue as integrative programs represented regular placement whereas holistic programs represented special placement.

Research on compensatory higher education suggested strengths and weaknesses in both models.[20] First, whereas the integrative (regular placement) model provided the opportunity for social and educational mainstreaming, it often provided little of the necessary educational foundation for success in the disciplines. Therefore, the underprepared student, often not possessing the requisite academic skills, was unable to handle college-level discipline courses without specialized attention within these courses. Furthermore, regular courses often provided no special mechanisms for remediation or the development of sound academic skills. On the other hand, holistic programs, while providing the integration of remedial and developmental strategies into all courses, represented a form of institutional tracking and labeling, which sometimes resulted in stigmatization and lowered self-concept. Although there are numerous studies of precollege special education in which the effectiveness of different types of placement was evaluated, little has been offered at the college level.[21] However, Roueche and Snow (1977), in their discussion of successful programs, suggested that the quality of services offered within each placement may be more important than the setting itself.

The major educational advocates of compensatory higher education stressed a number of philosophical and programmatic innovations that became the core of the reforms. First, Cross (1971) argued that the belief that all students can learn was the basic assumption of remedial efforts. That is, despite their serious educational problems and underpreparation, these students could and would learn under the right conditions. Second, in order for these right conditions to exist, colleges had to make fundamental shifts in their philosophy of higher education. Roueche (1972) argued that compensatory higher education rested on an egalitarian, anti-elitist philosophy, whereas colleges traditionally had meritocratic and elitist philosophies that stressed the student's requirements and curriculum, with only the qualified allowed to continue. Although stressing the importance of the retention of standards, he pointed out that these programs believed in meeting the student at his/her entry level and then raising him/her to the acceptable level of competency. Therefore, compensatory programs believed that, in order to be successful, colleges had to reject elitist assumptions and provide the services necessary to enable the underprepared student to succeed at college.

There has been significant disagreement over the proper educational placement of these students. Roueche and Snow (1977) concluded that despite the organizational differences a number of common features developed in most programs, including the existence of basic skills courses, tutorial services, counseling, and learning centers. Through the implementation of these types of services, compensatory higher education programs attempted to fulfill their educational mission of compensation as the first step in fulfilling their social mission of reducing social and economic inequality. The extent to which these programs have been successful is a major controversy in the sociology of education literature.

In the 1970s, liberal educational reforms were placed under both critical and skeptical examination. As part of the conservative attack on government spending, funding for various programs was cut back. Moreover, the effectiveness and goals of compensatory higher education were questioned. Conservative critics argued that the goals of equality of opportunity had been superseded by the attention to equality of outcomes, threatening the meritocratic selection process by destroying traditional academic standards (Heller, 1973; Mayer, 1973; Wagner, 1976). The result of these conservative trends was an erosion in the belief of higher education as a right and the partial return to viewing higher education as a privilege. Lavin, Alban and Silberstein (1981) pointed to the imposition of a tuition policy and the death of open admissions at the City University of New York as an example of this process.

The attack on liberal educational reform was not the exclusive domain of conservatives. Radical critics argued that liberal educational reform in general and compensatory higher education programs in particular were ineffective piecemeal solutions to problems outside the purview of the educational system (Bowles and Gintis, 1976; deLone, 1979; Milner, 1972). Furthermore, not only were these programs ineffective in reducing existing inequality, they also succeeded by failing (Apple, 1977). That is, educational reform programs were cooptive devices responding to legitimation crises

(Bowles and Gintis, 1976; Wolfe, 1977). Finally, critics concluded that these programs perpetuated the system of educational inequality initiated in primary and secondary schools by developing tracking systems at the college level (Gorelick, 1978; Karabel, 1972a,1972b; Trimberger, 1973).

Democratic-liberal evaluations disagreed with both conservative and radical criticisms asserting an increase in educational and social mobility for the recipients of reform (Ravitch, 1978). Furthermore, a detailed evaluation of the largest open admissions and compensatory effort in the United States, the program at the City University of New York, found evidence to support the perpetuation of educational inequalities, especially for blacks and hispanics; it also provided evidence of the successful opening of opportunities for various ethnic and minority groups (Lavin, Alba and Silberstein, 1981).

The conservative critique rested heavily on the defense of meritocracy and selectivity and the assertion that open access and compensatory higher education had diminished educational quality. The decline of standards hypotheses, however, rested less on the empirical investigation of compensatory programs and more on the moral perspective of those defending the sanctity of cultural standards. Christopher Lasch (1979:-221-261), echoing these feelings, pointed to the decline in educational and intellectual skills as part of a national trend that posed a threat to the sanctity of the culture. He suggested that the tensions between equality and quality resulted in the decline of the latter, and although he did not indicate that this trend was inevitable, he did bemoan the negative effects of democratization on the quality of educational pursuits. He argued:

> Yet the democratization of education has accomplished little to justify this faith (of its supporters). It has neither improved popular understanding of modern society, raised the quality of popular culture, nor reduced the gap between wealth and poverty, which remains as wide as ever. On the other hand, it has contributed to the decline of critical thought and the erosion of intellectual standards, forcing us to consider the possibility that mass education, as conservatives have argued all along is intrinsically incompatible with the maintenance of educational quality (1979:-221-222).

Arguing that mass education has resulted in a "new illiteracy" and the "spread of stupefaction," Lasch, by no means a conservative, eloquently supported what was the foundation of conservative opposition to mass education in general and open access to college in particular. As Lavin, et al. (1981:37–39) noted, the conservative opposition to open admissions and the assault on its continuation in 1975 rested in part on these types of elitist foundations. Thus, a major criticism of compensatory higher education was that it perpetuated the decline in standards and often passed unqualified students along without proper remediation.

The second source of criticism developed out of the critical perspective on education. Arguing that the role of education in American society is to reproduce social and economic advantages and therefore inequalities, radical critics, often supportive of the goals of liberal educational reform, were skeptical of their ability to succeed. Bowles and Gintis pointed out the limits and possibilities of open admissions programs and a way of understanding liberal educational reform in general:

> This reform [open enrollment] could very well meet the first objective [in the reduction of inequality] — the politicization of inequality. If youth of minority and blue collar families gained their share of higher educational credentials, the legitimacy of organizing production and social life hierarchically along class and race lines would be drastically undermined. The continued exploitation of labor and social oppression of minorities would increasingly come to be seen as rooted in the political power of dominant elites rather than in any cultural, biological or skill deficiencies of workers. But open enrollment does not necessarily generate a more equal distribution of educational credentials. Along with freer admissions policies have come a stronger internal tracking system within higher education and the proliferation of sub BA degrees. These symbolize the new educational stratification (1976:249).

Therefore, the authors concluded that although liberal educational reforms had the potential to reduce inequality if only through its delegitimation, they often never had this opportunity, as the educational mission was rarely accomplished. Radical critics suggested that open enrollment programs often created a higher level of educational stratification by implementing an institutional tracking system. As a result, many students were either tracked away from traditional BA programs into vocational tracks or cooled or flunked out before graduation. Numerous studies (Gorelick, 1978; Karabel, 1972; Pincus, 1980; Trimberger, 1973) supported the hypothesis that expansion of access led to the implementation of new forms of tracking at the postsecondary level, with minorities and working class students the apparent victims of these systems. Murray Milner (1972), in his study of the effects of expanded opportunities for minorities, concluded that equalization of educational results had not occurred, only the illusion of equality.

The illusion of equality, however, was an important aspect of the role of liberal educational reforms according to the radical perspective. The democratization of access was sufficient to legitimate the meritocratic ideology of inequality as open access had, in the eyes of significant numbers of people, provided all students with the opportunity to compete. Therefore, if large numbers of students did not complete their degrees this only reinforced the belief that the fault was their own. Moreover, as Bowles and Gintis pointed out, the role of education in legitimating inequality was continued at the college level as failing unprepared students blamed themselves rather than the institutions for not making use of the opportunity that a democratic society had provided. In this way, the liberal reforms at the college level had maintained educational inequality while supporting and legitimating a meritocratic ideology. As Bowles and Gintis argued:

> In many institutions, large numbers of students with drastically deficient high school backgrounds have been confronted by a hostile or indifferent faculty who are committed to a traditional academic curriculum. In these cases, widespread failure among the new students has probably reinforced discriminatory ideologies (1976:250).

In conclusion, the radical criticisms of open enrollment and compensatory education attacked not these programs' intent, but their effectiveness in reducing educational inequality and social inequality. The critical perspective suggested that for education to continue to fulfill its integrative function (that is, to reproduce inequality), open enrollment could not result in the equalization of results. Therefore, these programs led to the emergence of higher educational tracking and the reproduction of inequality at a higher level of the school system. These critics pointed to the low completion and high attrition rates and suggested, as Michael Apple (1977) argued about American education in general, that the schools "succeed by failing." Indeed, the conservative and radical criticisms of compensatory higher education, working from very different assumptions, both looked at the low completion rates of open enrollment students to justify their position.[22]

Conservatives used the same data to defend the importance of meritocratic selection processes and elite standards and demanded a return to selectivity. Moreover, the often poor performance of minority students within these programs was explained through a cultural deficit theory of educational achievement.[23] On the other hand, radicals pointed to the failure of these programs to ameliorate the problems for which they were created, resulting in the perpetuation of educational inequality. Like other liberal educational reforms of the twentieth century, their original intent became lost in their application. Critical theorists, unlike conservatives, rejected a cultural deficit explanation as a "blaming the victim ideology" (Pincus, 1983:138) and suggested that schools could not successfully alter conditions rooted in economic and social structure. As Fred Pincus pointed out, the educational problems of open enrollment students cannot solely be attributed to the individual weaknesses of students or to the inability of colleges to overcome differences and weaknesses prior to entry, but rather to an overall system of institutionalized racism.

Advocates of liberal educational reform, although acknowledging the complex problems facing compensatory programs, supported the hypothesis that compensatory higher education could make a difference. Educators such as Cross (1971; 1976) and Roueche (1972; 1977) reiterated the proposition that colleges could help students catch up through remediation. Furthermore, they believed that the constraints on success could be reduced under the right conditions. Therefore, the defenders of liberal reform rejected both conservative arguments about the inevitability and necessity of inequality and radical skepticism about the effectiveness of schools in reducing performance gaps.

The decline of standards hypothesis, according to the liberal perspective, made open enrollment and compensatory higher education a scapegoat for a much larger problem. The conservatives often failed to recognize that declining skills were not particular to compensatory students but to higher education in general. Although certainly not a defender of open enrollments, Lasch pointed out:

> But the conservative interpretation of the collapse of standards is much too simple. Standards are deteriorating even at Harvard, Yale, and Princeton which can hardly be described as institutions of mass education. A faculty committee at Harvard reports, 'The Harvard faculty does not care about teaching.' According to a study of general education at Columbia, teachers have lost 'their common sense of what kind of ignorance is unacceptable.' As a result, 'Students reading Rabelais description of civil disturbances ascribe them to the French Revolution. A class of twenty-five had never heard of the Oedipus complex, or of Oedipus. Only one student in a class of fifteen could date the Russian Revolution within a decade' (Lasch, 1979:223).

Thus, in a time when standards were declining in the most elite institutions, placing blame or centering on compensatory programs was both unfair and racist. Moreover, with more of the general student population arriving unprepared for college, the defenders of compensatory programs argued for their expansion rather than their demise. Finally, although small numbers of students did manage to proceed along without acquiring basic skills, the high attrition rates of these programs belied this as a common occurrence, thus rejecting a major aspect of the conservative critique.

The defenders of compensatory higher education likewise rejected many of the radical claims. Although they did not disagree that tracking often occurred and that educational inequality was rarely significantly reduced, liberals refused to accept the inevitability of such outcomes. Rather, they suggested that the problems faced by compensatory programs were immense, difficult and complex, but not insurmountable. Roueche and Snow (1977), in their exhaustive examination of a national portrait of compensatory higher education programs, concluded that these reforms can and do succeed. They cited a number of model programs that increased retention and graduation rates to the point where between 40 - 60% of the students completed the program and go on for degrees[24], and argued that rather than dismantle these efforts, the colleges should have constructed similar programs that were geared to success. The authors recognized that a large number of programs did not provide for the successful transformation of opportunity into results. Their study, however, supported the hypothesis that it was indeed possible. Therefore, Roueche and Snow rejected the inevitability of failure, cited numerous successes, called for continued examination of the factors leading to what they termed the educational redemption of the underprepared student, and implementation of these factors into more effective programs.

By the mid 1970s, however, the support for continued exploration into the development of successful programs began to decline. The fiscal crises of higher education resulted in a constant assault on all types of liberal educational reform. Many of the experiments that had been initiated only a decade before began to face considerable criticism and budgetary cutbacks. Compensatory higher education and open enrollment programs, with their higher rate of attrition, their lower rates of student performance, and their high economic costs (especially in terms of student financial aid) were especially vulnerable. However, as Lavin et al. (1981:309) pointed out, the reasons for the assault on these programs were only partly economic. In the conclusion to their study of the CUNY Open Admissions experiment they noted the severe curtailment of the policy in the 1976 fiscal crisis. Enrollment standards were raised, retention standards were strengthened and more rigidly enforced, proficiency exams were instituted for movement to the junior level and tuition was imposed for the first time in CUNY's history. The authors concluded:

> this contraction of opportunity was not the inevitable result of the fiscal crisis. The budgetary axe fell with greater force on CUNY than on any other service within New York City, indicating clearly that the concept of universal higher education is far from universally accepted (1981-:309).

Lavin et al. suggested that these events, in part, represented the rejection of the underlying foundations of liberal educational reform and a return to more meritocratic and elitist definitions of postsecondary education.

The CUNY action represented a trend during the mid 1970s into the 1980s. During this period, both liberals and radicals defended the continuation of these reform programs and opposed their curtailment. Despite their critique of open admissions programs as reproducing inequality, many radical theorists argued that in lieu of major extra-educational reforms the expansion of higher education opportunity was vital. Compensatory educators continued to argue for the improvement of existing programs and the possibility of effective remediation. Moreover, empirical studies like Lavin's, while demonstrating that these programs often fell short of their intended goals, also indicated that they had real benefits.

Compensatory higher education programs developed within the context of the larger liberal educational reforms of the 1960s and 1970s. In the 1980s, faced with a conservative backlash against liberal reform in general and liberal educational reform, in particular, compensatory programs battled to maintain their presence on four-year college campuses. As part of the ongoing conservative critique concerning the decline of standards and the need to restore excellence, compensatory programs faced significant opposition. In order to understand this opposition, we first must look at the educational reforms of the 1980s.

Educational Reaction and Reform: 1980s–1990s

By the late 1970s, conservative critics began to react to the educational reforms of the 1960s–1970s. They argued that liberal reforms in pedagogy and curriculum and in the arena of educational opportunity had resulted in the decline of authority and standards. Furthermore, they stated that the preoccupation with using the schools to ameliorate social problems, however well intended, not only failed to do this but was part of an overall process that resulted in mass mediocrity. What was needed was nothing less than a complete overhaul of the American educational system. While radical critics also pointed to the failure of the schools to ameliorate problems of poverty, they located the problem not so much in the schools, but in society at large. Liberals defended the reforms of the period by suggesting that social improvement takes a long time, and a decade and a half was scarcely sufficient to turn things around.

In 1983, the National Commission on Excellence, founded by President Reagan's Secretary of Education, Terrel Bell, issued its now famous report, *A Nation at Risk*. This report provided a serious indictment of American education and cited high rates of adult illiteracy, declining SAT scores, and low scores on international comparisons of knowledge by American students as examples of the decline of literacy and standards. The Committee stated that "the educational foundations of our society are presently being eroded by a rising tide of mediocrity that threatens our very future as a Nation and a people" (1983:5). As solutions, the Commission offered five recommendations: (1) that all students graduating from high school complete what was termed the "new basics" — four years of English, three years of mathematics, three years of science, three years of social studies, and a half year of computer science; (2) that schools at all levels expect higher achievement from their students and that 4 year colleges and universities raise their admissions requirements; (3) that more time be devoted to teaching the new basics; (4) that the preparation of teachers be strengthened and that teaching be made a more respected and rewarded profession; and (5) that citizens require their elected representatives to support and fund these reforms (cited in Cremin, 1990:31).

The years following this report were characterized by scores of other reports that both supported the criticism and called for reform. During the 1980s significant attention was given to the improvement of curriculum, the tightening of standards, and the move towards the setting of academic goals and their assessment. A coalition of American governors took on a leading role in setting a reform agenda; business leaders stressed the need to improve the nation's schools and proposed partnership programs; the federal government, through its Secretary of Education (under Ronald Reagan), William Bennett, took an active and critical role but continued to argue that it was not the federal government's role to fund such reform; and educators, at all levels, struggled to have a say in determining the nature of the reforms.

The politics of the reform movement were complex and multidimensional. Conservatives wanted to restore both standards and the traditional curriculum; liberals demanded that the new drive for excellence not ignore the goals for equity; radicals believed it was another pendulum swing doomed to failure and one that sought to reestablish excellence as a code word for elitism. Although the bulk of the debates and reforms in the 1980s were aimed at primary and secondary education, conservative attacks on higher education continued throughout the decade. On the one hand, these attacks centered on the curriculum and the putative leftist orientation of college faculty. Critics like D'Souza (1991) and Kimball (1990) charged that universities were places where the free exchange of ideas was impossible due to a radical orthodoxy and so-called political correctness. Liberal and radical opponents countered that conservatives' claims about the lack of free exchange of ideas was a mask for their attempt to reclaim a traditional vision of knowledge. On the other hand, based on the conservative claim that the American educational system produced mediocrity and that a decline in standards and knowledge was a profound problem, higher education programs aimed at equity were subject to considerable criticism. If, according to conservative critics like Hirsch (1987) and Ravitch and Finn (1987), there was a widespread decline in cultural literacy and our seventeen year olds did not know very much, then higher education had to take a stand. Rather than merely continuing to pass along "know nothing" students, higher education had to return to its traditional role of promulgating excellence.

In response to these charges, many universities placed excellence on the front burner and programs concerned with equity on the back burner. Many universities returned to core curricula, admissions standards and graduation requirements were often tightened, and, most importantly, as part of the widespread cutback during the Reagan and Bush administrations of social programs, funding for financial aid and compensatory programs was curtailed. Thus, the emphasis on academic excellence combined with significant loss of funding, left compensatory programs struggling to survive.

To some degree, compensatory programs became easy targets for those arguing that higher education had produced mass mediocrity. The arguments used against mass higher education in the 1960s reemerged, and critics suggested that such programs had systematically lowered admissions requirements and did not significantly make up for precollege deficiencies. Whereas the attacks on compensatory programs in the 1960s and 1970s were often aimed at the primarily minority and working class students in these programs, the conservative critics in the 1980s widened their scope. Mediocrity, they argued, was widespread and not reserved to minority and working class students, but was symptomatic of American education in general. Thus, as universities faced with declining pools of traditional age students in the 1980s reached further down into their applicant pool to survive, it became obvious that underpreparation was not simply a minority issue alone.

Interestingly, in the 1980s, as financial support for traditional compensatory programs declined (that is, for minority and working class students), many colleges and universities set up programs for underprepared students, many of whom were white and middle class. The contradiction between conservative calls for tighter admission standards and the economic need to admit students who were underprepared resulted in a significant irony. When it became necessary to admit underprepared students for financial survival, the hue and cry that accompanied open admissions in the 1960s disappeared. Moreover, in order to deal with the apparent contradiction between the call for excellence and the admission of underprepared students, some universities relied on a unique philosophical nexus of liberal and conservative ideas. One administrator, summarizing the need to balance equity and excellence, called for "democratic elitism," a system that would allow anyone into college, but allow only those who truly deserved it to graduate.[25]

Thus, in the 1980s, there were countervailing trends that defined the tensions between the call for excellence on the one hand and the need to recruit students on the other. Although some might argue that equity was still a significant concern, and on some campuses it was, the admission of underprepared students during this decade, in general, had less to do with concern for social justice and more with balancing budgets. The 1980s were not a good time for working class and minority students. Studies of community colleges (Brint and Karabel, 1989; Dougherty, 1987, 1992) indicated that, as the traditional educators of working class and minority students, they have been less than effective in providing access to four-year colleges. Furthermore, recent studies of African-American and Latino students in higher education in the 1980s (Allen, 1992; Thomas, 1992) pointed out significant barriers to the academic success of these students, especially in dominantly white colleges.

As we moved into the 1990s the question of access to higher education as a policy concern has reemerged. After a decade where questions of equity were overshadowed by an obsessive preoccupation with excellence, it is not clear that there will be widespread support for liberal educational reforms. Although much of the reform rhetoric speaks to issues of equity, especially as they relate to the improvement of urban schools, the current fiscal crisis significantly has limited postsecondary efforts to meet the needs of minority and working class students.

The fiscal crisis has already reduced these students' options. As public universities faced with significant reductions in state funding limit the size of their student populations, students from lower socioeconomic backgrounds have fewer choices.[26] Whereas middle class students are often capable of attending private universities, which continue to compete feverishly for paying customers, students who require substantial financial aid to attend private institutions are often prevented from attending postsecondary institutions. Additionally, the shift away from need based scholarships in many private institutions toward merit scholarships makes it difficult for underprepared students to attend private universities, unless they can pay full tuition. The contradiction between the call for excellence and the admission of these students (underprepared but financially able) has not been addressed for obvious pragmatic reasons. For the students for whom compensatory higher education programs first emerged, minority and working class students, the cruel irony of accepting underprepared students who can pay and curtailing access for those who cannot has not yet resulted in policies leading to increased access and opportunity.[27]

Allen (1992:42–43), commenting on the prospects for African-American students, stated:

> Far reaching, enduring change in higher education for African-American students will only come about when universities come to feel more keenly about their responsibility for changing the system of unequal societal relationships based on race. Universities must also become more proactive and deliberate in the actions taken to address barriers to African-American success in their institutions. Thus the challenge confronting U. S. colleges and universities now and into the twenty-first century is to achieve the promise of the high ideals of equality, representation, and solidarity in a culturally pluralistic society. If we fail to respond creatively and effectively to this challenge, not only will history judge us harshly, but this country will continue to suffer the negative consequences, such as the loss of its competitive edge in the world market, that have resulted from its failure to develop fully and utilize the talents of all of its people, without regard to race, gender, or class.

Allen eloquently addressed the policy concerns that were the basis of liberal educational reforms initiated twenty-five years ago. That he reiterates them today shows how much progress still needs to be made.

NOTES

1. For a discussion of the history of liberal educational reform see Bowles and Gintis (1976:Part III). For a discussion of the history of debates over liberal education reform see Cremin (1990:Chapter 1).

2. For a critical discussion of meritocracy and selection see Persell (1977:Chapters 3-5). In addition, for a detailed analysis of the issues relating to college selection see Karabel (1972b:30-44).

3. See for example, Lavin, Alba, and Silberstein (1981:Chapter 5) for a discussion of the effects of the open admissions policy on the composition of the student population at CUNY. In addition, Cross (1971:Chapter 1) provides a comprehensive portrait of the "new" students in higher education in the 1970s.

4. For detailed discussions see Hurn (1993:Chapters 5, 6) and Persell (1977).

5. The classic statement of this position appears in Davis and Moore (1945:249-299).

6. Although conflict theory and neo-Marxist theory share a number of common arguments there are significant differences between them. Conflict theory is a more multidimensional perspective and is based in part on the work of Max Weber. For a complete treatment of this perspective and its differences from neo-Marxist theory see Collins (1975).

7. For a detailed discussion of dialectical method and analysis see Boguslaw and Vickers (1977).

8. Bowles and Gintis (1976:104-108) provides a critical discussion of the role of education in the legitimation of inequality.

9. Wolfe (1977), provides a comprehensive analysis of legitimation crisis.

10. Two books illustrate these predictions very well: Heller (1973) and Wagner (1976).

11. For a detailed account of the types of developmental programs and methods that were implemented see Roueche and Snow (1977). In addition, Shaughnessy (1977), presents a personal account of the difficulties faced by underprepared students. Her description of the implementation of the CUNY remedial writing programs provides substantial evidence concerning the levels of educational disadvantage and the challenges and difficulties facing compensatory educators. For a poignant autobiographical account of the difficulties of teaching in these programs and the problems faced by underprepared students see Rose (1989).

12. See for example, Hurn (1993:Chapters 5, 6); Ogbu (1978); and Persell (1977).

13. See Hurn (1993:145-164) and Sadovnik, Cookson, Jr. and Semel (1994:Chapter 9) for detailed discussions.

14. The "Moynihan Report," (1965) raised controversial questions about the family and cultural deprivation. More recently, Lareau (1989) analyzes the relationships between family and school, using Bourdieu's concept of cultural capital.

15. Two central sources on cultural deprivation and difference theory are Riesman (1962) and Bloom, Davis, and Hess (1965). For a critique of these theories see Baratz and Baratz (1970:29-50).

16. For the classic statement of linguistic codes and education see Bernstein (1973a). For a critical and retrospective discussion of code theory see Bernstein (1990:94-130). For further critical analyses of Bernstein's work in general and code theory in particular, see Atkinson (1985); Danzig (1992:285-300); and Sadovnik (1991:48-63; 1994).

17. See Persell (1977:Chapters 1-3).

18. Ogbu (1978) provides a comprehensive analysis of the relationship between caste and inequality of educational performance.

19. See for example, Roueche and Kirk (1973) and Cross (1976) for a detailed account of the types of developmental strategies designed for the underprepared and disadvantaged college student.

20. Roueche and Snow (1977:Chapters 1–3) review the state of the art of developmental higher education and suggest a number of important factors affecting programmatic success. See also Rose (1989) for a discussion of the politics of pedagogy for underprepared students.

21. For a review of the precollege studies on educational placement see Bryson and Bentley (1980) and Carlberg and Kavale (1980:296–309). See Gartner and Lipsky (1987) for a discussion of the problems of special education placement.

22. See Lavin et al. (1981:Chapters 6, 7); and Roueche and Snow (1977:Chapters 1–2) for a discussion of the academic progress of open admissions type students.

23. See Hurn (1993:Chapter 5) and Persell (1977:Chapters 3, 4) for a complete discussion.

24. The data presented by Roueche and Snow is often unclear and does not present a conclusive picture of completion rates. Nonetheless, these figures represent the best approximation of these data.

25. This term was used in an in house document justifying the existence of a university's program for underprepared college students.

26. See Carter and Wilson (1992) for a discussion of these trends. Also, see American Council on Education (1988) for a discussion of minority participation in education and American life.

27. See Orfield (1992:337–372) for a discussion of the decline of financial aid and the limits to access in the 1980s. See also Orfield and Ashkinaze (1991) for an analysis of conservative policy in the 1980s and its effect on black opportunity.

3

THE EDUCATIONAL OPPORTUNITY DIVISION AT STATE COLLEGE: EGALITARIAN EDUCATION ON AN ELITE CAMPUS

The Main Campus: State College

State College is a four-year undergraduate college within a major state university system offering both professional training in the arts, leading to the BFA, and liberal arts programs leading to the BA. The School of the Arts consists of professional divisions of visual arts, theater and design technology, music and dance. The College of Letters and Science consists of the divisions of natural sciences, social sciences, humanities and, until 1983, educational opportunity.

State College, which officially opened in 1971,[1] was designed as an innovative higher educational institution offering an elite model of education within a public college. The State College liberal arts program, in its formative years, most closely resembled colleges such as Swarthmore and Reed, with junior examinations and senior theses and emphasized the undergraduate program as a training ground for "junior academics." The School of the Arts programs provides conservatory training for professional students and are extremely selective in their admissions. Moreover, the conservatory programs are almost entirely closed to non-professional students, creating two separate schools at State College, one in the arts and one in the liberal arts.

The most important feature of liberal arts education at State College during the years covered in this study was the combination of the elite nature of its programs with a set of "radical" educational innovations. The junior field examination and the senior theses required all students to demonstrate scholarly competence as the sole path to the bachelor's degree. In addition, individualized programs, small class size, an honors pass, no credit grading system, and an innovative academic calendar (12/4, 12/4 with the short term for special projects) were all implemented as radical educational alternatives.

The elite and radical quality of education at State College was the subject of continuous debate and controversy in the first 12 years of its history. Faculty critics of State College education argued that its radical facade disguised a conservative nature, and more importantly that it had failed to meet the mission of public education to maximize access and provide some programs which lead to specific career paths. These critics proposed alternative tracks to the bachelor's degree and the institution of some career oriented programs in pre-law, education, business, and social work. However, a powerful segment of the faculty defended State College's innovative structure and resisted any dilution of its scholarly standards or innovative methods.

As Grant and Riesman (1978) pointed out in their study of higher educational reform, the innovative reforms at many colleges and universities resulted in the continual definition and redefinition of the purposes of higher education. The development and implementation of educational innovation requires the defense of an educational ideology to legitimate the purpose of the college and the perception of its difference. This has certainly been the case at State College, where the *elite public college* image has been its central organizational philosophy. As Etzkowitz and Fashing pointed out:

> There seems to be a widespread assumption on the State College campus that the liberal arts program is qualitatively superior to any of the other state schools and most private schools. The President has been known to refer to it as the 'Harvard of the state university system.' This sentiment (without convincing supporting evidence) had led to the assumption among many faculty and students that the campus should occupy a special status among the several state university campuses. This status would entail, among other things, a level of support higher than for other campuses in order to maintain this differential. Such sentiments are shared by students who have already developed a sense of the elite status of the campus. Editorials in the student newspaper have frequently noted the original 'special commitments' to State College and have regularly argued that the college should have educational perquisites in the form of a lower student-faculty ratio, superior to other colleges in the state system (1977:10–14).

Although the creation of elite public institutions is not unique, at least in terms of high academic standards (for example, Wisconsin, Michigan, Berkeley), the combination of radical educational innovation and Swarthmore type liberal arts education posed a problem for the defenders of this tradition. Etzkowitz and Fashing (1977:8) pointed to the irony of a state college using public money to "sustain a dying tradition," while many private elite colleges moved closer to public models of higher education with a more career oriented curriculum.

The evolution of the educational program at State College further supported Grant and Riesman's (1978) description of the decline of innovation. While some programs steadfastly maintained their innovations, others like State College adapted to the demands placed upon it. By the 1981–82 academic year, the junior field examinations were eliminated in some divisions, the senior theses scaled down in some divisions, the academic calendar changed to a traditional 16/16 format, and the institution of an A–F grading system was adopted campus-wide. These changes were the result of emotional deliberations and lengthy conflicts. Although they did not change the character of State College, they certainly altered it. Nonetheless, State College could still be characterized as a public college with a perception of itself as an elite institution. While the battles concerning its elitism and its curriculum were on-going, its special character remained. It is within this context that the analysis of its educational opportunity division takes its central meaning.

Compensatory Higher Education at State College: Elite versus Egalitarian Education

The discussion of compensatory higher education stressed the question of the philosophy of higher education. Many critics of these programs pointed to the debasing of the meritocratic system and the inevitable lowering of standards. Others, defenders of remedial college education (Roueche and Snow, 1977), argued that colleges had to change their underlying assumptions about the functions of higher education and develop innovative organizational structures and processes to meet the special needs of the underprepared college student.

The elite versus egalitarian model is central to the analysis of the educational opportunity program at State College. The elite model stressed the defense of traditional standards of excellence and the importance of particular types of curriculum to a college education.[2] The elite tradition, while not necessarily opposed to compensatory higher education, firmly believed that students must fit into the standards and expectations of the college. The egalitarian model (the perspective that defends compensatory higher education) emphasized the social responsibility of higher education to ameliorate the educational problems associated with precollege schooling and suggested that colleges had to adapt to the needs of its population.

The existence of a compensatory program based on egalitarian educational philosophy on a campus defining itself as an elite public institution provides an important opportunity to analyze the conflicts and contradictions between these two adversarial systems. While an elite college does not by definition oppose a compensatory program, it certainly would define certain expectations for excellence and create a particular attitude about the type of education that occurs in its environment. As Roueche and Snow (1977) pointed out, the success of compensatory programs to a large degree was dependent on the level of institutional support that exists on the campus. Lavin, Alba and Silberstein (1981), Marshak and Wirtenberg (1981) and Gross (1978) all pointed to the conflicts within the open admission program at City University of New York surrounding the concept of academic standards. Despite institutional support for egalitarian ideals and the development of a system-wide program to integrate remedial programs while maintaining excellence, significant resistance and opposition existed, with many faculty believing that traditional standards were being destroyed. Since the level of institutional support was a major factor in determining the success of compensatory programs, and elite conceptions of higher education were likely to produce negative attitudes concerning their existence, then the conflict between the elite model of education at State College and the egalitarian principles of its educational opportunity program is a central theme in this analysis. As Etzkowitz and Fashing (1977) suggested, the emergence of an opportunity program on the State College campus provided a serious challenge to the college, as it would have to deal with students who did not meet its lofty educational expectations.

The Educational Opportunity Division

The Educational Opportunity Division (EOD) of State College was a separate two-year lower divisional compensatory program in the College of Letters and Science. It began as Coop College, the off-campus educational opportunity program jointly run by State College and two neighboring private colleges in 1969, and was located in a minority community about fifteen miles from the State College campus. For nine years it served a local community population, but by 1976–1977 declining enrollments, budgetary constraints, and state educational officials' pressure resulted in the move to the main campus.

The first nine years at Coop College provided the educational foundation for the division. Although the move to the main campus necessitated a shift in the student population from adult to traditional aged students,[3] the program that began at State College in 1978 was the result of years of conflict, debate and planning and, according to its faculty, was unique in its organization.[4] Moreover, the program was designed to ensure the successful preparation of the educationally and economically disadvantaged student.

Educational Organization and Philosophy

The discussion of compensatory higher education pointed to two differing models. The first, the *integrative programs* model, provided remedial and developmental courses, as well as counseling and tutorial support services to the underprepared student population, but mainstreamed these students into regular discipline courses from the freshman year. This type provides for *regular* placement of the underprepared student, with the educational opportunity program providing remedial and support services to enhance academic performance. The second, the *holistic model*, provided *separate* placement of the population into a homogeneous and independent unit of the college. Acting like a special education program at the college level, the holistic model provided a complete preparatory curriculum designed to mainstream students into the regular college with the requisite skills for success. The Educational Opportunity Division at State College was an example of this type of program.

The reasons for a separate division at State College were twofold. First, since the program developed as a separate division of the campus as Coop College it retained its separate character upon the move to the main campus. Second, the educational philosophy of the program supported the belief that underprepared students needed a specially trained faculty within all courses, with skills development and content integrated, in order to develop and strengthen their educational foundation. The purpose of this organizational framework was to avoid placing underprepared students in courses that were too demanding, given their educational deficiencies. Rejecting the belief that remediation (skills courses) and college level courses were separate, the Educational Opportunity Division stressed that the integration of academic skills and discipline content within all courses was the necessary ingredient in the development of the educational foundation, vital for the completion of the college degree.

This educational philosophy was critical of the integrative model of compensatory higher education. It suggested that placing students into regular college classes without developing their academic skills was begging for failure. As Roueche and Snow (1977:10) pointed out, to place a student with a ninth grade reading level into a course that demands the mastery of

Plato, Marx, Freud, etc. in the original texts was to set the student up for problems. Second, to believe that a few remedial courses could bridge the gap did not begin to respond to the needs of this population. Therefore, the EOD believed that a separate division that is committed to the needs of the underprepared student was the proper organizational framework. Pointing to the revolving door of academic failure characteristic of many compensatory programs, the division believed that the holistic model was best suited for success.

The holistic model employed by the Educational Opportunity Division had two major goals for its students. First, the division required that all students completed a 56 credit lower divisional curriculum designed especially for its particular population. Second, the division believed that one of its primary goals was to prepare its students for the successful completion of the college degree by providing the necessary educational foundation for success at State College. This latter goal was the most significant aspect of the division's mission. Its entire educational philosophy, organization and processes were geared to the dual task of compensating for precollege educational deficiencies and providing the necessary knowledge base for mainstreaming at the junior level. That is, the program was designed to place students directly into the junior year at State College, upon the completion of the division's requirements. In fact, the division actually served as a "community college" liberal arts transfer program on the main campus.

Student Population and Admissions

The Educational Opportunity Division recruited students from the metropolitan area surrounding State College. While the State College Admissions Office did some admissions work for the division,[5] the division maintained its own admissions process through the registrar's office. From 1978–1982, due to continued budgetary problems, the college reduced the division's recruiting budget and eliminated its recruiting position. By the 1981–82 academic year, the EOD director, the EOD registrar and the counseling office handled the majority of admissions work.[6]

State Educational Opportunity Guidelines strictly defined the admissions criteria for educational opportunity students. Since the state provided financial assistance to students designated as EOP students, the admissions requirements necessitated both *educational and economic disadvantages*.[7] While the majority of divisional students met these criteria, about 15% per academic year were admitted on the basis of educational disadvantagement alone. Although these students were full-time members of the Educational Opportunity Division, they were not considered EOP students for state auditing purposes, and by law were not eligible for any state EOP funds or special EOP services like the reading program, the counseling services, and the tutorial services.[8] In the following pages, therefore, *EOD* students refers to the students in the division who meet the State Educational Opportunity Program guidelines for EOP aid.

The state educational opportunity guidelines defined the concept of *inadmissability* as the major requirement for acceptance to the college's educational opportunity program. That is, a student had to meet both tests of educational and economic disadvantage *and* be declared inadmissable by the college's regular admissions office. Therefore, all students in the educational opportunity program had to technically be rejected by the State College admissions office before they were offered admissions to the EOD.

The EOD provided a series of criteria to judge the applications of prospective students. Since one of the admission requirements for State College was approximately an 85 high school average,[9] students with averages below this level were candidates for the division. The EOD, however, was not an *open admissions* program, as potential for academic success was a major requirement. Students with academic and psychological profiles that did not indicate the possibility of handling college work were not admitted. The State College self-study accreditation report stated the following concerning EOD admissions policy:

> In attempting to admit students who will receive maximum benefits from the program, EOD uses its own guidelines for admissions. All applicants to the EOD division must be educationally disadvantaged; an applicant's high school academic profile must fall short of standards required for admission to the College through the regular channels. The highest allowable high school average is 84, unless it is determined that the applicant's high school evaluations were weighted to conceal academic deficiencies. With few exceptions, the highest allowable average of the SAT is 450 (1981a:3).

The applicants were given a series of tests to evaluate the extent of their educational weaknesses. Included were reading, writing, and mathematics examinations which were used both for admissions decisions and for student placement. Finally, interviews with the counseling staff were required to evaluate the candidate's attitude toward higher education and commitment to academic success.

An examination of the freshman classes for 1978–1979, 1979––1980, 1980–1981 and 1981–1982 reveals that the division was admitting the population that the state's guidelines intended. That is, the program was offering educational opportunity to students who were educationally underprepared.[10] Secondly, although the state guidelines did not specify that their intent was to provide opportunities specifically for minority students, the program's administration often stated that this was an implicit intent, at least for those colleges with large minority communities in their immediate geographic location.[11] The admissions data for this period certainly supports the program's intent to fulfill this implicit goal and its success in meeting it. Table 3.1 presents admissions data for this period:

TABLE 3.1 SUMMARY OF EOD ADMISSIONS DATA 1978–1981

	Fall 1978	Fall 1979	Fall 1980	Fall 1981
Number	88	94	108	93
Race:				
White	7%	5%	4%	15%
Non-white	93%	95%	96%	85%
High School GPA	74.5	74.3	74.4	74.3
Reading Scores: California Achievement Tests	11.1	12.2	12.1	11.6

The data indicates that the program was accepting minority students with educational deficiencies. The comparisons of reading and writing tests results[12] for the entire college (given for the first time in 1981), while indicating some overlap, shows that EOD students were significantly below regular admissions students in reading and writing scores. The high school averages were approximately 10 points (on average) below the minimum admissions requirement for State College. Most importantly, the California Achievement Test scores, while indicating real deficits, did not demonstrate extreme overall deficiencies. While many open admissions programs admitted students with below 9th grade reading levels, the average levels of between 11–12 for all years show that a significant number of students was reading at or near senior high school level. While the program admitted students below ninth grade level, the overall data supports the program's intent of admitting students with the potential to succeed.

Educational Philosophy and Practice: The Achievement of Goals

The Educational Opportunity Division attempted to fulfill its dual mission of academic preparation and knowledge building through its curriculum, pedagogy and support services. The relationship between philosophy and practice was summarized in the writings of its faculty:

> The educational experience in the Educational Opportunity Division must provide a demanding program of study for its students. The program must address itself to the various teaching methods appropriate to the special needs of the population. It is incumbent that our students compensate for past educational difficulties by developing academic and intellectual skills within the division....The population educated by this division has not performed well when evaluated by traditional educational models and more often than not has failed to master the skills deemed necessary by our educational system. It is the mission of this division not only to improve the use of these skills, but to develop alternative models to succeed, where traditional models have not. Further, this division must simultaneously develop those skills particular to our population, many of which have been untapped and/or not subject to evalua-tion.... The goals of the division should lead to the formu-lation of methods that attempt to integrate traditional and innovative methods of educational achievement. In relation to the former, it is the task of our program to insure the ability of every student to master basic academic skills, such as reading and writing, and to require proficiency in these areas before the completion of the program. Further, our students must master college level abilities in research and paper writing. However, we cannot limit ourselves to

> these academic processes or to the notion of mastery of
> content and information, but should forge ahead in develop-
> ing an overall sense of intellectual process, and an appreci-
> ation and commitment to intellectual craft and the acquisi-
> tion of critical skills. That is, the division should not limit
> itself to the teaching of basic technical skills or to the
> mastery of content, but as importantly address itself to the
> critical process of educating in developing within students
> analytical and critical thinking abilities (1981c:5).

Therefore, the divisional philosophy transcended the remedial and developmental aspects of compensatory education and defined its goals in the
broadest tradition of liberal arts education.

The implementation of divisional goals, according to the faculty,
was in part achieved through its curriculum. The EOD philosophy suggested
that the dual goals of *compensation and preparation* and a broad *liberal arts
background* were accomplished through a series of academic requirements
combining skills and content in divisional courses and specific forms of
remediation in others.

The EOD curriculum was designed to meet its two major educational goals of academic compensation and preparation and the building of a
strong liberal arts foundation. Through an integrated curriculum offering
both skills and discipline courses, the program attempted to fulfill these
objectives. Unlike most compensatory programs where remediation in skills
courses was separate from college level discipline courses, the EOD offered
both separate remedial courses and college level discipline courses that
stressed the integration of skills and content. It was this *skills-content*
synthesis that provided an important core of the divisional educational
philosophy and was its major claim concerning its difference from other
programs. Therefore, it was not only the separate organizational structure
that supported the claimed difference, but its particular curricular and
pedagogical offerings.

The Skills-Content Synthesis

Probably the most important and yet misunderstood aspect of the divisional
educational philosophy was the concept of *skills-content synthesis*. While
most compensatory programs offer "remedial" or "developmental" courses
to build academic skills, the division believed that basic skills could not be
taught in isolation. Therefore, the division purported that all of its academic
courses (discipline courses in sociology, history, literature, biology, etc.)

combined the teaching of the content of the discipline with the teaching of basic reading, writing and where appropriate, mathematics skills.

The significance of the skills-content synthesis cannot be stressed enough, as it gave meaning to the division's insistence on a separate program with faculty in all disciplines. As we will see, the integration of basic skills into discipline courses raised the thorny issue of college level acceptability.[13] The division firmly believed that its discipline courses combined college level content with an emphasis on supporting the developmental skills offered in developmental courses.

The Three-Day Schedule and Teaching Load: Labor Intensive Education

A second feature of the divisional methods designed to maximize success was its longer teaching schedule. Whereas the State College classes met two days per week for 1.5 hours per class for four credits (3 hours/4 credits), the EOD classes met three days per week for 1.5 hours per class for 4 credits (4.5 hours/4 credits).[14] The purpose of this difference was summarized by a member of the program's faculty:

> In order to take students with academic deficiencies and prepare them properly for the junior level, we need more time. The three day teaching schedule allows us to cover the same amount of material in a semester (as the regular courses) but with sufficient time to bring the students up to an equal level.

Another faculty member addressed to this same issue:

> The three-day schedule is a core aspect of the program. It provides the time to combine skills and content. It would not be possible to do what we do in a shorter time period.

In addition to the three-day schedule, the division's faculty taught a heavier load than other State College faculty. Where regular[15] faculty taught five courses per academic year plus the supervision of senior theses, the EOD faculty taught six courses. When computing the differences in meeting times, this resulted in a sizeable difference in teaching load and hours per semester. The State College faculty taught between 6 and 9 hours per semester, while the EOD faculty taught between 12 and 13.5 hours per semester.

The heavy teaching schedule for the divisional faculty was

augmented by the labor intensive nature of divisional teaching. Because the underprepared student needed more assistance than class time allowed, faculty devoted considerable time to tutorial sessions. Additionally, every faculty member was required to be on campus four full days per week for this purpose, leaving one day free for office hours. In some disciplines, particularly English and mathematics, it was not unusual for faculty to schedule weekly tutorial sessions with every student.

These educational demands on faculty were central to the division's mission. It believed that only through the active participation and availability of its teachers could the underprepared student receive the necessary services to ensure academic success. The division's guidelines for promotion, retention, and tenure stressed these qualities above all other academic pursuits, with traditional professional obligations such as publications given secondary importance. These guidelines explicitly stated that the division's population required a teaching faculty and that the requirement for publication should be deemphasized in order to devote the required time to instruction. Some, in fact, felt that publishing and teaching in the division did not complement each other. As the program's director stated:

> I do not want a math teacher with a Ph.D. in linear modeling to teach in this program. He will get bored and his first interest will be his research. I want someone, regardless of credentials [meaning without a Ph.D.], who can and wants to teach basic mathematics to our students.

As we will see later, the conflicts between teaching and research, the heavy teaching schedule and the autonomy of divisional guidelines were sources of substantial conflict that raised central issues in the philosophy of higher education. For now, it is important to note that all of these aspects of the program were defined by its members as necessary to its educational mission and are examples of the implementation of educational practices that reflect a set of organizational goals.

The Educational Opportunity Division implemented its educational philosophy through its separate curriculum. The intent of the course offerings was to combine remediation and content through a complete liberal arts program. Students were required to complete 56 credits and a series of requirements in order to move to the junior level at State College. Upon admission to the program students were placed into sections and levels based on their admissions tests.

According to the 1981–82 curriculum section of the EOD handbook, the following curriculum was offered:[16]

The Curriculum of the program requires the following:

1.   All students must take the basic English
     and mathematics sequence:

English
Two semesters of course work (XEN101 and XEN102)
XEN 101 - Critical Reading and Writing

This is a basic introductory writing course that stresses the relationship between reading and writing. Students are required to write weekly papers of increasing sophistication from a set of reading materials. The English faculty stresses the importance of writing from reading materials rather than free writing. This course introduces the concepts of summary, analysis, criticism, comparison, and contrast and stresses organization in writing.

English 102 - Synthesis, Selection and Research
This course continues the introduction to college level writing and stresses the production of papers from a series of readings. The skills of comparison and contrast, integration, synthesis, and selection are covered in the first half of the course. The second part of the course introduces library research skills and requires the completion of a short (8–10 pages) research paper with full documentation and bibliographic citations.

Writing Workshops
The English Department requires writing workshops of all students with sentence-level deficiencies. These courses stress elementary rules of grammar and organization and are intended to eliminate basic skills problems.

Mathematics
Two semesters of course work are required (XMA101 and 102). Students with serious deficiencies in arithmetic (determined by the diagnostic placement test) are required to take XMA100. Students who major in math and science are required to take XMA103. Elective courses and math workshops are offered.

Mathematics Courses:
Math 100 - Math Concepts An introduction to basic arithmetic concepts. This course is designed to compensate for mathematical deficiencies and provide the foundation for further work in mathematics.
Math 101 - Elementary Algebra and Trigonometry
Math 102 - Intermediate Algebra and Trigonometry
Math 103 - College Algebra and Trigonometry
Math 107 (Elective) - Analytic Geometry and Pre-Calculus
Math Workshops

2.   All students must complete one year (two courses) in *three* of the following four areas: Language, Science, Social Sciences, and Humanities. These discipline courses are designated as *skills intensive*, that is combining content and skills.

Language
Introduction to Spanish I
Introduction to Spanish II
Introduction to French I
Introduction to French II

Science
One semester of Physical Science and one semester of Life Science. Science majors may be exempt from these two courses and substitute Introductory Biology I and II and/or Introductory Chemistry I and II. Placement is based on placement scores.

Humanities
The distribution requirement is two courses. The Division offers a variety of lower divisional courses in history, literature, writing, and philosophy.

Social Sciences
The distribution requirement is two courses. The Division offers a variety of lower divisional courses in political science, psychology, and sociology.

3. *Communication Skills*

Students with reading deficiencies (determined by the reading inventories given to incoming students) are required to take Communication Skills in order to attain college level reading skills. Students must repeat this course (non-credit) until they attain college level proficiency.

4. *Freshman Orientation: College Survival Skills*

The objective of this seminar (non-credit) is to impart both learning and personal adjustment skills to entering students. Every entering student must take this course.

5. *Research Paper*[17]

A major research paper, which is acceptable to an instructor in an appropriate discipline, is required before a student is approved for junior status.

Curricular Methods: Toward a Successful Developmental Education

The division's curriculum was designed to offer students a broad sequence of courses designed to build a solid foundation for college work. However, it was the special methods within these courses that the proponents of the program saw as its major strength. The skills-content synthesis, the extra class time, the intensive tutorial system, and the special emphasis on *writing* in all appropriate courses was a central claim of divisional methodology.

The division's statement to the New York State accreditation committee reflected its special concern with a methodology appropriate to its population:

> The methodology and its consequences become apparent when they are discussed in relation to various academic areas.... In foreign languages increasing grammatical complexities are avoided. Basic grammar (which the students need badly) is stressed. There is a great deal of oral drill which permits the student to become comfortable with the spoken language. The grammar reinforces sen-

tence level work that is done by the English faculty. A primary aim of the language program is that students should become sufficiently proficient at elementary communication so they can use language as a tool for other studies (1981a:12).

In Humanities and Social Sciences instructors pursue several goals: to introduce students to the discipline, to acquaint them with a certain body of knowledge, and to develop the understanding and thinking skills in each particular discipline. Writing assignments are frequent. Students begin with writing short papers in their first semester, and progress to research papers in the more advanced courses. A number of instructors in the program (Humanities/Social Sciences) also teach in the English sequence, which makes for close coordination between skills work done there and the demands made in the discipline.

The Natural Science program also stresses methodology. Since the method of science is inductive, laboratories are of primary importance. Here students learn to observe and record. Confidence and control emerge when they are able to work through an independent approach to a problem. In addition to the use of the laboratory, there is a body of knowledge to be mastered which requires the student to read for information, to retain it and to integrate it with lecture and laboratory material (1981a:12-13).

Mathematics and English present the student with an array of skills which may be called for in various disciplines. Both areas offer a sequential series. The student enters at the appropriate level determined by a placement exam. By and large, discipline courses for incoming students draw on skills practiced at the beginning of Math and English sequences; courses for sophomores use the more advanced skills (1981a:14).

In Mathematics, while computational skills are sharpened and the habit of precision is acquired, students also learn to think through a logical sequence of steps and observe their thought processes. While they master alternative algebraic methods, they move towards concepts that are increasingly abstract. Students' perspectives are sharpened when they see that there are several mathematical methods which will achieve a single goal. Besides the obvious application to the natural sciences, and other quantitative areas, these skills often carry over to paper writing, in particular paper planning which requires a series of logical steps and the ability to move comfortably from general to specific (1981a:14).

Similarly in English, while sentence skills are addressed at each level, students are asked to move towards increasing complexity in both thought and execution. The student learns that there are various kinds of reading which are suited to several disciplines. Writing, too, must respond to a demand. With practice, the skills become adaptable, fluent, and under student's control. With writing skills in hand, a student should be able to undertake sustained independent tasks with assurance (1981a:15).

These statements illustrated an educational philosophy that attempted to develop a curriculum and methodology to fulfill its educational goals and meet the special needs of its population. This philosophy resulted in what the faculty considered an integrated curriculum with the skills taught in one subject reinforced and augmented in other subjects. Both curriculum and methods were designed to prepare students for the demands of the independent work required at State College.

The Counseling Office

The research on student performance in compensatory programs demonstrated that the disadvantaged learner faced more than educational problems.[18] Although there was little consensus in the research, a variety of themes may be discerned:

1.   The disadvantaged student was handicapped by poor academic skills and this plays a significant role in his/her ability to succeed at the college level.

2.   While skills problems were considerable, the psychological and economic problems faced by these high risk students were equally

responsible for educational failure. On the psychological level, poor self-concept and fear of failure and/or success were often barriers to academic success. On the economic level, financial problems were often major factors in student attrition.[19]

3.   Therefore, proponents of compensatory higher education stressed the importance of support services to help students deal with these problems (Roueche and Snow 1977).

The Educational Opportunity Division addressed these issues through its counseling program. The Counseling Office consisted of two full-time general academic counselors (GAC) who dealt with the complex relationship between psychological and academic problems. Although the counselors dealt primarily with academic progress, they attempted to grapple with students' psychological and economic problems as well.[20] Every student was assigned a counselor and the counseling staff attempted to meet with every student at least once per semester.

Faculty Committees and Meetings

In addition to regular teaching, advising, and tutorial responsibilities, the division's faculty comprised its two major committees, the curriculum committee and the committee on academic performance (CAP). Although the division's administration had final decision-making power, the division was run by the faculty. The Director's office took responsibility for admissions, and the complex bureaucratic monitoring required by state educational opportunity law; the faculty controlled curricular and educational decisions through its committee system. The faculty met in committees twice each month; in addition, the entire EOD faculty met on a monthly basis, with a State College faculty meeting scheduled once each month. In addition, departmental meetings of the division's programs (English, Language, Math/Science/Humanities/Social Sciences) were held as needed. Once every semester, town meetings with students were held. The core of divisional business was introduced, debated, and resolved[21] at faculty and committee meetings.

The Curriculum Committee was the central mechanism for the review of educational policy and instructional methods. This committee was charged with developing and approving courses, scheduling classes, crediting courses,[22] and evaluating their appropriateness for the division's population. The committee also assumed responsibility for articulation with other divisions concerning the integration of curriculum on a college-wide basis.[23] In theory, the committee was responsible for the discussion and implementation of methods and pedagogy, but did not function in this respect.[24]

Although State College has an academic progress committee, the Educational Opportunity Division had its own committee to monitor student performance and progress. The Committee on Academic Performance consisted of faculty and counseling staff and was charged with the evaluation of every student's progress. The Committee reviewed each student's folder on a semester-to-semester basis to monitor academic performance (satisfactory progress[25]) and the fulfilling of requirements. In addition, the committee sent out letters of warning, probation, and dismissal for students with academic difficulty and commendations to students with high academic records. Moreover, the committee reviewed candidates for completion of the program and recommended students for the transition to junior level. Although the work involved in these processes was extraordinary,[26] the division believed that only through its own separate academic progress committee could it provide the close attention that students in the division required.

The Holistic Program: Toward A Successful Compensatory Program

The Educational Opportunity Division considered itself a complete program in terms of meeting the needs of the underprepared student. Through a curriculum designed specifically for its population, a faculty committed to teaching disadvantaged students, and an integration of administrative, counseling, and faculty efforts, the program hoped to close the revolving door characteristic of these types of programs. The division was a holistic model in that it provided the entire experience for its students, including remediation, instruction in disciplines, counseling and advisement. The basic premise was that underprepared students needed this type of total effort to prepare them adequately for educational success.

The preparation of its students for the completion of the college degree was an important goal of the program. The concluding comments of the division's self-study report summarized this point:

> A student moving through the program is pressured in all courses to achieve control of skills in addition to acquiring a body of knowledge and a sense of the approach that a particular discipline takes to it. Further, it is hoped that by the very structure of the program self-motivation and independent achievements are enhanced. All academic

subjects and counseling experiences reinforce each other in these respects. After much hard work the student should discover that strategies that are fruitful in one course will be fruitful in others. To the degree that these become internalized as part of the permanent learning experience, they are the strategies which will allow the student to approach each new educational experience with confidence and with the expectation of success. When the student has mastered these strategies and has acquired a liberal arts background suitable to a sophomore, EOD has achieved its objective. The student is ready to move on (1981a:15).

Although the completion of the EOD program and the subsequent completion of the B.A. were important divisional goals, the EOD did not support the evaluation of success based only on these traditional measures. Rather, it believed a "value added" concept of higher education was as, or perhaps more, appropriate. As one faculty member stated:

Given the place our students begin it is inconceivable that the majority will graduate. However, if we keep them two or even one year and transmit skills, concepts, a love of knowledge... if we in any way touch and improve the quality of their lives, then we have been, I think, successful.[27]

The Educational Opportunity Division and State College: Interorganizational Relationships

The relationship between the Educational Opportunity Division and the rest of the State College community was an important part of the division's history. The existence of a separate compensatory program whose student population was predominantly black posed a number of interesting questions. Moreover, the division's commitment to the goals of egalitarian education on a campus designed around an "elite model" further complicated the relationship between the opportunity program and other constituencies on the State College campus. These relationships comprise a central story in the development of the opportunity program at State College. At this point, however, it is necessary to outline the basic structural and organizational relationships between the division and the various parts of the main college and to outline the various sociological questions that need to be addressed. Table 3.2 (below) outlines the organizational structure of State College:

The Educational Opportunity Division was a separate division of the College of Letters and Sciences. Its faculty served on all campus-wide committees and represented divisional interests in college policy making. The articulation between the division and the rest of the main college is central to understanding the evaluation of the program since its move to State College in 1978. These interactions revolved around a number of central issues:

1. Cross Registration: although the divisional policies required that students complete 56 credits before moving to the regular divisions, this changed from 1978–1982.[28] As we will see, the subject of cross-registration (EOD students taking courses outside of the division) became the subject of considerable controversy, consternation and debate, and the regulations concerning this process changed in the five-year period. In short, in 1978, upon moving to State College, EOD students did not cross register. By 1981–82, students could cross register after the completion of 24 credits in the division in good academic standing.

2. Integration and duplication: from the outset of the EOD's move to the main campus, the question of separation was a major issue of discussion between the division and other segments of the college, especially the administration. The major questions centered around the need for a separate model of compensatory higher education, the duplication of courses,[29] and possible avenues of integration between divisions.

3. The needs of underprepared students: as the questions of integration intensified, the needs of divisional students became an on-going theme in interorganizational discussions. The conflicts between elite and egalitarian models were most apparent in this realm, as divisional faculty consistently questioned the commitment and ability of State College faculty to educate an underprepared population.

4. Academic quality and credentialism: the questions of academic quality and faculty status were implicit to all interorganizational relations. While these issues were not often raised directly, their sensitive nature was always an undercurrent to discussions of integration. In terms of academic quality, the issue of college level courses was the primary theme, with State College faculty often skeptical about the rigor and demands of EOD courses. In terms of

credentialism, the EOD guidelines concerning teaching quality over scholarly achievements was the subject of some tensions. Moreover, the tenure of some EOD faculty without the Ph.D. was another issue relating to this theme. These issues became most pronounced when integrative strategies were discussed.

TABLE 3.2 ORGANIZATIONAL MODEL OF STATE COLLEGE

Administration

President

Vice President for Academic Affairs	Vice President for Finance
College of Letters and Sciences	School of the Arts
Dean of Letters and Sciences	Dean of Visual Arts Dean of Theater Dean of Dance Division of Music
Division of Natural Sciences Division of Social Sciences Division of Humanities Division of Educational Opportunity	Division of Visual Arts Division of Theater Division of Dance Division of Music
Divisional Faculty Committees	Divisional Faculty Committees

College Wide Faculty Committees

L&S EPC (Educational Policies Committee)	Arts EPC
L&S PPC(Personnel Policies Committee)	Arts PPC

Faculty and Students

The core of any program is the people in it. Any discussion of the educational and social processes of the division must begin with a profile of its lifeblood, the students and faculty. One of the major shortcomings of many sociological analyses of education is their treatment of social actors as determined parts of on-going social and historical processes. For example, as Featherstone (1976) pointed out, Bowles and Gintis' major work on the radical interpretation of education in the United States almost entirely ignored the two major groups within the schools, students and teachers. Moreover, in looking at social process without examining the subjective and intentional actions of members, these analyses often confused outcomes with intent.[30] As London (1978) demonstrated, the analysis of actors' meanings is a central task of sociological analysis and therefore a study of an educational organization must examine its main actors.

Students

The social, psychological, and educational characteristics of the disadvantaged and underprepared college student have been the theme of considerable research in compensatory higher education.[31] Although this study does not directly concern itself with an empirical analysis of these questions, a discussion of the program's student population is necessary in order to understand the processes related to the division's evolution.

The move to the main campus resulted in a shift in student population from an adult to traditional age group.[32] From 1978–1982, the division admitted students with a median age of 19; 42% male and 58% female. Moreover, as the admissions profiles demonstrate, the students had a history of economic and educational disadvantage. While these objective characteristics are important to our analysis, the subjective perceptions of the students themselves and of the faculty about the students is crucial in understanding the program.

The program's students came to the Educational Opportunity Division from urban public high schools in the metropolitan region of State College. A sample of divisional students responding to a questionnaire[33] provides data on the student population.

First, these data support the fact that the program admitted students who meet the profile in the educational opportunity program guidelines. The admissions data demonstrate that the program's students were economically disadvantaged and educationally underprepared. In addition, state EOP guidelines required a history of educational disadvantage, including the parents' lack of a college background. The questionnaire data support this requirement, with students reporting that 21% of their mothers and 30% of their fathers completed less than 12 years of schooling, 37.2% of their mothers and 16% of their fathers completed high school, 22% of their mothers and 12% of their fathers completed some college and 9% of their mothers and 7% of their fathers completed college.

The students enrolled in the Educational Opportunity Division either on the recommendation of their high school guidance counselor (28%), a friend or relative (15%) or through the recruitment efforts of the division (30%). However, many students did not know or did not understand that the Division was a separate program.[34] 33% percent reported that they were aware of the separate divisional structure, while 65% stated that they were unaware of this organization. Of these, 18% reported that they found out at freshman orientation, 9% during advisement, 9% on the first day of class, and 27% sometime during the first semester. While the reasons and consequences of this will be discussed later, there were three possible factors for this: 1. the division's recruiters and the admissions office did not inform students and/or intentionally misled them, 2. students did not understand or misunderstood the information, 3. the regular admissions office used the EOD as a "dumping ground" for minority students, with all students checking the EOP box on the application form (many thought this box was for opportunity program financial aid) and not for a separate program, placed in the division. There is evidence to support all three points. First, interviews with students suggested that some recruiters never told them about the separate organization; second, other students, in retrospect, reported that they were told, but did not understand the implications. Third, the EOD admissions personnel report an indiscriminate tracking system in regular admissions that channelled all students checking EOP to the program, regardless of educational or economic disadvantage. This is supported by students who stated that they checked the EOP box and wound up in the EOD. While all of these arguments will be examined later, it is important to note here that a majority of the division's students was unaware of the separate divisional structure upon entry into the program.

The underpreparation of students was a central assumption of the division and its educational methods. While admissions test results, high school averages, reading and mathematics levels, and writing samples documented a pattern of educational deficit, the students' perceptions of their abilities was also important. Questioned upon entry to the program, 4% considered themselves excellent high school students, 43% good, 41% average, 10% fair and 3% poor. In addition, 15% stated that they were very prepared for college, 65% somewhat prepared and 20% not prepared. These perceptions of incoming students suggest some discrepancy between subjective and objective reality and are central to the understanding of student reaction to their subsequent college experiences.

Finally, the question of student attitudes about college and the development of a student culture needs to be explored. As London (1978) demonstrated at a community college, the development of an anti-school culture can be a dominant aspect of community college life, with students developing a consistent pattern of anti-intellectual attitudes. Moreover, the need for career relevance and the distrust of irrelevant academic concerns was a central theme of London's ethnography. Although this study will not provide an in-depth analysis of student culture at this juncture, we must examine the attitudes of incoming students concerning their education and goals, for these significantly affected their reaction to the program's educational processes.

Most EOD students came to college to better their lives. Although most did not understand upon entry the meaning of a State College education or of liberal arts education in general, they all stated that a college degree was necessary for success. In addition, most of the students stated that they wanted professional careers and planned to continue their education at the graduate level. An examination of the admissions folders indicated that law, medicine, social work, business, and education were all listed as aspirations. The irony of this was often defined by students, whose essays displaying these aspirations were often poorly written and sometimes barely literate. An example of this was contained in a student's admissions essay:[35]

> I come here so I become a doctor. I wants to finish my college at State and applys for medical school. I understands to work hard I begin to succeed and this are the first step. I wants to be a doctor to help me people and returns to my community practicing medicine.

Although the purpose of a compensatory program is indeed to give this type of student the opportunity to make up for these deficiencies, the pattern of discrepancies between the perceptions of students about their skills and the demands that were placed upon them to fulfill their aspirations (and their ability to meet these demands) is an important aspect of understanding the difficulties in educating the underprepared population. In summary, a profile of incoming students suggests the following:

1.   a level of academic underpreparation.
2.   high educational and occupational aspirations.
3.   a discrepancy between level of skills preparation and student perceptions of weaknesses.

4.   a lack of knowledge concerning the ins and outs of college
        education and the meaning of liberal arts education.

As important as the students' own perceptions of themselves was the
faculty's definition of its student population. Research on teacher perceptions
and expectations, while inconclusive, suggested that teacher definitions may
have some effect on educational processes and outcomes (Persell, 1977;
Sadovnik, Cookson, Jr. and Semel, 1994:Chapter 9). Although the question
of teacher definitions will be explored in detail elsewhere, a brief discussion
is required here to understand the development of divisional curriculum and
methods.

Of importance, was the relationship between the division's definition
of its students and the justification of a separate division with appropriate
methods. Although the division did not claim that regularly admitted
students did not have some of the same qualities, they maintained that
educational opportunity students as a group were qualitatively different in
both skills level and affective characteristics.

The following statements from the accreditation self-study report
revealed this definition of the program's students:

> Admittedly, it is not unusual to find students anywhere who
> are bright, even motivated, and yet ambivalent about being
> in school. What distinguishes the EOD student is the
> degree to which negative feelings about school, about the
> mainstream American society whose values the school
> reflects, and about the student's own self impede the
> student's ability to perform with any sort of *consistent*
> success (1981a:4).

Commenting on the profile of students, the report continued:

> EOD faculty perceive certain constellations of affective,
> cognitive and social behavior running through the division.
> Engaging as EOD students may be, these underlying
> behavioral difficulties present obstacles to academic
> achievement. In the affective area, a low self-image is
> probably the primary tract. Along with it goes a short
> attention span and a tendency to procrastinate. There are
> problems with planning for the future and anticipating the
> consequences of action or inaction. By and large, EOD
> students have difficulty in delaying gratification. They are

predominantly passive and tend to blame external forces for their deficiencies, thus taking little responsibility for initiating any action on their own behalf. These students do not understand that they are supposed to move in the direction of controlling their own lives. Their expectations about college are vague and unrealistic. They have goals, but little sense of the practical sense and the hard work necessary to reach them. On top of all these problems (and perhaps because of them) they have various and often serious, problems with authority (1981a:6).

Focussing on their academic weaknesses, the report stated:

Their high school experience has not provided these students with learning strategies. They have difficulties in differentiating between teaching styles and spend too much time trying to figure out 'what the teacher wants.' High school did not help them to develop methods for approaching new and various academic materials. EOD students do not know how to memorize a body of material in a short period of time. They lack application. They are unsure when they have 'really learned' something. Nor have they had experience in applying basic academic skills to the solution of more advanced academic problems. Each new task requires a fresh start (1981a:7).

The report continued:

Cognitive behavior is also unequal to college level performance. The student's world view, background of general information, and language and quantitative skills are apt to be woefully inadequate. EOD students frequently have trouble reading beyond the factual or narrative level. They do not easily discern sequence, main ideas, or inference. Oral presentations tend to be formless and awkward, skimming merely the surface of the material. Standard oral patterns are not well developed. In the quantitative areas, as in others, students have trouble working with sufficient rigor. They do not know how to push themselves through the solution of knotty problem. They aren't sure when a thought sequence is logical. And in the basic skills areas, particularly in reading, writing, and mathematics, fear and

> anxiety attend the practice and further obstruct progress
> (1981a:7).

And finally, the report commented on the social factors affecting its students:

> Socially, as well, EOD students have some learning to do.
> Many of them come from poverty level homes where the
> adults have limited education. Thus, these students tend to
> associate themselves with a non-academically oriented peer
> group. It takes time and encouragement to change this
> social image. When they come to State College, EOD
> students have trouble knowing how to fit into the social
> environment that is new to them (1981a:7).

This profile of the division's students was based upon faculty, administration and counselor's experience with the population. It is important to note that these descriptions supported the cultural deprivation theory's profile of the culturally deprived student. Although considerable controversy has raged over the validity of this perspective in terms of both its alleged racist bias and the failure to empirically support its assertions,[36] this is not the significant issue at this point in the discussion. Analysis of the validity of the report's assumptions and assertions is indeed necessary,[37] nevertheless, the important point was the existence of a particular theory of the division's students that was well developed and stated.

The existence of a "cultural deprivation" model of its students was an important aspect of the division's educational organization, curriculum and methods. As some studies of compensatory higher education suggested, the purpose of these programs was to eliminate "culture of poverty" values and to inculcate middle class values. Although the appropriateness of such a strategy is open to question, it was clear that this transformation was implicit to the program's goals.[38] Moreover, according to the EOD it was the existence of a population with these educational and affective handicaps that necessitated its separate divisional structure and specialized curriculum. Speaking directly to these issues, the report stated:

> What makes the EOD a unique program is not its stress of
> basic skills, although remediation is a primary focus of the
> program. Rather, EOD's uniqueness lies in the willingness
> of its staff to confront with patience and understanding
> basic attitudes that are resistent to the learning process and
> that, while common among all student populations, are

much more prevalent among EOD students and much more likely to emerge as dominant personality traits. What EOD offers is a period of transition, during which students can strengthen their skills, but more importantly learn to deal honestly and confidently with academic challenges. The program is unique in its willingness to offer students who are, on one hand, often exceptionally curious about learning, and on the other hand, often paradoxically resistant when it comes to satisfying their curiosity, the time and guidance that will allow a fair proportion of them to adjust successfully to academic life (1981a:10).

Based upon the belief that its students were significantly different in degree and perhaps in kind from regularly admitted students, the EOD justified its separate organization and curriculum by the special needs of its population. Only through a separate program with a faculty and staff dedicated to the development of successful compensatory strategies did the division believe that the underprepared student could succeed in college. It was toward this end that the division's educational philosophy, curriculum, methods and practices were designed.

In addition to faculty perceptions of students, EOD student perceptions of themselves were equally important. Moreover, the discrepancies between student and teacher perceptions were a central aspect of the confusion many incoming EOD students felt. Interviews with EOD students, faculty, and EOD counselors office suggested that adjustment to college life was a central problem for this population, with both educational and social factors presenting numerous difficulties.

In an educational context, EOD students struggled to come to grips with the discrepancy between their aspirations and skills. During the first year, most EOD students became painfully aware of their educational shortcomings and reacted in a variety of ways. Some blamed their high schools, others rejected the "underprepared" label placed on them by the EOD and still others accepted the institutional label and worked hard to ameliorate their educational problems. What was clear from lengthy discussions with EOD students, however, was that the first year presented a number of painful definitional experiences in which the EOD student confronted his or her academic weaknesses. For many students who arrived without a real sense of deficiency, this certainly had some profound social psychological effects.

While the goal of the EOD program was to assist EOD students to accept a realistic self-portrait and make use of the educational program to maximize their potential, students often reacted angrily or ambivalently to what they perceived as negative labeling. In fact, many EOD students reacted against the EOD and blamed the division for their problems, as opposed to adopting the educational values transmitted by the faculty and staff. Moreover, according to many students, their confusion about their self-worth not only resulted in anger but in an ambivalence toward school work and a fear of failure. The existence of a "delay and avoidance" syndrome, where students failed to complete significant portions of their assignments was widespread and both EOD students and the counseling staff suggested this was a reaction to confusion and identity problems; that to some extent seemed to be reactions to the institutional labeling process.

Although adjustment to the educational demands of college was an important feature of the EOD student experience, the transition to the social aspects of campus life were equally important. Particularly, the problem of minority status on a white college campus was a critical problem. EOD students were asked to assimilate into the dominant white culture and problems of cultural conflict and racism were central features of their experiences. It is important to note here that EOD students expressed feelings of alienation and confusion in their first year about their relationships with non-EOD students, particularly white students. It was clear from discussions with these students that problems concerning integration presented important dilemmas. The EOD provided a ready-made cohesive structure. However, it was a segregated one and therefore students were often, in their own words, "confused about whether to stay isolated in the EOD or risk strangeness outside." More importantly, since EOD students were racially segregated educationally (in the EOD) but integrated socially (in housing), a number of complex reactions occurred. These problems are discussed in more detail later on.

In conclusion, EOD students came to State College with many educational problems and faced a complex set of adjustment factors. Moreover, while the EOD was structured to help them deal effectively with these situations and to inculcate a "successful" educational value system, interviews with students suggested significant problems in this respect.

EOD Student Academic Attainment and Achievement

Throughout its history at State College, EOD student academic achievement was of paramount concern to the division. As the following chapters will illustrate low student achievement and retention rates that increased as students moved into the college mainstream became significant aspects of faculty debates about divisional philosophy and practice. This study will not provide an in-depth empirical analysis of EOD student achievement,[39] however, the following section provides a brief discussion.

Table 3.3 presents EOD attainment data for 1978-1981 admissions classes:

TABLE 3.3 RATES OF COMPLETION BY YEAR (1978-1981)

Class	N	Comp 2 Yrs	Comp 3 Yrs	Comp EOD[1]	Comp 4 Yrs	120 Cred.	Grad
1978	88	55 (.63)	48 (.54)	40 (.45)	37 (.42)	24 (.27)	14 (.16)
1979	94	51 (.54)	38 (.40)	33 (.35)	27 (.29)	25 (.26)	15 (.16)
1980	108	55 (.51)	42 (.39)	36 (.33)	28 (.26)	24 (.22)	15 (.14)
1981	93	53 (.56)	36 (.39)	31 (.33)	25 (.27)	23 (.25)	16 (.17)

For these four admission classes (the first four years on the State College campus), 56% of the students completed 2 years at State College, 43% completed 3 years, 36% completed the EOD program (all program requirements, including an independent research paper), 31% completed 4 years, 25% completed at least 120 college credits, but did not complete all graduation requirements, and 16% graduated from state college within 6 years. Implications of these and related data will be discussed more fully in the concluding chapter. At this point it is important to note that with approximately a third of its students completing four years of college and less than 20% actually graduating from State College, the ability of the EOD to help its students successfully translate access into success was constantly under question. Given the level of student educational underpreparation and economic disadvantage, it may be the case that the division was doing a credible job. This is a matter of interpretation and judgement. What is clear, however, is that with its students from 1979 to 1981 receiving an F or NC (no credit) in 42% of their courses and in 1981-1982 an average GPA of 1.74 once grades were instituted (Sadovnik, 1983), that EOD student

---

[1]Completion of 56 credits, all distributional requirements, and the independent research paper.

achievement justifiably was a matter of concern and a significant problem.

The Faculty

The shaping force of any educational organization is its teachers, especially at State College where faculty prerogative was an important aspect of decision making. The governmental process of both the main State College programs and its Educational Opportunity Division actively depended on faculty participation; in fact, the faculty almost exclusively shaped the educational program at State College through the Educational Policies Committee and in the EOD through the Curriculum and CAP Committees.

Both programs of study, in the regular programs in the Letters and Sciences and in the Educational Opportunity Division, reflected the educational philosophies, personalities, and politics of its faculty. The different histories of each program, the reformist roots of EOD at Coop College and the "innovative radical" roots of State College resulted in major differences in educational outlook and philosophy that go beyond the elite versus egalitarian conflict. Although there was great diversity among faculty in each program, there was a dominant "personality" that defined each program and that shaped its evolution. Moreover, it was these differences that often contributed to the interorganizational conflicts that defined the politics of State College.

A large proportion of the faculty at State College (total = 160 faculty, during the period of this study) were original faculty members and helped to shape their educational ideal into a living system of higher education. When State College was founded in 1969, a large number of its original faculty were young, idealistic, innovative, and radical junior faculty who wanted to shape the institution in their image of educational reform. Working with a small number of senior faculty, they devoted themselves to the creation of a "utopian educational community," combining professional work in the arts with high quality intensive study in the letters and sciences.[40] The Letters and Sciences faculty wanted to develop an alternative public college where students of high motivation and independent energy could work closely with faculty members in exploring the significant questions of culture, art, and science.

The Letters and Sciences programs at State College developed in the experimental images of its faculty. For the most part Ivy League educated, of upper middle class background, and holding doctorates from the best graduate schools in the country, they were committed to upholding the highest standards of the academic enterprise. Yet, as "children of the 60s," they fervently held the era's political ideologies and supported its educational innovations.[41] What emerged from this group was a program defined by rigorous academic standards (junior exams, senior theses) and innovative and non-traditional organization and pedagogy (small class size, a short term for special "unique classes," an honors-pass-no credit grading system, and independent study). In fact, State College combined the elite educational program of a Swarthmore, with the independent curriculum of a Sarah Lawrence, and the innovative radical ideas of a New College or Santa Cruz.[42]

While the first thirteen years of its existence saw a gradual change in State College education, the changes involved a great deal of emotional debate and turmoil. The dominant segment of the faculty had its roots in the educational ideals of its founders, and the retention of what Etzkowitz and Fashing (1977) call a "dying tradition" shaped faculty debates. Although one could point to a number of differing political and educational philosophies within the State College faculty, the collective personality resided in the elite-innovative traditions of its original faculty. And while an increasing number of faculty and administration called for greater curriculum structure and the introduction of more career oriented programs, the faculty was still dominated by individuals with a fervent belief in quality liberal arts education without the "debasements" of the business world.

State College politics reflected the best and worst in participatory democracy. Decisions were reached at monthly faculty meetings which were characterized by endless debate and little action. The faculty guarded its prerogative to implement educational policy by carefully weighing and usually rejecting alternative governance strategies. At the same time, decisions sometimes took years to reach and often were reintroduced and redebated. The politics, like the educational organization, was a reflection of a faculty with a disdain for hierarchical authority and a mistrust of structure, either educational or political.

The Educational Opportunity Division, like State College, retained a large proportion of its original faculty from Coop College and, like the larger campus, was a reflection of the dominant political and educational philosophies of its members. In both cases, the retention of an original faculty led to a continual evocation of historical precedent, tradition and roots as the basis for debate. The past was always referred to as the guide to the present and the program's history and struggles were constantly used to defend particular actions. More importantly, the EOD faculty thought of the program in "parental" terms, as they had given birth, nurtured, and struggled to develop it. This collective perception of intimacy was especially important in discussing the decline of the division, as many faculty suffered from the kinds of emotions that typify parent-child separation or perhaps the death of a loved one.

Like the State College faculty, the EOD faculty (N = 19 in 1978;

N = 13 in 1983) may be defined as a diverse group with a dominant tradition. The diversity resulted in continuous debates over educational philosophy, methods, political strategy, and organization. The dominant tradition was the outcome of the resolution of these controversies and resulted in the overall flavor of the program. London's (1978) discussion of the political perspectives of community college faculty is especially useful and reflected the diversity within the EOD.

A small percentage of the faculty (N =4) reflected what London called the conservative perspective (1978:119-121). Within the EOD, this perspective was characterized by the following:

1.   Student problems were the result of individual weaknesses in character and motivation.
2.   Students had to be expected to live up to educational demands and to take responsibility for their academic and personal lives.
3.   While the social class background and race of the division's students were important, they were not and should not have been excuses for failure.
4.   Underprepared students needed a highly structured program with heavy demands and faculty had to be unbending in upholding requirements.
5.   A mistrust of the elite character of State College and a fervent belief in the integrity of the division and its faculty.
6.   A fervent opposition to integration with the mainstream programs and loyal defense of the EOD as an autonomous unit of the college.

The largest segment of the faculty (N = 11) belonged to the liberal perspective (London, 1978:121-135). Within the EOD this perspective was be characterized by the following:

1.   Student problems were seen as part of larger social problems, and while students had to learn to take responsibility for their lives, the economic, social and educational disadvantages specific to the population had to be addressed.
2.   The solution to these problems was to change the values and attitudes of students by helping them to adopt "middle class" educational values.
3.   The program had be structured to meet the needs of its students, that is, flexible enough to meet the students at

their level and demanding enough to prepare students for the rigors of college life.

4.   A "missionary impulse" and "liberal ideology" (London, 1978:127) to democratize higher education, to educate and provide opportunities to those who historically would not have them.

5.   A deep belief in the purpose of higher education and the conviction that all students can learn under the right conditions.

6.   A strong belief in the separate model of the division, a mistrust of the elitism of State College, but willingness to discuss integration.

7.   A concentration on the educational outcomes of the program, but little discussion of the overall nature of higher education in American life. Goals were seen as educational, with the assumption that educational success will translate into a "better life."

A small percentage of the faculty (N = 4) could be described by the radical perspective (London, 1978:135–139), although those who best met the characteristics concerning political consciousness and the use of the classroom for praxis were gone by 1978. None of the faculty who were part of the program from 1978 (at State College) met the formal descriptions of political radicalism, but fell somewhere between the liberal and radical perspectives. Therefore, these faculty are best described as liberal-radical and were characterized by the following:

1.   Student problems were seen within a broad social, educational and institutional context.

2.   A distrust of liberal ideology, meritocracy and cultural deprivation theory as explanatory systems.

3.   An ambivalence about academic standards, and a concern for the broader social and economic implications of their use. As one of these faculty members stated:

It is a mistrust of the political uses to which academic standards have been subjected in the current controversies. That is, it is not whether you believe or disbelieve in standards, and it is not whether you invoke them yourself; it is certainly possible to be painfully aware of the limited contributions students have to make when they are deficient in essential skills, just as it is possible to be equally aware of how the ingenious products of these students' creative impulses make these same standards restrictive and inappropriate to an appreciation of what they have to say. The point is that "standards" are too often used to ward off those instances that sanction an opposing point of view.

4.   An identification with the State College program and its educational philosophy but an uncertainty about its appropriateness for the division's population.

5.   A distrust of the separate model of the division and a partial support of integration.

6.   A belief that the experiences of disadvantaged students should be used as "motivational" and pedagogical devices.

In conclusion, both the State College and EOD faculties may be defined as diverse groups with dominant traditions. Each faculty was to some degree reflective of the educational philosophy of its programs and to a certain extent there were fundamental differences in outlook between the two groups.

Given the characteristics of the EOD and other State College programs, the nature of the EOD student population, and differences between EOD and regular college faculty, it was not surprising that the EOD's move to the State College campus in 1978 resulted in considerable conflict.

NOTES

1. The main campus was completed in 1971. The EOD, which opened in 1969 as a joint effort of State College and two neighboring private colleges, became the official educational opportunity program of State College (with the withdrawal of the cooperative arrangement) in 1971.

2. Grant and Riesman (1978) provide a comprehensive discussion of elite and egalitarian models of higher education.

3. Due to the location of State College and its inaccessibility by public transportation, commuter students found it difficult to attend. The adult population from Coop College, with family responsibilities, could not become residential students. While a small number did in fact commute, the move to State College completely changed the program's population.

4. In addition to being the only educational opportunity program in the state that was a separate division, the faculty believed its unique methods and philosophy separated the EOD from other opportunity programs.

5. The relationship between the EOD and the State College admissions office was a source of controversy throughout the program's history on the main campus, with the EOD charging it with not having a commitment to the recruitment of minority students.

6. Despite their often herculean efforts, this arrangement was not satisfactory, and enrollments began to drop by the 1982 admission year.

7. The State EOP Guidelines state: Students sponsored by EOP allocations must meet *economic* and *educational* eligibility criteria. The basic criteria for determining educational disadvantagement are: (1) nonadmissibility under the college's normally applied admission requirements, (2) identified potential for successful completion of an academic program at the college.

Economic Criteria (1978–1981)

Number of Members in Household	Gross Annual Family Income
1	$ 4,780
2	$ 5,920
3	$ 7,540
4	$ 9,050
5	$10,440
6	$11,710
7	$12,870
8	$13,920
9	$14,850
10	$15,660
11	$16,350
12	$16,920

*The gross income may be raised by $1,000 for each additional member of the household attending a postsecondary institution on at least a part-time basis.

**In addition, 15% of the EOP population may come from families whose income exceeds these guidelines but still meet the *educational disadvantagement* criteria.

8. The admission of non-EOP students into EOD posed a number of problems. First, as enrollments declined the division admitted more non-EOP students (based on underpreparation alone) and began to go over state guidelines regulating the number of non-EOP students. Second, the division permitted these students to make use of all its EOP services (that is, those paid by state EOP, not college funds), even though this technically violated the spirit of EOP funding. Third, as the movement toward integration developed, the pressure to open EOD courses and services to underprepared regular admissions students increased.

9. Remarkably, State College did not have readily available data on this. However, according to the admissions office an 85 high school was average the approximate cut-off point for Letters and Sciences students; art students were accepted based on a portfolio or audition.

10. The important question then is the extent to which a separate division for officially designated underprepared students resulted in a negative labeling process. This question is addressed more fully in Chapter 7.

11. State College is in a metropolitan region with a very large minority population and recruited extensively in the high schools in these sections.

12. This analysis is presented in Sadovnik (1983:Chapter 8).

13. Many constituencies did not believe that EOD courses deserved college credit equal to that received in regular division courses.

14. State College violated the Carnegie Commission recommendation for crediting (as do many colleges) courses with the equivalent of one credit per weekly contact hour. However, the college claimed that each course required sufficient independent work and outside contact through conferences to justify the overcrediting. While there is evidence to support the former, none exists to suggest extra student-faculty conferences except in EOD, where overcrediting was not a problem.

15. The distinction between regular and EOD, in terms of students, faculty, and courses, was a reflection of the language used at State College. While it connoted a distasteful comparison, that is, were EOD students, faculty and courses then by comparison *irregular*, it was used occasionally in the text both to convey the reality of language use and for lack of another less offensive description. Moreover, it is used primarily as a designation of *placement*, that is *regular* versus *special*.

16. This section relies on the EOD Curriculum Handbook, 1981 (and is augmented by the author's editorial comments and amplifications).

17. This requirement, after considerable controversy, was abolished in 1981–82. See Chapter 4 for a detailed discussion.

18. See Roueche and Snow (1977) for a detailed discussion of the emotional psychological problems faced by these students.

19. Even with complete financial aid packages, the costs of education posed serious problems for EOD students. In addition, bureaucratic problems with the financial aid office (many of which are caused by

student delay in completing forms) forced some EOD students to withdraw from school.

20. In 1978, the division had its own clinical psychologist; however, budget cuts eliminated the position by 1980. The college, however, had an overall counselling service.

21. However, resolution sometimes took months, or years.

22. The crediting of courses involved negotiation with the State College administration and at times the state education department. For example, in 1982 the state overruled the EOD and required that it remove credits for a group of remedial offerings, including Math 100 and the skills workshops ruling that they repeated high school. This issue was a controversial one throughout the program's history, as many other of its courses conceivably could have been viewed the same way. The Curriculum Committee's role was to document how courses that indeed appeared equivalent to high school courses were in fact different and *worthy* of college level credit.

23. This became a central function in 1982–83.

24. See Chapter 5 for a discussion of the opposition to this role.

25. The definition of satisfactory progress has changed over the years as the grading system changed from Honors/Pass/No Credit to A – F. Under the old system 12 credits per semester was considered satisfactory. Under the new system a more complicated system of grade point average (2.0 by the sophomore year) was implemented. The key issue revolved around the need for different criteria (from the rest of State College) for EOD students, especially in the freshman year, in order to give the students an opportunity to catch up before being judged for probation and dismissal.

26. Over the years, members of CAP constantly referred to the difficulties in handling the extraordinary work load.

27. In addition to the large deficits upon entry, many EOD faculty pointed to the nature of the State College curriculum as barriers to the graduation of EOD students, and therefore insisted that completion of the EOD program is a better measure of programmatic success and a more realistic objective.

28. While students still needed to complete EOD requirements before *officially* moving to the upper divisions, by 1982 students began to cross-register into lower and sometimes upper divisional courses in the regular divisions as early as their second semester.

29. The EOD offered discipline courses that often duplicated regular divisional offerings (for example, introduction to sociology in both EOD and the sociology department). Although the division attempted to legitimate this through its skills-content synthesis, the administration argued it was unnecessary, costly, and not justified.

30. That is, just because a particular outcome exists does not mean it was the result of conscious or rational planning.

31. The literature is extensive. One ERIC search for 1978–81 revealed over 10,000 articles on this question.

32. This resulted in a population with different focuses, perceptions and needs.

33. The entire questionnaire appears in Sadovnik (1983:Appendix).

34. Sadovnik (1983:Chapter 9) discusses the importance of this knowledge and its relationship to EOD student feelings about the division.

35. This is an extreme case. However, it is representative of the severe writing problems many EOD students had upon entry.

36. The debate over the culture of poverty and cultural deprivation is an important one. The major issues concern the existence of deficits or differences and secondly, the extent to which deficits, if they do exist, are the cause of poor educational performance or poverty or are in fact the product of social and institutional constraints. See for example, Persell (1977:Chapter 3) and Ogbu (1978) for critical discussions of these issues. For a detailed analysis of the relationship between structural economic changes and issues related to the culture of poverty see Wilson (1987). For a poignant journalistic account of controversies surrounding the culture of poverty thesis see Lemann (1991). Finally, for an analysis of social policy issues see Jencks (1992).

37. That is, to what extent did EOD students actually exhibit these characteristics? While this study does not directly test these as hypotheses, it does suggest that, in part, the characteristics did exist for many students.

38. That is, the faculty stated in a variety of settings that this process was vital to success.

39. See Sadovnik (1983) for a detailed discussion.

40. However, from the outset the School of the Arts had been almost totally separate; despite efforts to integrate the Letters and Sciences and the Arts (mostly by L & S), the Arts faculty maintained that separation was vital to their ability to offer professional programs.

41. At State College, the H/P/NC grading system, independent study, not formal requirements, and an experimental calendar (long and short terms 12/4 12/4 which was eliminated in 1979) were all examples of these innovations.

42. Grant and Riesman (1978) present an in-depth history of these innovations, with the discussions of New College and Santa Cruz especially relevant.

4

COOP COLLEGE AND THE TRANSITION YEARS AT STATE COLLEGE (1969–1981)

The Educational Opportunity Division at State College: The Off Campus Years

The Educational Opportunity Division of State College (EOD) began in 1969 as the off campus educational opportunity program of the newest college in the state system. Coop College, as it was initially called, was a cooperative effort of the state college and two neighboring private colleges, and was located in a minority community about fifteen miles from the State College campus. Coop College was a reflection of the educational times, a program designed to take college to the people, situated in a community whose population was educationally and economically disadvantaged and designed to provide access to this population.

The state educational law required that all branches within the higher education system provide a program to assist the educationally and economically disadvantaged. The off-campus Coop College served this function for State College. Although there was some concern by State College faculty that Coop College was not really what the EOP guidelines had in mind, the arrangement seemed to satisfy both state officials and the State College administration, at least during the early years.[1]

From 1969–1978, Coop College provided educational opportunities for minority students within its local community. This educational experiment was indeed a reflection of the times, with its "take the college to the people" approach neatly supporting the liberal educational reforms of the period. Coop College began as a separate two-year program providing testing, diagnosis, counseling, tutoring, and a developmental curriculum to its students. Although the program was designed as the first two years of the State College program, and Coop College students were admitted directly to the main campus for the upper divisional program, very few students actually completed their degrees at State College.[2] While the neighborhood program was accessible to the minority and working class population, State College was not. Although situated in an affluent section of the county which could be reached by automobile in only fifteen minutes, it presented a difficult commute by public transportation and posed particular handicaps for the Coop population.

Because Coop College served a special population, its educational development evolved in relation to its needs. During its nine years in the community, the program served primarily adult minority students. Although the program recruited some of its students from the local high schools, adults returning to college comprised the majority of its students. In many ways fitting the model of the educationally disadvantaged population described by K. Patricia Cross (1971), the Coop College population combined extreme educational deficiencies with acute economic hardships. The common thread for all students was the belief that higher education provided the avenue for upward social mobility and a better life for themselves and their families. As one student stated, "That poster (this refers to an advertisement for the program) made me decide to make a complete new start. I talked it over with the boys (four sons) and they encouraged me to try for a college degree."[3]

The main challenge for Coop College was designing an educational program to meet the difficult educational needs of its population. Over its nine-year history the faculty experimented with a variety of curricular and pedagogical strategies to prepare underprepared students for the completion of their college degrees. The ecological design of the program made it, by definition, an experimental program within the state university system. Whereas educational opportunity programs traditionally were situated on the college campus, with educational opportunity students integrated into the regular curriculum from the freshman year, the separate geographical location of Coop College required a totally separate program. This separation made Coop College the only separate educational opportunity program in the state university system and the development of its educational program reflected this distinctive structure.

The history of Coop College has been described by its original faculty members as a period of experimentation and turbulence.[4] The many philosophical and educational conflicts led to the evolutionary development of a highly structured two-year lower divisional curriculum intended to fulfill two major educational objectives: 1. to provide developmental and skills building courses in order to prepare educationally disadvantaged students for the completion of the college degree, and 2. to provide a comprehensive and well rounded liberal arts education at the lower divisional level. During its nine year history, Coop College developed what its faculty considered the best approach to the teaching of an underprepared population.

The program that developed at Coop College stressed the vital interplay between the academic and social components of education.

Recognizing that the barriers to the completion of the college degree were social and economic, as well as educational, the program built a structured cohesion to its educational processes. The concept of the teacher-counselor emerged as an important aspect of this structure, with faculty members serving dual roles in an attempt to help students deal with the academic, social, economic, and psychological problems posed by their complex situations. By the final years as Coop College, the Educational Opportunity Division had developed the type of holistic program[5] its faculty thought vital to the success of its student population.

In 1976–1977, the future of Coop College was a major issue. Although many faculty members expressed satisfaction with the separate geographical location, pressure mounted to bring the program to the main campus of State College. A number of reasons contributed to this pressure:

1. Declining enrollments and budgetary constraints: by 1976–1977 the educational reform market was expanding while, simultaneously, the available economic resources were declining. The development of opportunity programs at neighboring colleges created a climate of competition for educationally disadvantaged students. The institutionalization of compensatory higher education as a reform combined with the decline in the traditional college age student population made the recruitment of special populations vital to the survival of most colleges.[6] This competition for the disadvantaged population resulted in a dwindling student population at Coop College.[7] Additionally, the fiscal crisis of the period contributed to an overall decline in available funds for all college programs, especially experimental ones. The combination of declining enrollments and the high cost of maintaining a separate physical plant made a move to the main campus a logical administrative decision.

2. Affirmative Action Pressure and the State College Commitment to Egalitarian Education: Although Coop College certainly served the type of population mandated by the Educational Opportunity Program Guidelines, its separate geographical location posed a number of questions for the State University Office of Special Programs and the State College faculty and administration. Many faculty members at State College and certainly the administrative hierarchy of special programs argued that Coop College provided an opportunity for State College to legally avoid its commitment to disadvantaged students. As Etzkowitz and Fashing stated:

This innovative 'take the college to the people' program,

however worthy it is in and of itself, raises several issues about the nature of the program at the main campus and of State College's real interest in the Coop college. For example, it has been charged in faculty meetings that the Coop College is treated as a 'plantation' of State College and that the existence of the Coop College allows State College to maintain an elite educational model and not have to deal with the variety of students who might not fit into that program. With no EOP program at the main residential campus and the Coop College open only to those within the community area or in commuting distance to it, potential EOP students from other parts of the state are automatically excluded from attending State College (1977:18–19).

Therefore, many members of the State College community viewed Coop College as a means by which the main campus could avoid a rigorous commitment to the ideals of egalitarian education, with the token off-campus program satisfying state educational law.

Second, the racial composition of the main campus became the subject of pressure by state education officials. In 1976–1977 and 1977–-1978 the main campus had an underrepresentation of minority students,[8] with the Coop College population its major source of minority enrollment. Critics of this composition charged that the main campus was segregated and the "plantation" center did not really fulfill the mandate for an integrated public college population. Thus, pressure developed to move the off-campus educational opportunity program to the main campus.

The combination of declining enrollments, the high cost of Coop College, and the allegations of elitism and segregation at the main campus resulted in the decision to move Coop College to the main campus. The 1977–1978 academic year marked the transitional period, with the 1978–1979 academic year slated for the actual move.

The transition to the main campus initiated a series of educational debates that would define the coming years. The conflicts between an egalitarian model of higher education and the elite model of State College were a major concern for faculty at the main campus and within the Coop program. This theme concerning the commitment of State College to the disadvantaged student population became the major educational concern of the Educational Opportunity Division and forced the State College faculty to look closely at its own educational philosophy and mission.

The apprehension of the state college faculty was expressed by Etzkowitz and Fashing:

The question of State College's relationship to students with a background other than that would fit them in a mini-Ph.D. program must now be directly confronted by the administration and faculty at State College since the state educational bureaucracy is putting pressure on the Coop program to move to the main campus. State College would then have a program that admits EOP students on the same basis as any other state campus, but there is substantial fear that the program would be far less successful on campus. There are a variety of reasons offered, but the elite charac-ter of the campus program, probably the most formidable barrier to success is rarely confronted directly. Whether the transfer takes place or not, the proponents of an elite model as the sole path for State College will no doubt face their first serious challenge since the college opened especially since a majority of those who go beyond Coop's first two years do not choose State College (1977:19).

Therefore, even as the transition was being debated, the conflict between the egalitarian concerns of a compensatory higher education program and the demands of an elite model of higher education was being raised.

The transition was no less a concern for Coop College faculty. While the budgetary and administrative imperatives were clear, three major questions emerged within Coop College:

1. The commitment to the community: a number of program faculty thought that the cooperative-community model was the most effective program for disadvantaged students and that community based education was both educationally and socially sound. They feared that the move to the campus would remove the major avenue of educational mobility for community residents and eliminate the opportunities for the present student population, as they would not be able to commute to State College; nor could they become residential students, given their family responsibilities. The strategy proposed by the advocates of maintaining the off-campus program suggested the strengthening of recruitment efforts and presentation of a healthy program with good enrollments to the State Office of Special Programs.

2. The conflict between elite and egalitarian education: Just as the State College faculty perceived the discrepancy in educational goals, the Coop College faculty and administration perceived difficulties

in merging the program with the main college program. In addition to the loss of its special character, the program would find itself on a campus perceived as having little interest in developmental higher education. Moreover, the creation of a separate opportunity program consisting primarily of minority students on the state college campus would pose new challenges and problems for the program.

3. The change in student population: the move to the main campus would result in a change in the program's population. While every effort would be made to assist Coop College students in transferring to the main campus, the future population would not come from the same adult population. The residential character of the main campus would require the recruitment of a more traditional aged disadvantaged population who would reside on campus. The shift in population combined with the new problem of black students living on a white campus increased the fears concerning the transition.

Despite these fears, the reality of declining enrollments, high financial costs and the educational pressure of the state bureaucracy resulted in the decision to move Coop College to the main campus of State College in 1978-1979. The first period in the Educational Opportunity Division marked the end of one era and the beginning of another. In fact, this period represents the first *rise and fall* of this educational reform program and its *reemergence* in a new form. Representative of the educational period, the Educational Opportunity Division began as a community experiment, was a victim of the declining enrollments and budgetary crises of the mid-1970s and continued as an integrated part of the main campus. This last process denoted the institutionalization of compensatory higher education as an accepted part of higher education in the 1970s. It spoke to a vague commitment to the reforms of the 1960s and early 1970s. Perhaps it represented the realistic appraisal by postsecondary institutions of the declining college population with the necessary college-level skills and the need to provide some services for a growing student population without these skills, whose attendance was vital to healthy enrollments.

The Transitional Years and the Search for Divisional Identity: 1978-1980

The arrival of the Educational Opportunity Division at State College in 1978 signified the beginning of an important educational experiment. Faculty within the division and the main college viewed the transition with some fear and reservations. Could a compensatory program succeed on an "elite campus"? What kinds of support could the division expect? How would the change in student population affect the program? Could underprepared students survive at State College? How would the large incoming minority student population affect the middle class white population at State College?

The anticipatory fears did not prove to be without foundation. The next five years were filled with promise, turmoil, conflict, and critical educational and organizational problems. The decision to integrate the program with other segments of the State College divisions in 1983 and to retain a small integrative educational opportunity program marked a final decline in the division's history as an autonomous unit. The important task is to trace the processes leading to this event.

The fears of the Division were hidden by the anticipation of a promising partnership with the State College community. At the first faculty meeting of the year the director of the program spoke to the theme of old traditions and new beginnings. The old traditions referred to the tested methods and practices of a proven faculty; the new beginnings reflected the new environment and student population. The tone was optimistic and called for the infusion of the successful spirit and energy that defined Coop College. However, an anxious and apprehensive tone defined the director's description of the EOD's relationship with the college. On the one hand, he hoped for a smooth transition and supportive relations; on the other hand, he feared problems, both for faculty and students.

The theme of the day became clear: State College, long a symbol of elite education, had to adjust to the division's presence. The hidden farm system was no longer hidden and the college would never be the same. More importantly, the director spoke to the division's future in terms of the future of higher education. With declining national test scores, lowered freshman reading and writing skills and, most crucially, a decline in the traditional college age population (white, middle class) the division's population would certainly be the wave of the future. The division sat at an exciting crossroads. It could become a model for compensatory higher education at a time when its expertise and services were in heavy demand, or it could fail to penetrate the elitist walls of the State College campus.

Educational Philosophy, Ideology, and Collective Identity

The concepts of ideology and collective solidarity are central to the analysis of organizations. Swidler (1979) in her study of alternative schools pointed to the use of ideology as the bonding feature of the educational community.

The belief and continual reliance on ideological commitment both defines the organization's identity and holds its members together within a collective spirit. The Educational Opportunity Division at State College arrived in 1978, with a firm educational philosophy that became its organizational ideology and a faculty who, despite its differences, supported the divisional identity. That is, a central part of the division's image was the presentation of a "unified self," of the division as a collective unit.

The organizational ideology stressed a number of related issues:

1. The necessity of a separate division to meet its special mission: often couched in the rhetoric of the civil rights movement and of liberal educational philosophy, the mission of the division to provide access and opportunity to minority students was constantly embraced.

2. The uniqueness of the division: as the only separate model of its kind in the state system, the divisional identity solidly supported its special nature.

3. The expertise of its faculty: the program stressed its special methods and talents for successfully preparing its special population. These included its curriculum, tutorial system, faculty-teacher contact, faculty training and concern, and most importantly, the *skills-content* synthesis. "We are experts in this type of education," became a standard phrase in the invocation of the ideology of expertise.

4. The program's history: the connection between ideology and history was an important one. The special identity and expertise of the division were reflections on its history at Coop College. The retention of a large segment of its original faculty and staff contributed to the use of history as a defining tool. The faculty and staff constantly referred to its long history in various contexts. This was used to support the ideology of expertise.

The existence of an organizational ideology defined the program in its early stages at State College and contributed to the program's strong sense of collective identity. During the first two years on the main campus this solidarity would be constantly tested by the various organizational and educational dilemmas that defined this period.

The Separate Divisional Structure: The Seeds of Discontent

Although the division's philosophy stressed the importance of its separate divisional structure, this feature of the program proved to be its single most controversial feature. In the first two years at State College, the issue was not put explicitly in terms of separation versus integration, but the seeds of discontent emerged. This period was marked by the constant questioning of the program by its students and their claims against divisional policies, curriculum, and campus social life.

The transition years were marked by the constant evaluation and reevaluation of the program. Coming to the main campus with a strong commitment to the structure of its program, the division's faculty responded defensively to the pressures brought to bear on it by its students. This period marked the development of the first seeds of intraorganizational discontent, with the faculty intensely debating the claims brought by students.

The definition of educational problems within the division was initiated by its students. The initial claims centered on two interrelated issues, the separate structure of the division and the EOD students' perception of racism on the State College campus. The importance of their relationship cannot be overemphasized, as the students merged the problems of divisional structure and institutional racism into one issue and addressed it in this manner.

Willie and McCord (1972), in their study of black students on white college campuses, outlined the difficulties faced by minority students with issues relating to integration versus segregation. Their study concluded that black separation was due to white racism rather than black desires for exclusivity. That is, most black students retreated into the protective environment of separation to avoid the effects of racism and the conflicts associated with assimilation. At State College, the students connected the issues of racism and divisional separation, and their discontent defined much of the conflict during this period.

The division's students displayed confusion, anger, and resentment over their treatment on the campus, and these feelings were expressed by challenging institutional racism at State College and the division itself. First, although the EOD students were placed in a separate division of the college (that comprised 95% of the State College's minority population), they lived in integrated residential arrangements with the rest of the college community. Thus, EOD students were segregated educationally and integrated socially. Tensions emanating from this arrangement led to extreme conflicts between the students and the division.

In particular, the infusion of a sizeable black population into the dormitories created numerous tensions and frustrations. Black and Latino students complained that they were "abused" by the white students in their dorms. Controversies over music and cleanliness erupted on a daily basis. In particular, black students charged that white students ignored them and degraded their culture.

Music represented a major issue in the conflict. Black students complained that disco and soul music were not given equal time at dances, parties, and in the dorms. They argued that the domination of punk, new wave, and rock-n-roll represented a disregard for their needs and a debasement of their culture. This topic was constantly aired and debated in classes, meetings, and in conversations between students. As one student told me:

> At dances, all we hear is new wave. For every one disco record, they play nine of theirs. It really makes me mad. I mean we go here too and we like our music.

Another student echoed this concern:

> When we demand equal time for our music, they act like they're doing us a favor. They cannot understand that we like our music; they find our tastes weird, but they can't understand when we don't like their punk music.

A second point of controversy, cleanliness, surrounded housing arrangements. Many of the division's students were repelled by the habits and attitudes of their white roommates and considered them irresponsible. The key factor in these conflicts concerned attitudes about cleanliness. EOD students constantly complained that their white roommates were "pigs" and refused to take responsibility for cleaning the rooms. As one student told me:

> You would not believe it. She is a pig. She never cleans, she never washes, she leaves everything a mess. I can't live in a zoo.

Another student voiced this same feeling:

> You have to wonder about their upbringing. Either their parents did everything for them or they are just plain dirty.

A third student went even further:

> It's not just that she won't clean the place, but she resents

my keeping the place clean. I have asked for a change in
housing, but the office says we should work it out.

The issues of music and cleanliness were symptoms of the larger
racial tensions that existed in EOD's first two years on campus. A resident
assistant in the dormitory described the events:

> The first two years that the EOD program was on campus
> were tense. Students from the program seemed confused
> and angry. 'Regular' students were often hostile and conde-
> scending. There were a lot of incidents between black and
> white students.

While the racial tensions in the dormitories were important issues,
the hostility and anger of EOD students transcended the quality of campus
life. The issue of racism was never voiced in isolation, but always directed
to the organization of the division. The key to student feelings revolved
around their perceptions of their place on the campus and the feelings of
inferiority associated with the division.

One of the major concerns of EOD students was what they considered the imputation of stigma by non-EOD students. During the transitional
years, the campus was not fully aware of the division, its meaning or its
purpose and EOD students often heard many negative remarks about their
status. "Regular" students remarked that they were here on a free ride, less
capable, stupid, etc. A constant complaint aired by the division's students
during this time was that other students made them feel inferior.

In addition to the labels placed upon them by fellow students, EOD
students complained that the institution's bureaucratic structure was racist.
Students constantly alluded to the office of financial aid and the bursar's
office as the main villains. They felt that the bureaucratic rules and
regulations were somehow directed against them and that the staff were
often condescending and arrogant. More importantly, the students defined
all bureaucratic entanglements as racist, and did not distinguish between real
examples of prejudice and the ordinary disenchantments of bureaucratic
organizations. Minority students defined all bureaucratic constraints as
aimed at them, not as the problems faced by all students regardless of race.

A significant feature of student discontent centered on the issue of
financial aid. Many regular students defined the EOD as the place that
minorities get money. Some of these students, according to the division's
students, resented what they perceived to be a free ride and publicly
proclaimed these feelings. Divisional students reported that the college's
financial officials treated them with hostility. One student reported:

> That white lady in the bursar's office snidely said, I pay for my kid's education, be thankful and don't complain (about waiting for your stipend check).

Another student summarized these feelings:

> They make us wait on line for our book checks like welfare recipients and treat us the same. Both white students and the staff treat us like we're getting something for nothing. And standing on line just makes it all the worse. My God, it's like 125th Street and Lenox on the first of the month, all the blacks waiting for food stamps. Here we wait for book checks.

The perceptions of racism and the racial tensions on campus resulted in the solidification of the EOD student population and their mobilization around these issues. The issue of divisional separation became an organizing theme for claims against the division. That few students in the first two admissions classes understood the purpose or nature of the division, or in fact knew that they would be placed in a separate division upon their arrival at State College, exacerbated their discontent. Students demanded to know why they were in the division, why they were treated differently from other students, why they had to take different courses from regular students and why they were not told of the separate divisional structure prior to their acceptance of the college's offer of admission. More importantly, they made the connection between the social tensions on campus, their perceptions of racism and the divisional structure and equated these problems with the division. Consequently, students projected their anger at the division and equated their problems with the division itself.

The scope of student claims making activities in the first two years, while not demanding a change in the divisional structure, centered on clarification. They demanded that the faculty address the issue of racism on campus and explain the purpose of the division. What they in fact were doing was asking for answers to their questions and an end to their confusion.

During the transitional period, the division responded by making counterclaims that defended the program's mission, philosophy, and structure. While the administration and faculty did not reject the students' claims, they attempted to reduce tensions by legitimating the division itself. Faculty debates during this period did not question the division's organization, but rather searched for intraorganizational solutions to the problems voiced by its students.

Faculty meetings and town meetings provided the major forums for these discussions. At faculty meetings, the division discussed the educational and social problems facing the program and its students. At town meetings, the faculty and students discussed the problems and attempted to come up with reasonable solutions. These interactions helped to define the division's identity and test the strength of its foundation.

Significantly, during this transitional period, the question of divisional separation was not an issue for the division's faculty and administration. The overwhelming majority of the program supported the divisional separation as the superior model for its population and, therefore, little discussion of any shortcomings as a model existed. Rather, the faculty attempted to come to grips with the serious social problems facing its students and searched for answers within the divisional structure. The director of the program, consistent with his office's objective for defending the needs of the disadvantaged student, took student claims about racism seriously and engaged his office in finding acceptable solutions to these problems. He initiated discussions with the housing office, the bursar's office, the financial aid office, and the college's central administration to alleviate tensions and resolve conflicts. His theme was clear: the campus had to recognize the existence of minorities as a reality and institute remedies to institutional and individual cases of racism.

While the program's director acted on the administrative level, the faculty's concerns reflected the educational goals and philosophy of the program. Since the faculty was primarily concerned with the educational success of its students, the claims of its students became framed as educational questions. Some faculty accepted the claims as valid and suggested they pointed to important student needs. Others, however, did not and suggested they unnecessarily detracted from the division's educational mission. Nonetheless, faculty seemed somewhat confused by the clamor. The taken for granted aspects of the program, products of intense thought at Coop College, now became the subject of debate. Reluctantly and painfully, the faculty began the task of responding to student needs by looking reflectively at itself. The consensus was that the program's structure was sound, but the new younger population posed somewhat different educational problems, and the move onto the main campus intensified these problems. The faculty moved to meet these problems by informing its students about the special nature of the division and their special place in the college. Thus, the faculty responded to student claims by defending itself. Their counterclaims were not so much a rejection of the students, but a legitimation of themselves and the attempt to incorporate student needs into the present divisional structure.

Two distinctive perspectives emerged during this period and formed the basis for intraorganizational debates in the years to follow. The first, representing the views of liberal and liberal-radical faculty members supported student claims and sought viable programmatic solutions. The second, representing the views of conservative faculty, rejected student claims and saw them as excuses for poor academic performance. During the transitional period, the issues of racism were at the root of these differences. Liberal faculty suggested that the racism on campus should be a central divisional issue and was essentially an educational as well as social problem. Recognizing that the emotional and psychological perceptions of its students were important factors in educational performance, these faculty supported student feelings and presented them as important concerns of the faculty. These faculty raised the issues of racism often and supported the open airing of student claims at Town Meetings. Conservative faculty, however, opposed the continual discussions of what they perceived to be "non-educational" issues and as one faculty member, summarizing his perception of this view (as summarized in meeting minutes) noted:

> My colleague suggested that while racial discrimination has always been and persists as a problem, he cautioned against providing an excuse for failure. The more serious problem, according to him, is the poor motivational and attitudinal problems of our students reflected in poor attendance and academic difficulties. He stated that the problems our students face are problems of inferiority, not particularly race and that while the faculty should be willing to discuss instances of racial prejudice, the emphasis should be on academic performance. Connecting the two, he suggested that high academic performance will improve students' perceptions of themselves and reduce inferiority and help to alleviate many academic and social problems faced by our students.

Therefore, this period marked the introduction of a major theme in the program's evolution: the analysis of student performance and the attempt to understand the high rates of failure of the division's students. Moreover, it witnessed the development of a split in the faculty between liberals who defined the social and psychological factors as a key to improving student performance and conservatives who rejected these explanations as missing the point: that students must take responsibility for their own success rather than use them as an excuse for failure to do this.

If the faculty was split over the degree to which it should give legitimacy to student claims, it was not divided over the need to respond to the educational needs of its students. The faculty became resolute in its belief that its students could succeed and that the divisional structure offered the best possible avenue for this success. Town Meetings provided the forum for the faculty to convey this message through its response to student challenges. Their message was clear. The separate division was essential to student educational success.

The EOD organized the Town Meetings to answer student questions and to respond to their problems. The faculty viewed these meetings as an opportunity to educate students to the division's requirements and to socialize incoming students to the purpose of the program. Students viewed them as an opportunity to address problems and state their grievances. The meetings served both purposes and functioned as an avenue of tension management, with students making claims and the faculty responding to them.

The tone of the meetings was often angry and always emotional. Moreover, the meetings were structured to produce a paternalistic quality, with faculty instructing students about the program and giving expert advice on their queries. It was not unusual for faculty and students to have very different perceptions of the meetings, with the faculty leaving with positive feelings about the effectiveness of the session and students leaving with negative feelings about being dismissed or lectured to. What was clear, however, was that despite the failure to resolve many issues, these meetings set the stage for the continuing debate between students and faculty as well as between the faculty itself.

The Town Meetings served as the primary arena of student claims making. During the transitional period, students presented their concerns over racism and their questions about the division. Students wanted to know why they were in the division, what the purpose was and wanted specific features of the divisional requirements explained. In summary, the division's students wanted to know why they were being treated differently from other students.

The faculty responded to these questions with a defense of the divisional structure and a clarification of its purposes. Their main point stressed the special needs of the division's population and the necessity of the division in meeting these needs. Faculty members pointed to the academic deficits and difficulties of the students and the special attention offered by the program. They pointed to the special nature of the division and the fact that the students should have considered themselves lucky to receive special attention.

The messages relayed to the students at the Town Meeting attempted to turn negative perceptions of the division into positive ones. The concept of "different but as good" emerged to reduce the EOD population's fears of stigma and negative labeling. Students received positive reinforcement, but also honest appraisal. The faculty did not attempt to cover up the purpose of the division; students were informed that they were placed in EOD because they did not meet the college's entrance requirements and the purpose of the division was to improve their skills and prepare them for academic success.

The Town Meetings served a number of important functions:

1.   Socialization: Students were initiated to the basic requirements of the program and educated about the meaning of EOD. This served a critical purpose as it represented the first opportunity for many students to find out the answers to many troubling questions. The meetings served to clarify many misunderstandings about the nature of the division.

2.   Tension Management and Divisional Solidarity: The faculty attempted to develop a cohesive spirit among students by reducing their anger and creating a positive orientation to the division. The positive aspects of the program such as tutorials, extra-help, positive reinforcement, and individualized education became the legitimating ideology of its existence. While students brought serious questions about differential treatment to these meetings, the faculty attempted to reduce the conflict by pointing to the positive aspects of difference. Different did not have to mean inferior, but rather it meant privileged; that is, privileged to be in the EOD and have its services at your disposal. By the second and third year, the involvement of second-year and third-year students became a vital part of this process, with "socialized" upper class students functioning to inform new students. Their stories always pointed out the help they received and their debt to the division. Although this process did not eliminate the conflicts concerning the divisional structure, it did manage the various tensions and most students left with a more positive view of the division's potential.

3.   Academic Success and Responsibility: A primary goal of the Town Meetings involved the faculty's presentation of its expectations of and for its students. The faculty indicated that every student could succeed at State College and that the EOD provided the means to this achievement. The division would provide every opportunity for its students, leaving it up to the individual student to take advantage of the program's special features. This message clearly placed the responsibility for success squarely on the shoulders of the students

by saying "we (faculty) all do our part, but you make the difference." More importantly, the corollary to this stated that students should spend less time complaining about the division and more time studying. This implied that the continual conflict over the program was a major cause of student problems, not the program itself. Reflecting a conservative approach to the solution of social problems, the faculty defined the individual, not the structure, as primarily responsible for positive educational outcomes.

The Second Stage: Loosening the Boundaries

During the 1980–1981 academic year, the walls of the division began to bend and the concept of integration with other parts of the campus became a topic for consideration. The question of difference once again propelled the discussion of divisional autonomy. Moreover, students again pressed the claims about important differences in the EOD program. While the first stage saw the general challenge to divisional autonomy, the second stage reflected a questioning of specific features of the program, its requirements and its curriculum. Beginning in 1979–1980 with an emotional debate over the division's grading policy and continuing in 1980–1981 with debates over the division's attendance policy, cross registration and curriculum requirements, the division was forced to take a serious look at itself. Moreover, the reality of EOD student performance, including low retention, high absenteeism and high rates of failure[9] became an overriding concern of the faculty and an important feature of these debates. The division's students continued to mount serious challenges to the program. At the same time, they were not performing well in the program. These two facts were linked together to form the basis of continual debate, agonizing and anguish. If nothing else was clear, the commitment of the faculty to its mission stood out. Although it did not have ready answers, the faculty demonstrated a willingness and concern for the students. The solution to their educational and social problems became a major theme of the period.

The Grading Policy
During the 1979–1980 academic year, EOD students challenged the division's grading policy, citing the difference between EOD and State College grading procedures. State College used an Honors, Pass, No Credit grading system with narrative evaluation for all students. Whereas the EOD used narrative evaluations, the grading system included only Pass, No Credit and Fail; no Honors grade was permitted and a distinction between No

Credit, for students who completed all work at below passing level, and Fail, for all students who did not complete the coursework, was made.

The difference in grading policy underscored substantial conflicts within the EOD. For students, the issue represented a continuation of the essential debate over the division: why does it treat its students differently from other students at State College? Moreover, the inability of EOD students to receive an Honors grade represented to the students a public statement of their inferiority. For faculty, the grading issue spoke to the heart of the division's identity, raising the concepts of difference and college level courses. The latter issue hit a sensitive and complex problem that transcended the grading policy, as some faculty believed the honors grade should not be given for skills or remedial work.

The students presented their position clearly and passionately. They stated that: 1. all EOD students should have the opportunity to earn the honors grade, as could all State College students; 2. the specification on the narrative evaluations of a Fail box, with the denotation for EOD students only, was a primary example of the negative labeling of EOD students and the imputation of inferiority.

The faculty was divided. Although the entire faculty agreed that the Fail box with its negative denotation should be removed, the issuance of honors was a thorny issue. Some faculty believed that EOD students should have the opportunity to earn honors, and they viewed the grade as a motivational tool. To do otherwise was to stigmatize and present an image of low expectations to the students. For others, two principles guided their opposition to the honors grade: 1. to give honors in a remedial level course debased the grades; students in these courses should have been graded on a Pass/No Credit basis because, for example, an honors in a basic arithmetic course has little meaning; 2. based upon past experience, EOD student performance could not warrant the grade, so it should not be instituted (to avoid giving students unrealistic goals). Finally, a small segment of the faculty opposed the honors grade out of a general opposition to grading and competition. This minority had more in common with the spirit of the State College educational philosophy, but little to offer this debate outside of an adversarial spirit. Finally, a large segment of the faculty would have preferred a complete break with State College and the adoption of a traditional A-F grading system.[10]

The following statement summed up the entire debate, as well at the pro-Honors position:

the EOD problem demands immediate resolution and so, at least for the time being, the *grade of Honors should be awarded within the EOD.* It stands to reason that this would in no way compel a faculty member to utilize such a grade. Is this not also true regarding the grade of Pass?

Indeed, if we continue to recognize Honors as the highest grade available for a course taken at the College, it is conceivable that some instructors might never find the occasion to apply it. On the other hand, no instructor should be denied the potential for its application.

If honors were awarded within the EOD, there are likely to be many students who would never receive it. It is hoped that this criticism applies equally to the regularly admitted students. If not, what is so important about the grade of Honors? In fact, nobody is disadvantaged by not receiving the grade. Honors, like any other grade is not guaranteed to any student. Of course, if it is earned, it should be awarded. The existence of the grade guarantees only the opportunity to earn it. To be able to recognize this is a basic part of the education of any student, be he EOD, or regularly admitted.

Finally, I must state that I cannot find justification for the agony which our faculty has been enduring with respect to the grade of Honors. Therefore, every teacher serving the College is bound, in conscience at least, to make use of that grade when and where it is clearly deserved. To discover, however frequently, that no one in a particular class is capable of attaining that grade is quite understandable. But to preclude the awarding of the grade as a matter of individual or faculty policy is a) prejudicial to the students concerned, b) degrading to the particular course. In the first case, every student entering the EOD is being told from the outset that he or she does not possess the potential for hard work and outstanding achievement; in the second, the EOD course is presented as an anomaly: a college course which is not a college course. Obviously, neither case is tolerable.

Why then this interminable anguish over the grade of Honors? One explanation seems to come to the fore. As a faculty we seem, in this matter, to be moved on the one hand by a sense of inadequacy and, on the other, by a yearning to be accepted into the campus elite, its mythical existence notwithstanding. I hope that I am wrong. Because such a situation can only serve to aggravate the feeling of inferiority which seems to be affecting some of our students. It can demoralize our faculty and it can, ultimately, spell the death of the EOD (1980).

In an exhaustive and emotional statement this particular faculty member not only summarized the major pro and con arguments, but spoke almost prophetically to the subsequent decline of the division. Again, at the root of the problem was the divisional identity as a separate division and the negative labels associated with its differences by student and faculty. Could the division retain its special identity and in turn justify its existence, or would it move closer to the identity of State College?

While the faculty debated these philosophical and educational issues on a number of levels, the students were unimpressed with the intricacies of their deliberations. At a Town Meeting for the express purpose of resolving the grading issue, the issues were heatedly debated. The students demanded equal treatment and the faculty expressed their divided opinions. Finally, in a very close vote, the faculty adopted the Honors grade by moving to the same grading system as all other divisions. The deciding factor seemed to be the desire to avoid continued stigmatization of EOD students. While many faculty believed that the unique character of the division was left intact, if nothing else, the decision moved the division closer to the State College divisions. Although it did nothing to affect the divisional structure at this juncture, it presented an important step in breaking down the walls that separated the EOD.

The Attendance Policy

Just as the student claims making over the honors grade challenged the differential treatment of EOD students, the attack on the attendance policy took on a similar theme. Likewise, the faculty debates on its attendance policy transcended the single issue and in fact became a referendum on student performance. Moreover, the ongoing debates really concerned themselves with the faculty's analysis of its population's education weaknesses and the proper educational environment to remedy such problems. In the final analysis, however, the debate over a unified attendance policy was firmly grounded in "cultural deficit theory," with a large segment of the faculty attributing poor educational performance to attitudinal rather than cognitive problems. Finally, these debates reflected a faculty who were deeply troubled and concerned with the educational problems of its students and who were searching for educational solutions to a complex set of problems. Emotional debate, intense differences in perspectives, and the frustration of all characterized the various meetings concerned with the issue. The issue reemerged throughout the 1979–80 and 1980–81 years. In June, the faculty finally abolished its uniform policy, leaving the matter to each individual instructor.

The division had a compulsory attendance policy from the time it moved to the State College campus. Students could not exceed the equivalent of two weeks of classes (6 absences in a semester), that is, seven absences resulted in automatic failure. All faculty were required to keep formal attendance records,[11] and to inform students of the attendance policy during the first class.

EOD students reacted to the policy with anger and hostility. They argued that EOD classes were the only ones on the campus to require attendance and that the reading of the roll reminded them of high school. Their challenge represented an overwhelming belief that the division patronized them and treated them as children. Moreover, they believed that unlike the descriptions of other State College classes gleaned from non-EOD students, the EOD was structured, authoritarian and not really college-like in its atmosphere. The question of college level respectability did not limit itself to the content of a course, or the methods of instruction, but related to the ambiance of the classroom, as well.

Once again, the faculty's response to student claims was a divided one. Political and philosophical divisions within the EOD manifested themselves in heated and sometimes endless debate. At the center of the controversy stood the larger issue of educational policy and student performance. During this period, the Committee of Academic Performance documented high rates of absenteeism, lateness, and failure. Moreover, individual instructors were painfully aware of the attitudinal and motivational problems besetting many divisional courses; students also complained about the low motivation of many EOD students and the lack of academic rigor in many classes. By the 1980–81 academic year, a general malaise had infected the program, with the academic performance and low motivation of its students as central issues of concern.

The attendance debate reflected the division's attempts to come to grips with these problems. Many of the faculty connected low performance rates directly to poor attitude and argued that failure to attend classes was the major cause of failure. Others noted that poor attendance existed when a compulsory policy was in fact in effect. Those in favor of its retention replied that the problem was not the policy, but the faculty's inconsistent application of its requirements. They charged that only some instructors really enforced the policy, others ignored it, and still others bent the rules to fit individual cases. The problem, they argued, was that students were confused about the lack of uniformity. As one instructor noted:

> How can I expect students to respect the rules when some
> of us do not. Students come to me and say, 'But my other
> teachers are passing me.'

The divisional conflict reflected the different political perspectives of the faculty and their related educational philosophies. The older, conservative faculty supported the retention of the policy and strongly believed its abolition would mark the imminent decline of educational standards. For these members, the policy evoked their own passionate opposition to the State College program with its permissive educational atmosphere. What EOD students needed more than anything else was structure, as well as the enforcement of educational standards. Many of these faculty came from parochial (Catholic) educational backgrounds from elementary to graduate education and strongly believed in structure, discipline, and rigid academic requirements for all students, but especially for the underprepared learner. The younger, radical-liberal faculty were strongly against the attendance policy on opposing philosophical grounds, and spoke fervently against its retention. These members, many of whom were products of the educational innovations of the 1960s, were more comfortable with A.S. Neill than with St. Thomas Aquinas, and opposed the highly authoritarian nature of the program. More importantly, the young faculty, having more in common with their State College colleagues, intensified the division between the EOD's conservatives and the main programs, as the intraorganizational debate became a metaphor and a projection of interorganizational conflicts.

The central issue of the debate involved the epidemiology of student failure. Conservatives argued that poor study habits and motivation were the major deficits in the population and that divisional students had to learn to accept responsibility. Liberal faculty, who tended to move between both poles, bemoaned the effect of the unmotivated on the tasks of the division. A clear theme in this debate redefined the mission of the division in terms of opportunity; that is, the program gave disadvantaged students the opportunity to make up for their educational deficiencies, but they had to take responsibility for using the services.

The radical-liberal faculty did not disagree with the fact that lack of motivation represented a serious difficulty undermining the program. However, they argued that the conservative response treated symptoms and not causes. The program's psychologist commented that a complex set of cultural and psychological factors underlied students' attitudinal difficulties, and that changing behavior was far more complicated and difficult than setting external requirements. The program's sociologist noted that the student population had a history of poor relationships with highly structured and authoritarian high schools and the program's attempt to reproduce these relations of authority would exacerbate, not eliminate, student ambivalence. Although these faculty agreed that structure and expectations should be high, they considered the program's approach to represent a "blaming the victim" ideology. Moreover, they considered the analysis of the external social and psychological factors as more important than the enforcement of structured attendance requirements.

While the debate between the conservatives and radical-liberal wings defined the controversy, the liberal wing of the division controlled the majority of votes, and it was their movement between the poles that lengthened the discussions. These faculty shared conservative disdain for the unmotivated student, but also believed that the problems could not be solved by demanding compliance to external rules. They searched for a process of transforming the undisciplined student; or, as some critics of liberal educational ideology would suggest, of making minority students into "white middle class students."[12] The tone of their discussion certainly supported this view as they constantly spoke in terms of changing behaviors and instituting a process to teach students to take responsibility for their academic lives.

The liberal educational philosophy from which the division originated permeated these proceedings. The concepts of internalization of responsibility versus external authority became a major theme for months. Despite the differences of opinion the overall feeling emphasized the student as the major factor in determining academic success and described attitudinal factors as more problematic than the population's educational and skills deficiencies. The latter could be overcome with hard work and application; the former would make their solutions impossible.

Twice during the 1980-81 academic year the faculty voted to retain its compulsory attendance policy. By the end of the year the issue was still a hot one. At the year's final meeting, the director, noting continual student opposition to the policy, continued high absenteeism, and inconsistent application by divisional faculty, asked for the abolition of the attendance policy. This request, as we will see, was part of a more drastic proposal from the division's administration to legitimate student challenges and move in the direction of integration with the entire campus. The faculty, unable to offer solutions to the larger educational issues, voted to abolish the attendance policy. Once again, the separate and different character of the division was gradually declining. The conservative faculty bemoaned this vote as a prelude to further disintegration; the radical-liberal faculty did not see it as a victory, but as the initiation of continued discussion of the program's central problems; the liberal faculty hoped to move on to the real tasks of educating its students, and to continue to explore solutions to both the social and educational problems. As an issue, the attendance policy represented these larger concerns and, during the 1980-81 academic year, the discussions of performance and curriculum, all framed around the theme of divisional separation, became the focus of all divisional discussions.

Independent Research Paper

No other single issue defined the division's difficulty in developing what it considered the appropriate curriculum for underprepared students than its deliberations concerning the independent research paper requirement. From 1978-1981, the division required that all students complete an acceptable research paper (minimum fifteen pages), approved by both a faculty member in a discipline (for content) and in the English Department (for organization and grammar), before moving to the junior year. This requirement had two purposes: 1. to demonstrate writing and research competencies reflecting junior level abilities, and 2. to prepare for the independent skills required for the State College senior thesis.

The division's faculty strongly believed in this requirement, but the continued difficulties in administering the requirement and the large number of students who failed to complete the paper by the junior year resulted in an ongoing debate over the policy. Throughout the 1979-1980 and 1980-1981 academic years the issue emerged as a major curricular problem and one that spoke directly to the notions of educational standards, student responsibility, and educational preparation. For over a year and a half the discussions centered on how to best administer and carry out the policy, but by Spring 1981, like many of the policies that originally defined the division, the faculty voted to abolish the requirement entirely. The reasons for this decision were complex, but they were all framed by the issue of educational obstruction. EOD students perceived the research paper as another divisional constraint to their progress. Because it became a symbol to students of divisional barriers to upward transition, the faculty felt it had no other recourse but to remove it. More importantly, the abolishment of the requirement represented the inability of the faculty to come to grips with its mission, as the debates certainly revealed.

Originally, the English Department supervised the independent research paper requirements. In fact, the English requirements for completion of the EOD program included English 101, 102 and the independent research paper. The English Department introduced students to library research skills and the research paper in English 102, with the submission of a short (eight page) research paper, the final requirement of this course. The independent research paper requirement was intended to be just that, an independent project. Students were supposed to choose a discipline instructor, propose a topic, and complete the paper. The paper would then be submitted to both the instructor and an English instructor for the approval of content, organization, and grammar. This requirement presented a number of serious dilemmas that brought into focus the essential problems of compensatory higher education.

The first problem concerned the implementation and supervision of the paper. Ideally, students could select any 200 (sophomore) level course in a discipline and write a paper for the course. However, since not all 200 level discipline courses required a research paper, and since all students in a given course did not want to fulfill the requirement in that class, the completion of the paper presented some difficulty. First, if all 200 level courses required a research paper for all students, it would be possible for students to complete the requirement within any EOD sophomore course. Although this might have appeared a simple solution to some, it became the subject of considerable consternation. Some discipline instructors, on grounds of academic freedom, balked at any divisional edict requiring the assignment of a research paper. An instructor, they argued, must have autonomy over his/her course requirements and division wide definitions of course curriculum were unacceptable. Others argued that the requirement of a research paper allowed students to get around specific course requirements and readings by writing a paper on a related topic, but not including some of the course's important topics or texts. The faculty rejected the solution of requiring both a research paper and a final exam on course content, as too heavy for EOD students.

The failure to establish one method of implementation resulted in chaos for both faculty and students. Because the division never really clarified its position, students did not really understand the purpose, intent, or method of completing the paper. Moreover, the English department, by offering a one credit independent research paper course, added to the ambiguity and confusion. This course was intended only for students who required additional help with research skills. However, it posed a particular problem as students without these needs complained they were being short-changed. For example, a student writing a research paper to fulfill a political science course requirement received four credits (for the course), but a student also enrolled in the independent research paper seminar received the same four credits for the discipline course, plus the extra credit for the seminar. Therefore, the more needy students received an extra-credit for essentially the same work. The idea of giving all students one credit for the paper did not receive much support as it granted an extra credit to the students in a course who used a research paper to fulfill the divisional requirements, but not to the other students in the class. In theory, all students would receive an extra credit just once, so it would all even out;

however, in practice it became impossible to justify and administer.

The continued uncertainty and ambiguity within the faculty was only intensified by the difficulties in administering the policy. Without a clear understanding of the requirement, students did not complete it on a timely basis. They often chose to complete the paper in a discipline course, delayed until it was too late, and because the course did not require a research paper, the student then chose to take the final examination instead, or just not write the paper, if it was not a course requirement. Some instructors handled this by requiring all students to complete the paper as one of the course's requirements; others did not allow shifting from the paper option. In addition, some students were permitted to complete their requirement within English 102, if they produced a quality 15 page paper. While this helped the more able students, it just added to the confusion. There were just too many ways to proceed and no clear policy — it became an administrative and curricular nightmare and its solution did not seem possible.

The second, and perhaps more crucial issue concerned the level of acceptability. The necessity for two faculty signatures, grading both content and writing resulted in many problems. Often papers passed on content, but failed on writing. This led to endless rewrites and the failure to complete the requirement. Additionally, students could not understand how a paper that allowed them to minimally pass a discipline course (with a C or D — although the lack of grades intensified the problem, since the P did not make the point as a D could) could not fulfill the independent paper requirement. By the 1980–81 academic year it became clear that no standard of acceptability existed, with many passing papers clearly below the standards of State College. This touched a particularly sensitive issue as the division did not want to stand accused of passing along unprepared students, yet it faced continued charges by students of obstructing their progress.

For the entire year the faculty debated the issue in a variety of forums. The curriculum committee spent countless hours on the establishment of a reasonable policy, and the faculty as a whole debated their proposals with no consensus. The English faculty and the Humanities-Social Science faculty all held separate meetings to resolve the dilemma. Finally, at the end of the fall semester, in disgust, the coordinator of the English program distanced herself from the matter by declaring it "a divisional, not an English matter." The coordinator of the Humanities-Social Sciences, who represented those most in favor of the requirement, moved in and accepted responsibility for setting the policy. Although the division did not adopt a policy at this time, a major change had occurred: the independent research paper now became a divisional rather than an English requirement and fell under the auspices of the disciplines.

The spring semester picked up where the fall semester had ended, with the coordinator of the disciplines trying to develop a rational system. The director announced that all 200 level instructors should require a research paper and this would solve the problem. Moreover, he implied that if the faculty was not prepared to gear their courses to student needs and the program's goals, then they ought to re-evaluate their commitment to the program. The faculty reacted with hostility to his implications and rejected the proposal. The debate continued.

The discussions moved from the question of implementation to the question of the realistic nature of the requirements. If it was a question of administration, some argued it could be solved. However, if the completion of the paper posed an unrealistic demand on students still incapable of meeting its requirements, then students should be given more time in the division. This introduced a significant issue that symbolized the faculty's frustration: how do you adequately prepare disadvantaged students when the time pressures are often contradictory to this goal. Perhaps students needed three full years in the division to make up for their skills deficits; however, the students' perception of the division as obstructing their progress was only enhanced by this feeling. The continued backlog of students who had fulfilled all their requirements but did not possess the skills to complete the research paper was a source of frustration and embarrassment. How did they get this far? What can we do at this date? All of these represented very delicate problems.

Some of the faculty insisted that it had to come up with a solution that retained the research paper, so that students would move to the junior level with adequate preparation. Others insisted that students technically remain in the division until they completed the requirement, even while cross registering for all their courses. One conservative faculty member argued a somewhat contradictory position of defending standards, but abolishing the requirement as elitist. In an emotional statement that summarized the entire faculty's frustration he stated:

> The problem is not EOD, but little Oxford (State College). We are too conscious of the senior thesis, which is an elitist requirement, in any case. Our students cannot write sentences or paragraphs and we are debating research papers. What is needed is a complete revamping of the English sequence, with an emphasis on grammar, not research. And if it takes our students three years to complete the program, so be it.

The faculty realized he had hit a critical point, nevertheless, they reacted angrily and rejected this claim. Although many students retained skills deficiencies, keeping them back would not solve the problem, but only intensify their feelings of imprisonment. Finally, after almost two years of seemingly endless debate, the faculty gave up and abolished the requirement. The action was part of the Spring 1981 abolition movement and symbolized the continued weakening of divisional requirements and boundaries. It represented both a response to student claims of imprisonment, but more importantly the frustration of the faculty in dealing with student weaknesses and their inability to successfully help them to be ready for the transition to the junior year. In fact, it was part of a larger debate on the entire divisional curriculum as a response to student claims of imprisonment by divisional requirements.

Challenges to the Curriculum

Over the first three years at State College, the EOD students continually challenged the division's curriculum on a number of grounds. First, they argued that many EOD courses repeated their high school curriculum and that taking these courses was demeaning. Moreover, because the courses were heavily geared to skills, many students charged that the courses did not provide intellectual stimulation and challenge. In addition, they suggested that the poor motivation and attendance of many students reflected these problems more than any inherent attitudinal defects. Finally, some students claimed that the divisional requirements obstructed their academic progress and kept them entrapped within the division for longer than they cared to stay. These perceptions combined to form a constant vocal challenge to the curriculum, with students' demands for, at the least, a liberalized cross registration policy.

The faculty's response to these claims reflected its traditional concerns with educational preparation and philosophy. At the beginning of the conflict, most faculty rejected the student arguments and defended the necessity of the requirement. The invocation of "history" became the legitimating ideology, as the division pointed to the time tested methods of the past. It had worked diligently at Coop College to construct an appropriate curriculum, and the faculty was confident of its practicality and necessity. However, the faculty response pointed to the educational deficits of its students as justification, by arguing "if you did not need skills courses, you would not be in the division." Therefore, to the faculty, the curriculum realistically reflected the entering level of its students and, while students rebelled against this distinction, the faculty felt that the EOD population needed the types of courses it offered. The initial response was somewhat paternalistic, with the faculty deflecting student claims by telling them, "we know best what is good for you."

The charge of divisional obstructionism also met with initial faculty rejection. As one faculty member stated:

> If they could handle the regular courses, they would not be here. The purpose of our courses is to prepare them and make up for their skills deficiencies. By definition, it must take them longer to finish. EOP funding recognizes this and allows our students five years to complete the degree, one year for catching up and four more to finish. The problem is our students just don't recognize the need; they want to be treated like everyone else, but they are not. At some point, they will realize this and thank us!

Moreover, the faculty handled the students' claim concerning the level of the EOD courses and their repetition of high school in a similar manner:

> The point is they did not do well in these courses in high school, so they must make them up here. If they had mastered algebra and writing skills, and biology and chemistry at the high school level, they would not need us. Certainly, our first year curriculum in some ways duplicates the academic track of a good high school, but our kids did not successfully complete the academic track, or only marginally so, and one cannot state that they graduated from good high schools. Our admissions and placement tests determine the course level for each student; if they have the skills they do not belong in the course; if they have no skills deficiencies, they do not belong in the program.

Thus, the initial faculty response defended the curriculum and posited the problem as one of "misplacement." The program would be careful, in the future, to tighten its placement process (that is, making sure students entered at their proper level) and to allow students who were obviously misplaced in the division to accelerate into the mainstream programs. In this way, the division would serve its intended population and eliminate some of the tensions resulting from student discontent.

The problem of student misplacement represented the much larger issue of admissions policy.[13] During the first three years on campus, the director noticed some irregularities in the admissions process and attempted to clarify the procedures with the State College Admissions office. The EOD had its own admissions policy, separate from regular admissions, with its own set of procedures, interviewing and testing. In addition, for its first two years on campus (before budget cuts eliminated the position), the division had its own recruiter working out of the admissions office. While the EOD program recruited and admitted students independent of regular admissions, the two offices were supposed to coordinate activities. That is, EOD sent the folders of students who clearly met regular admissions standards to regular admissions, and regular admissions sent its rejections who met state EOP requirements to the EOD.

In practice, a number of problems emerged. First, it seemed all students who checked the EOP box on the central application form were immediately sent to EOD, regardless of educational disadvantage.[14] This led to the placement or at least transfer of applications of most minority applicants to the EOD. Many of these students who checked the EOP box for financial, not educational reasons, found themselves in the EOD. Second, the regular admissions office seemed to forward the applications of marginal[15] minority students to EOD, but either accept borderline white students or reject them without forwarding their applications to EOD. This informal policy[16] had significant consequences. First, it often resulted in the admission of some borderline minority students into EOD (students, who in theory were admissible to the program who did not meet regular admissions standards), whose educational deficits were not as glaring as the rest of its population. Second, many borderline white students were admitted directly to the regular program. These processes resulted in many EOD students feeling misplaced and more importantly stigmatized. They realized that the community equated the EOD with minority status and with educational deficiencies, but also realized that many of their white roommates, outside of the division, were not more intelligent or skilled than they were. On an educational level, these students often felt entrapped and unstimulated; on a social and political level, they clamored for reform.

The faculty understood this problem and sought to redress it through tighter admissions policy, better placement and the individual, case by case, response to student claims. However, the faculty rejected the idea that the problem was widespread, for if that were the case, the division's very existence seemed threatened. Sticking to its guns, the faculty viewed the majority of its population as in severe need of remediation, and sought to allow speedy cross registration for those truly without need. For example, one student who clearly impressed a number of faculty with her competent skills, and who clearly was misplaced and bored in all her classes, was granted permission to cross-register for all her courses by the second semester. However, the faculty viewed this as the exception, not the rule.

A more serious charge presented by students concerned the EOD courses themselves. Arguing that they were repetitive in level and atmosphere to high school, the students challenged their necessity. Although all courses were mentioned, the math and science curriculum received the heaviest complaints. Students said they were insulted by the level of Math 100, a course in arithmetic concepts, Math 101 and 102, courses they argued were the equivalent of ninth or tenth grade algebra, and Life and Physical Science courses, which again, they charged were not even equivalent to high school biology or physics.

The level of required courses was only part of the problem, as the time requirement necessary to proceed to "college level" created numerous other problems. Since many EOD students intended to major in the natural sciences,[17] they viewed the EOD requirements as seriously obstructing their path to the major. For example, an entering student might be required to take Math 100, 101, 102, 103, and 107 before reaching the required calculus course taken by regularly admitted students in their freshman year. Likewise, some students might take Physical Science, Life Science, Introduction to Biology I, II, Introduction to Chemistry I and II before being permitted to enroll in regular General Biology I, II, and Chemistry I, II that regularly admitted prospective science majors took in their freshman year. While this indeed represented the most extreme case, and while it did not happen often, it did occur at times, and often for students who did not need all of the courses. The fact that, in some cases, these students could not begin their science major until the junior year and would have to stay six years at State College to graduate resulted in the perception, if not the reality, of obstructionism.

The Curriculum Committee took the responsibility for examining these problems, and began with a consideration of the Math and Science programs. The Math-Science faculty reacted defensively to being singled out, and initially dismissed student claims. They offered a simple response: 1. students were placed in courses based on testing and only those in severe need had to take all of the courses, 2. EOD science students had to take Math 103 and 107 and Introduction to Biology I, II and Introduction to Chemistry I, II — those with skills deficiencies had to take the prescribed courses in preparation for these, 3. EOD students, by definition, could not handle the regular calculus or General Biology and Chemistry I, II and the entire purpose of EOD courses was to prepare them to successfully handle these courses, 4. therefore, the EOD Math-Science curriculum was the necessary component of the disadvantaged students' program, and if it took six years for the student to graduate, then this was what was required, and 5. without the background these courses provided, the students would certainly fail out of the rigorous science program.

While the Curriculum Committee did not seriously challenge the

Math-Science faculty's defense of its requirements, the Committee did push for some reform. First, the Committee proposed that all prospective science majors begin with EOD Introduction to Biology and Introduction to Chemistry (skipping Physical and Life Science). Second, they proposed that students with proper skills move more rapidly in the sequence; for example, from EOD Introduction to Biology I to regular General Biology II; from EOD Math 103, directly to regular Calculus. Although the Math-Science faculty had reservations, they agreed to carefully monitor student placement and progress and to implement discussions with the Natural Science faculty about using EOD faculty recommendations to waive the General Science course requirements based upon excellent performance in EOD introductory courses. Although no specific policy emerged, the spirit of addressing student claims evolved from the discussions.

A more crucial issue emerged from these discussions, and although it did not receive considerable attention at this point, it would become central to the politics of integration that developed in the 1981–1982 academic year. The repetition and duplication of courses, for example, Introduction to Biology in EOD and General Biology in the natural sciences, pointed to the issue of college level acceptability. The Natural Sciences did not accept the EOD course as equivalent and, therefore, students had to take their courses. The acceptability of EOD courses as "real courses" caused both the faculty and students considerable anguish and defined a central perceptual and educational problem of compensatory higher education. The claims to difference and the deficits of EOD students used to justify the program resulted in the regular divisions defining EOD courses as remedial and below college level. The contradiction, however, was that the EOD claimed difference to justify its existence, argued its students could not handle regular State College courses, but at the same time, demanded equal status (crediting) and recognition of some of its courses, at times as equivalent. Although the EOD based its demands on the various levels of its courses, the rest of the college did not always understand these distinctions. Therefore, both students and faculty were locked in a definitional bind, to claim to be both different and equal, but to receive little or no recognition. This would become a critical issue in faculty interactions in the coming years. At this point, the students perceived these definitions as further examples of their stigmatization. More importantly, it left them confused and angry about their place on the State College campus.

If the Math-Science issue was the most evident, it did not constitute the only challenge, but rather symbolized student claims. By the end of the 1980–1981 academic year, students angrily denounced the majority of EOD requirements, including two courses in three disciplinary areas, freshman orientation, the independent research paper, etc. In addition, the large number of students with 56 credits, but one or more requirements outstanding, led to the CAP's rejection of their applications to move to junior status. Moreover, the division could not continue to require these students to take divisional courses, as budgetary cuts limited EOD offerings, but more importantly, the students who anxiously awaited their transition to the regular divisions, balked at taking any more courses. The only solution was to let students unofficially move to the junior year taking almost all their courses outside the division, and completing the requirements at the same time. All of these events resulted in the continued perception of entrapment and more importantly, to the continued withering of the legitimacy of division boundaries, if not the boundaries themselves.

Curriculum and Cross Registration

During the 1980–81 academic year, the faculty grappled with numerous curricular issues, but none as important as the divisional cross registration policy. Like the grading and attendance policies, the discussion of cross registration was initiated by student claims and, in a similar fashion, the debates spoke to the heart of divisional difference and separation. However, as a single process, cross registration represented the most significant issue as it would directly result in the initiation of forms of integration with other college divisions.

Discussions about the cross registration policy, as most of the discussion during this period, was framed by the concern over EOD student performance. While the faculty was acutely aware of the problems its students were having within the division, the spectre of underprepared students in regular courses raised serious educational problems. Cross registration meant mainstreaming, and the faculty concerned itself with the multitude of issues related to this concept.

The apprehension over cross registration, however, was not limited to educational problems, but related to organizational identity and survival. While the division certainly pursued their students' best interests, with the concept of readiness and preparation central features of all discussions, the faculty understood that a liberalized cross registration policy opened up the floodgates toward more total integration and could eventually threaten the division's very existence. Moreover, from a purely administrative vantage point, cross registration would send EOD students out into the college, increasing other division's FTE's[18] and decreasing them in the EOD. In a period of budgetary constraint, and with a college administration that was extremely enrollment conscious, the numbers game could not be overlooked. Thus, the cross registration discussions featured all of the major themes relevant to the division's existence, such as:

1. divisional identity and separation;
2. mainstreaming;
3. the needs of the student population;
4. organizational survival;
5. the relationship between EOD and other divisions.

Upon the move to State College, the original EOD requirements mandated that students take their first 56 credits within the division, before qualifying for junior status. The intent was to insure that the underprepared student receive the special attention, curriculum and pedagogy of the EOD as the preparation for the upper divisional curriculum at State College. Implicit was not only the belief that the division provided the best program for its students, but that State College could not and would not meet their needs. Within this context, the division's perception of State College and its faculty as elitist and insensitive to the needs of the underprepared population defined all discussions of the matter.

During the first two years at State College, as we have noted, the EOD students consistently challenged all forms of divisional separation, arguing that it was stigmatizing and degrading. At the same time, the program's administration and faculty responded to these claims by defending the educational necessity of separation. The cross registration issue spoke directly to this conflict between social and educational functions, and the faculty proceeded to debate both aspects of the question.

The students demanded the liberalization of the cross registration policy and asked for a system that permitted EOD students to take courses in any division of the college. Once again, their challenge, fueled by perceptions of differential treatment and relative deprivation, pointed to the rigid structure of the program and its unfair requirements as compared to the regular programs, which had little or no requirements. Moreover, the college's adoption of a unified freshman experience for all regular admissions students, through the newly created Freshman Studies Program,[19] intensified the separation of EOD students from their fellow classmates in other divisions. While the entire freshmen class took a common year long course stressing the interdisciplinary study of Western civilization, the EOD students felt isolated in their program. It is true that many of these students felt they could not handle the material, but others thought they deserved the opportunity. More importantly, the students felt they were robbed of an important collective experience: the seminars, whatever their educational value, did provide a collective endeavor for freshmen (and, in fact, the program was instituted to provide a sense of community for incoming students on a campus where lack of community was a common complaint), and EOD students reacted negatively to their inability to share these common experiences. Their reaction all too clearly emphasized the division's central dilemma: how to provide the best educational program for its students, but avoid the systematic isolation and separation of its population and the declining spirit and self-concept seemingly a product of such isolation.

In addition to the social disadvantages of divisional separation, many students questioned the educational efficacy of the EOD curriculum and methods. These claims went to the heart of the division's mission and required the faculty to examine the educational effects of the program. Many students charged that the EOD courses were patronizing at the high school level and did not provide either stimulation or challenge. They suggested that the poor performance of EOD students and high absenteeism were a consequence of these shortcomings, and students wanted the opportunity to enroll in what they considered the real courses at State College. Moreover, many students claimed that the overall malaise pervading the EOD program spread through the population, negatively affecting the students' growth, both intellectually and socially. More than any other single issue, then, this required a complete analysis of the program, a process that would begin in 1980–81 and reach systematic proportions in the following year as the State College accreditation process was to begin.

The faculty understood the necessity for a clear policy regarding cross registration. Throughout the past year, although students were not supposed to cross-register, an ad hoc policy had permitted it on a case by case basis. By the middle of the 1980–81 year, the faculty could not prevent the tides of discontent from weakening its walls, so they debated the adoption of a sensible policy to ensure both that students' needs were met and divisional survival protected.

The cross registration debates evoked considerable emotions and tensions at both curriculum and faculty meetings. The discussions centered on issues related to divisional separation and mainstreaming. Although the faculty had moved away from the support of total separation, and recognized the need to mainstream its students earlier than the junior year, the question of when to allow cross registration emerged as a central concern. The faculty pointed to its mission to prepare its students for State College and in doing so suggested the positive and negative aspects of mainstreaming. Nevertheless, since students would be expected to eventually handle regular classes, they should have a taste of them at the lower divisional level. Since students had pointed to considerable differences between the EOD classes and the upper divisional courses at State College, the faculty believed some exposure to the regular programs might be accomplished through cross registration into selected lower division courses. Secondly, the faculty did recognize the social disadvantages of separation and felt that the gradual integration of its students would ease some of the tensions. Therefore, the faculty understood the educational and social value of cross registration for its students, but also recognized the problems inherent in the process.

The negative aspects of a liberalized cross registration policy, according to the faculty, were related to the concepts of preparation and readiness. However, these issues were framed by an overall distrust of the State College programs and their ability to provide a proper educational environment for the disadvantaged student. Pointing to the large class sizes in introductory courses, the absence of a commitment to the division's population, and the elitism of the State College faculty, the EOD faculty were very apprehensive about cross registration. The majority of the faculty still believed that a separate division provided the best system for their population, but the pressures against complete separation made this impossible to defend. The key then involved the implementation of a policy that would provide some of the positive aspects of integration, while simultaneously retaining the important characteristics of divisional autonomy. Furthermore, the EOD sought to avoid the problems they foresaw due to the lack of concern and expertise outside the division.

The ideology of expertise comprised a significant part of these deliberations, as divisional autonomy was legitimated by the faculty's invocation of its own special talents. Using the argument that for over 10 years they had experimented with the appropriate methods for underprepared students, the faculty defended its autonomy by imputing its special character. This presentation of its special character was not only used to define the division's particular place on the campus, but represented the underlying differences between EOD faculty and State College faculty. While at this point no overall attitude about the college's faculty existed, the majority of the division's members either distrusted or were openly hostile to their colleagues in other divisions.

The Roots of Interorganizational Conflict:
The Different Missions of EOD and State College

At the heart of interdivisional conflict were the two different missions of the EOD and State College programs. The EOD, committed to its definition of compensatory higher education, felt the State College programs, with their commitment to innovation and elitism were essentially incapable of meeting the needs of EOD students. As in the other intraorganizational conflicts, the EOD faculty became divided along political and philosophical grounds. The conservatives scorned the State College elitism, deplored its lack of structure, discipline, and rationality, and saw no reason to integrate with other divisions. They referred to State College with remarks like "little Oxford" and fervently believed any form of integration would be disastrous for the students and the EOD. Furthermore, they could not understand student problems about the division and felt that EOD faculty needlessly compared themselves to their colleagues in other divisions, and that these negative comparisons and perceptions by EOD faculty were partially responsible for the division's malaise. Their perspective was clear: the EOD was superior to all other programs on campus, its faculty the most committed and hard working, and its existence as a separate division worth defending. The clear path for the division according to these faculty should be the strengthening of divisional autonomy and the rejection of claims for cross registration and integration.

The radical-liberal faculty presented the opposing viewpoint and often acted in what they believed was representative of student claims. These members, some of whom were original members from Coop College, while others were new to the program during the State College years, were somewhat skeptical of the ideology of expertise and far less hostile to the State College faculty and the concept of integration. They had much in common with the college's young faculty and, while understanding the difficulties endemic to cross registration, did not see them as insoluble. More importantly, the radical-liberals strongly supported student claims concerning isolation and social stigma and supported liberalized cross registration for these reasons.

Consistent with previous conflicts, the resolution of the cross registration issue rested with the majority, the liberal faculty. While the solutions always involved some integration of conservative and radical-liberal perspectives, the liberal faculty integrated their points into its own vision of the program. The overall concern of these faculty, at this point, was the adoption of a sensible policy incorporating the positive aspects of cross registration, with protection against the negative features. The liberal faculty shared some of the mistrust for the State College faculty, but were far more willing to acknowledge their ability to work with EOD faculty to meet the needs of its students. Moreover, they concerned themselves with the reality of student claims. Although they all supported divisional separation in theory, the realities of student pressures necessitated some liberalization. Furthermore, these faculty fervently believed in the ideology of expertise and were cautious about loosening the barriers. This feeling was clearly stated by one liberal faculty member, whose ideas, while not necessarily shared by this constituency, seemed to define the heart of the division's approach. In speaking to the relationship between the EOD and the new Freshman Studies Program, she stated:

1.   The academic part of the Freshman Studies Program is not suitable
        for EOD freshmen because:
        a) of the number and length of the readings, and
        b) of its essentially non-disciplinary nature.[20]

2.   EOD students should share in the social experiences of the
        Freshman Studies Program, while taking all their first year
        courses within the EOD (1982b:1).

Therefore, by the middle of the 1980–81 academic year the
majority of the faculty moved to support some forms of integration, but
were opposed to any enrollment of its students in the educational aspects of
the Freshman Studies Program. The liberals, however, did not rule out the
liberalization of cross registration in other types of classes.

During the Fall semester of 1980, the past year's debates culminated
in the adoption of a liberalized cross registration policy. The policy included
a compromise between the conservative's total opposition and student
demands for the elimination of all restrictions. It stated:

In general, EOD students should not register for courses in
other divisions before their second semester. Second,
students may cross register if:

1.   they are completing the EOD requirements, and

2.   they have not failed any course or received an Incomplete grade in
        any course in the preceding semester.

3.   they have passed an EOD course in the same discipline (if possible)
        or in the same area (social sciences, natural sciences, etc.).

4.   they have the permission of the faculty member who taught the
        EOD course, or the permission of the coordinator of the area in
        which he/she seeks to cross register.

5.   they have the approval of their faculty advisor.

In most cases EOD students should cross register for
courses only up to the 200 level. No student should cross-
register for more than two courses in any given semester,
not including Physical Education or Art courses. In
exceptional cases, permission to cross register must be

granted by a committee consisting of the director, the
faculty advisor, and one member of the Committee on
Academic Progress.

As a compromise, the policy left divisional autonomy intact and
temporarily assuaged student challenges. However, as we will see, its highly
bureaucratic formula led to severe problems of enforcement and the
subsequent ignoring of its complicated features by faculty.

By the Spring 1981 semester, the division was at a crossroads. The
past year and a half saw the liberalization of the cross-registration policy,
the debate over attendance, the implementation of a freshman study skills
course to provide EOD students with motivational and attitudinal support
and the overall loosening of divisional boundaries. Nonetheless, student and
faculty morale was decimated by the problems of motivation, poor student
performance, continued student challenges to divisional separation, and
constant budgetary constraints on the entire college, and particularly on the
division. Moreover, the cross registration policy proved impossible to
monitor, resulting in haphazard advisement and student discontent. At the
last scheduled faculty meeting of the Spring 1981 semester the director took
bold strides to respond to these problems by proposing steps that would
move the program closer to integration.

Citing the continued challenges of its students concerning racism,
their desire to move out of the division, their view of the division as
obstructing their progress, and the student attack on divisional requirements,
the director proposed the following:

1.   the abolition of the attendance policy,
2.   the abolition of all cross-registration restrictions.

Arguing that many of the division's students felt imprisoned by the division
and that a feeling of oppression and separatism pervaded its walls, the
director urged a complete loosening of divisional barriers. While he stated
his philosophical opposition to these moves, he stressed that it was necessary
to protect EOD students. If students indeed perceived the divisional structure
as counterproductive no matter how much the faculty supported the
division's continuation, as director he could not support any program that
obstructed student progress. He did not wish to disband the division, only
to open the gates. In addition, he felt the reduced pressure would strengthen
the division and might result in the students taking a more realistic
assessment of the division's positive contribution. Stressing the need to
abandon its protective structures, the director pointed out that EOD students
had to learn to face responsibility in the real world, and the free movement

into all courses represented a first step.

The Politics of Integration: The Decline of EOD

The director's recommendations for the loosening of the restrictive divisional boundaries were the result of three years of frustration and conflict. After arriving at the State College campus with reservations, but nonetheless positive expectations, the program had navigated troubled waters. Continued challenges by its students, internal disagreements among the faculty, and the continued budgetary problems in the state university system all provided the impetus toward some form of integration. In addition, the problems of student performance and retention required the faculty to engage in continual self-examination. The director made it clear that he was not abandoning the separate divisional structure, but was reacting to a situation that called for some immediate action. While he was not at all certain that his moves would produce favorable results, he believed they would reduce the tensions produced by student challenges.

The faculty called an emergency meeting after the semester ended to discuss the director's proposals. Perhaps exhausted from the year's battles and in one faculty member's words "burnt out," the faculty did not seem to have the energy or desire to rekindle old debates. Nonetheless, the entire future of the division seemed at stake, and the faculty did not take the task at hand lightly. Although the overall tone of the meeting was collegial, the general atmosphere was not one of resignation. The director's proposals did not go over well and did not receive considerable support. The majority of the faculty still fervently believed in the division's separate identity and felt the continued loosening of its boundaries would be detrimental to the division and its students. The discussions placed the major emphasis on the needs of EOD students, and most faculty opposed unrestricted cross-registration. In a compromise move, the faculty voted to table any motion on unrestricted cross registration. However, they approved the following statement defining the intent and spirit of the divisional policy:

> As a general rule, incoming freshmen should not be allowed to cross register. Students with exceptionally strong skills must have permission of the coordinator of the area they wish to crossregister. The curriculum committee should reexamine all of the cross registration rules this fall. Any revisions of the rules should be made well in advance of Spring registration, and our student body should be informed of the new regulations.

The division's faculty chose not to make a hasty decision, but to carefully examine the issues in the coming year. The work, however, could not wait until the Fall semester, as two important events would begin in September. First, State College's new President would begin his first year as the college's head administrative officer and second, the Middle States Accreditation Committee would complete its evaluation of all State College programs. The beginning of the new administration marked an important crossroads for all constituencies at State College. After two years of administrative uncertainty, the 1979–1980 year marked by turmoil, the censure and subsequent resignation of its President, the 1980–81 year defined by its acting President as a time of stability but little change or innovation, the arrival of a new administration would certainly set the stage for a critical appraisal of all programs. In a time of continued budgetary crisis, declining enrollments, and an overall college attrition rate that was highest in the state system, the State College program needed leadership, and the faculty expressed apprehension about what this leadership would mean. In addition, the accreditation review required the production of a large self-study report outlining the college's strengths and weaknesses. In all respects, the entire college would experience a period of critical self-examination and appraisal, and the coming year would be crucial in determining the future direction of the college and all of its programs.

The Educational Opportunity Division had particular reason to be concerned over these events. Over the past three years the college budget crisis had affected this division more than any other on the campus. The division arrived at State Campus with 19 faculty lines, including a full-time admissions recruiter and a counseling psychologist. By the 1981–82 year the division lost 5.5 lines, including the recruiter and the psychologist. Moreover, the budgetary constraints seemed to always place the EOD in a particularly vulnerable position, with its low student-faculty ratios, declining enrollments, and the duplication of discipline courses.[21] Although the director always defended such features (with the exception of declining enrollments) as necessary to the division's mission, growing pressure from the campus community over the division's separation began to emerge. While the 1980–81 academic year did not produce any direct administrative threats to the division, with the acting President choosing to leave these types of decisions to his successor, the division's director and staff felt particularly vulnerable, and the mounting pressure from within did not help matters. The collective solidarity that had defined the EOD upon its arrival had eroded, along with the divisional boundaries.

The EOD had been particularly concerned with the selection of the new President. The division's faculty representative spent long sessions interviewing prospective candidates on their support of compensatory higher education. Although the candidate she felt was most likely to support the division did not get the post, she expressed an anxious anticipation about the new President. While he was coming from another state school with an educational opportunity program, and stated his support of this program as Dean of the college, he was not familiar with the concept of a separate division. The EOP program at this former institution was an integrative program, and although he supported the concept of an educational opportunity program, he would not commit himself to EOD's form.

The summer of 1981 became crucial in preparing for the accreditation review and the arrival of the new President. A faculty committee (consisting primarily of original faculty) set about to write the EOD section of the self-study report and, in doing so, to clarify the division's mission, identity and purpose. The guidelines for this report emerged from two sources: 1. The EOD faculty, who wanted a review of the program with respect to its continued internal problems. Rather than passively support the director's recommendations to break down its walls, the faculty chose to use this opportunity to review and clarify the program by retaining its strengths and providing alternatives to its weaknesses. 2. Administrative input: the academic review committee, chaired by the Assistant Academic Vice-President (the former Dean of Social Sciences, and Professor of Sociology) drew up a number of specific questions for the EOD section. These questions clearly pointed to integration of some type as the future direction of the EOD. In addition to questions about the program's history, the move to State College, and the changes that occurred in this process, the suggestions revolved around two important themes: a. the effectiveness of the present divisional structure, and b. the articulation and integration of the division with other segments of the college. Toward the latter, the committee posed the following questions:

1. are EOD students different from regularly admitted students in degree or in kind? If they are different, in degree only, should EOD courses be open to weak L & S students?

2. to what degree should EOD remain separate academically?

3. how much can the division loosen up around the edges?

4. should the college push for more exchange of faculty?

Thus, the movement for some type of integration came from three directions: 1. internally from student claims, 2. internally from faculty responses to these claims, and 3. externally, from the college administration and faculty. At this point, no clear plan existed; however, the EOD faculty understood that to survive it had to act to redefine itself within the college's budgetary constraints and to do so quickly. The accreditation committee took this as its major task and prepared itself to complete its self-study over the summer.

At the final faculty meeting of the Spring 1981 semester, the faculty began to seriously consider the question of integration. The conservatives still actively opposed the concept, however, the radical-liberal coalition moved in this direction. At this meeting, the introduction of a new direction (partially in response to the academic review committee guidelines) emerged, and although its form appeared undeveloped, it reflected what would be the division's direction in the coming years. Instead of supporting the director's wishes to loosen the barriers by *integrating out*, the faculty introduced the concept of *integrating in*. This concept would prove to be essential to the division's future and reflected the continued belief in the division's identity and mission. Moreover, it would become the central response to the accreditation questions and the framework for the division's self-study.

In an undeveloped form, the idea of *integrating in* was proposed by a senior faculty member, one of the strongest defenders of divisional autonomy and its mission. While she rejected conservative opposition to any form of integration, she, more than any other member of the faculty, espoused the importance of a separate division and the expertise of the EOD faculty. Moreover, her visibility on the campus as one of the divisional representatives to the Educational Policy Committee and her writing on skills-content synthesis made her an active spokesperson for what she considered the division's special place on the State College campus. Although the division's faculty did not always feel that she represented the collective will of the division, her importance cannot be understated. She continually imputed the divisional ideology, both internally and externally, and was instrumental in reminding all parties of the historical roots and educational philosophies that made the division *different*, and the educational realities that she felt made these differences necessary.

In a brief position paper to the division's faculty presented at this meeting, she introduced the concept under the heading *Articulation of the EOD with the Freshman-Sophomore Program*:

Problem

1.   The Freshman Studies Program is the only
      experience which freshmen have in com-

mon, and EOD Freshman should not be excluded.

2.   The academic part of the program is not suitable for EOD Freshmen, because of the number and length of the readings and because of its essentially non-disciplinary nature.

3.   The Freshman Studies program is only one course, and all students need courses in the disciplines which will supplement the training in skills which the Freshman Studies Program offers, both on the freshman and sophomore level.

4.   Students in other divisions have begun to ask for courses similar to EOD courses.

5.   As the Freshman Studies Program begins to take in more students, notably from the Arts divisions (where academic criteria for admissions do not operate), it will be faced with the needs for skills work on a level it has not yet attempted to address.

Solution

1.   The EOD faculty have had 12 years of experience in developing a program of skills courses which could be opened to students from other divisions who need them.

2.   The EOD faculty is also highly experienced in teaching discipline courses with a high skills component, which could be offered to students in other divisions.

3.   To safeguard the interests of the EOD student population, enrollment in classes by students in other Divisions should be

kept to 1/3 of the total class size.

Implementation

1.   Diagnostic tests given to entering fresh-
     men should determine how many need
     EOD courses in English and/or Math.

2.   The different Boards of Study would
     discuss and approve courses in the disci-
     plines open to students from other divi-
     sions.

This solution would fill a need which cannot be filled by
the Freshman Studies Program, would help structure the
sophomore year, would end the isolation of EOD students
on campus, would amend the EOD's distorted image, and
would help to use faculty effectively and efficiently.

Thus, she pointed to a new direction for the program and incorpo-
rated a number of critical points. Moreover, in addressing effectiveness and
efficiency, she presented a solution in line with administrative concerns.
Integrating in, that is, opening EOD courses to all students, would allow for
the retention of the EOD and offer its expertise to the entire community.
Although there were many problems to be clarified, particularly with respect
to state EOP guidelines[22] the proposal was supported in theory by the
faculty. Most importantly, the proposal struck at the elitism of State College
by suggesting that its regularly admitted students were not that different
from EOD students, and as a group did not possess the kinds of academic
skills assumed by State College requirements. The EOD could fill a
necessary void, helping to prepare all students for State College.
     One final issue emerged at this meeting concerning divisional
separation and isolation. Responding to student claims about isolation and
racism, the faculty wondered why the majority of EOD students were black
and Latino. Reiterating a charge of an institutionally racist admissions
policy, the faculty demanded an investigation into the general admissions
policy of the college. If it were true that all minority applicants had been
channelled to the division and white students either rejected by the college
and not offered admission to EOD, or accepted as marginal students to the
regular programs without regard to proper placement in EOD, the division
wanted a change in attitude and policy from the admissions office. For the

EOD, this admissions policy spoke directly to the problems facing the program, for part of the minority students' claims against the division reflected their belief that they were negatively labeled and stigmatized by the separate divisional structure, while they knew many regularly admitted students suffered from similar educational deficits. The division proposed two policies to remedy the situation: 1. the acceptance through regular admissions of more qualified minority applicants, and 2. the acceptance through EOD of more educationally and economically disadvantaged white students.

While these recommendations intended to racially integrate both the EOD and regular programs and thereby reduce the process of equating EOD with minority students (and subsequently labeling minority students as inferior), the director and some faculty had some reservations. The historical mission of Coop college and EOD had been to provide educational opportunities specifically for minority students, and the director took this responsibility seriously. Although state EOP guidelines did not specify the program's intent as specifically for minority students, and although many state programs served a white working class population, the EOD saw its mission in terms of its minority population. Citing its original roots in the civil rights movement of the 1960s, the director stressed the importance of keeping in touch with its early goals. Whereas he understood the problems endemic to the program's racial segregation, he did not want to stop serving what he defined as its intended population. With these reservations in mind, the faculty voted to increase its non-minority population through active recruitment efforts and to carefully mandate the continued admissions of minority students. In this way, some of the negative effects of labeling and stigmatization might be reduced, and the separate divisional structure left intact. Combined with a practice of integrating in, the faculty felt it had developed a rational outline for its future that would save the program as a separate division, but make it available to a larger constituency. Again, the problems of losing touch with the original population were mentioned, but three years of pressure from students and faculty mandated a change in course. What the faculty proposed amounted to the retention of the program, with a number of strategic variations. The faculty accreditation committee charged with integrating these proposals into a written self-study document began its work in the summer.

NOTES

1. Not until the mid-1970s did the off-campus setting begin to pose problems.

2. Less than 10% transferred to State College.

3. This quotation is taken from EOD promotional literature.

4. According to one faculty member, by the time the program moved to State College, the major disagreements about race and education within the faculty had subsided with what he termed the radical-activist wing leaving the program.

5. Holistic refers to a complete and independent program for the disadvantaged students combining remediation, counseling, tutoring, and discipline courses.

6. By the 1970s, colleges began to compete for non-traditional students in order to maintain their declining enrollments.

7. By the mid 1970s, enrollment problems posed a serious threat to the survival of Coop College.

8. The main campus had a student population that was over 90% white.

9. See Sadovnik (1983) for a detailed discussion of these trends. The important point here is that the faculty perceived these as major problems.

10. The EOD faculty began to lobby for a change in the State College grading system and helped to initiate the change to letter grades in 1981.

11. These regulations were required by state educational law since educational opportunity students receive stipends. These records were audited by the state office of special programs, and students not attending classes regularly were threatened with a loss of funding, although no cases of this have been brought to my attention.

12. In many ways this is analogous to the assumption behind compensatory education at the elementary level, such as Project Head Start.

13. A complete analysis of the problems addressed here is provided in Sadovnik (1983:Chapter 8).

14. This is based on allegations by the EOD admissions staff.

15. Marginal is defined as students slightly below the State College admissions requirements.

16. There is no evidence to suggest it was widespread; more importantly, the data on EOD student admissions profiles does not support the hypothesis that prepared students were admitted to the EOD. However, the perception that this was happening is the important social-psychological issue.

17. These students had serious problems in meeting the standards of the regular natural science programs. Sadovnik (1983:Chapter 8) documents their poor performance in regular division courses in the natural sciences. The important point here is that the faculty believed that EOD students needed more preparation and the students viewed this as obstruction.

18. FTE refers to full time equivalent enrollments.

19. This course was introduced to combat the high attrition rate at State College by providing a "community" experience for incoming students.

20. The author believed that freshman courses should be framed around specific academic disciplines.

21. The State College administration attacked the idea that the EOD offered introduction to sociology, introduction to history, etc., as did the regular divisions. They believed EOD students should have been placed into

the regular courses, thus saving money by ending duplication. The EOD stressed the need for a skills-content synthesis absent in non-EOD courses. The administration, as the fiscal constraints worsened, would not accept this logic.

22. The major problem concerned admitting more than 15% non-EOP students into courses funded through state EOP funding.

5

INTEGRATION, NEGOTIATION, AND THE RESPONSE TO CRISIS (1981-1982)

The Politics of Decline

The summer of 1981 provided an opportunity for the Accreditation Committee to prepare its statement for the college self-study and, in doing so, re-examine the program and plan its future direction. The statement reviewed the years at Coop College, the transition of State College, the problems facing the division and its future direction. Its main points may be summarized as follows:

1. The move to the State College campus required some fundamental shifts in the original structure of the program.

2. Continued isolation and separation hurt the division, its students, and the college.

3. However, if the college still believed in its moral and legislative commitment to disadvantaged students, the retention of the separate divisional structure was indeed necessary.

4. The division could serve an expanded function on the campus by offering its courses to all students with skills problems. As the college enrollment problems resulted in the general decline in the skills of all incoming students, the EOD could provide a vital function to the entire campus constituency.

5. Although the division was willing to open up its doors, it maintained its right to exist as an autonomous division and defended the superiority of its model of compensatory higher education.

Therefore, the accreditation self-study report reflected the ongoing movement toward integration and at the same time defended the division's separate identity. To the authors of this document, the concept of integration did not mean the dissolution of the division, only its more efficient use. Relying heavily on the integrative proposals presented at the final faculty meeting of the previous semester, the division chartered a course of action intended to preserve its existence by expanding its functions. In this way, it was hoped that the dual problems of isolation and budgetary constraints would simultaneously be addressed.

The 1981–1982 academic year marked the first year of the college's new President. In an attempt to understand all of the college's various constituencies, meet the faculty, and learn about the programs, the President scheduled a meeting with each division. In addition, the meetings would serve as his platform to give his impressions of the College's strengths and weaknesses, as well as his preliminary thoughts on the direction the college would be taking under his leadership. While it was clear that the President wanted to get to know each program before making any concrete changes, the faculty understood that continued budgetary constraints created an atmosphere of urgency. The EOD faculty and its director perceived this first meeting as critical in defending the program's place at State College. Moreover, they sensed that a positive presentation of the program would be vital to the division's future.

The division took this meeting very seriously. Goffman (1959) presented a dramaturgical analysis of everyday life and suggested that team performance is often vital to the public presentation of an organizational identity; and the preparation and interactions surrounding this event may be viewed from this perspective. The entire week before this meeting, the faculty met to discuss strategy and ideas. These meetings represented an organizational backstage (Goffman, 1959:112) where the division developed a script for its presentation. Who should talk, when should they talk, should the President or the division begin, how much should be revealed; these questions all became subjects of serious deliberations. The faculty decided it best to let the President begin so as to allow the division time to interpret his position and react. The chairperson of the Curriculum Committee was selected to respond to the President by presenting the summary of the program, its educational philosophy, and its special identity. The entire process aptly supported a Goffmanesque view of impression management, with the division engaging in an elaborate team performance enacted to portray itself as positively as possible and, to extrapolate the real intentions of the President as opposed to his actual statements. The division, through this staging and planned performance wanted to control the interaction to its own advantage.

In his opening statement to the division, the new President acknowledged his interest in the EOD, commenting on his own experience in developmental education, teaching remedial English at the University of

Kentucky. Addressing the extremely deficient backgrounds of those students from the coal mining communities of Appalachia, he stated his understanding of the difficulties facing the EOD faculty. In addition, he commented on the Educational Opportunity Program at his former college and his support of this program as Dean. He praised the EOD program for its rational curriculum and noted that the rest of the State College programs should have been so structured. Calling himself "something of a traditionalist," he said that the EOD had one of the curricula in the college that "made the most sense," because of its structure, prerequisites, and sequence of courses.

Like all good politicians, the President began with the good news and then proceeded to the problematic. Noting the finite resources of the college, he stressed the importance of efficiency and effectiveness. Noting that he did not quite understand the separate divisional structure and stating that the EOP program at his old college was integrated and effective, "he promised that he would support the program, but said he could not promise that he would support it in its present form and its present resources." He concluded by raising the following questions for EOD:

> The program as it exists seems sensible and structured, carrying a conviction of what students ought to have. However, some of the offerings seem to duplicate what is offered elsewhere. Should the EOD faculty be interrelated more fully with faculty in the disciplines? Are you satisfied with this? Why are we not pooling our resources?

In keeping with the script, the chairperson of the Curriculum Committee responded to the President. He explained that duplication did not actually exist because of the special nature of the EOD courses. He defined the EOD philosophy of skills content synthesis — that for skills to be taught effectively they must be addressed in all courses — and added that there already was some articulation between EOD courses and those in other divisions. Furthermore, he stated that the division was willing to discuss opening its services to non-EOD students, if it could do so without destroying its original mission and commitment to minority students. This presentation of organizational self reiterated the direction that began to take shape in the previous spring and was defined to the President:

1.   the educational philosophy and pedagogy of the division,
2.   the legitimacy of its separateness,
3.   the expertise of its faculty,
4.   its willingness to open its doors,

5.   its commitment to its original mission and population (that is, if opening doors meant serving white middle class students at the expense of minority students, the division would reject integration).

Thus, through the imputation of an ideology of expertise, commitment, and tradition and the invocation of a little 1970s civil rights rhetoric, the program sought to defend its existence.

The remainder of the meeting consisted of a discussion of these issues. On articulation and integration, the President commented that many students in the mainstream have basic skills problems and asked that the division define the difference between such students and EOD students. One faculty member suggested there would be "considerable overlap," a difference in degree, a difference in attitude.[1] He added that the division had found that it could only address the particular problems of its students in a programmatic package. Another faculty member noted that while the division would welcome association with other programs, there were constraints on the faculty's time. He stated, "we carry a heavier course load and our classes meet more frequently." The President then raised the issue of joint appointments with other divisions to eliminate duplication. One faculty member responded by noting that while this, in theory, would be acceptable, it could lead to the deprivation of the EOD student population, who represented the program's first commitment. On the future of the EOD, the President offered a commitment "to explore those elements of the program that should retain their original form and those that should be integrated."

The new direction of the EOD took shape at the meeting with the President. After three years of challenges to its separate divisional structure by students and, at times, by its own faculty, the movement toward increased integration was clearly indicated at the meeting. Although most divisional members still supported the separate programmatic structure and saw integration as a way of retaining this model with modifications, the spectre of extinction remained an unpleasant undercurrent.

The faculty's reaction to the meeting indicated continued differences over the division's future direction. The conservative members held on to the concept of divisional autonomy and regarded the President's message as evidence of his support for the superiority of the EOD curriculum. Basing their interpretation on his praise for its rational and structured curriculum, they suggested that the EOD curriculum might become the model for a revision of the entire college program (not in terms of level, but in terms of structure and requirements). According to this group, the best direction would be the continuation of the program as it existed, with an effort to increase enrollments. If the division could increase its incoming class to 100 students and lower the high attrition rate, that is, stabilize the EOD enrollment picture, the division would be in good shape.

The other members of the faculty, the liberals and radical-liberals, did not share this view, either in terms of its defense of the status quo or its optimistic portrayal of the division's position. First, the division's movements toward greater integration, both by cross registration in and out, were responses to severe internal and external pressures. To suggest that higher enrollments would eliminate these factors, in the opinion of some faculty, was shortsighted and ill-conceived. Second, the budgetary constraints and administrative concerns over duplication and cost-efficiency would demand increased integration, whether the division wanted it or not. It seemed crystal clear to this segment of the faculty that the division would have to actively shape its own future. To passively support the status quo and do nothing would allow the new administration to step in and determine the future direction of the EOD. This essential difference in political strategy between defense of the status quo on the one hand and active reshaping of the division within an integrative format on the other became the central theme of intraorganizational conflict.

The faculty and director's analysis of the meeting with the President reflected an important process in interorganizational interactions. Drawing upon a symbolic interactionist perspective on the negotiated reality of social order and the problematic nature of meanings, we can examine the interactional and definitional processes that define organizational life. The important feature of this meeting and many other interdivisional sessions to follow was the process by which members attempted to make sense of the definitions and meanings that were presented. Both the President and the division's members constantly presented a particular definitional statement and similarly attempted to interpret the other's intended meaning. Although some understanding always took place, more often than not the overall definitions of meaning attributed to one another were different or inconsistent with the intended meaning of the presenter. Because each party often relied heavily on a particular ideology, codified in a symbolic linguistic code, the negotiation of reality may be better described as ambiguous rather than orderly. Nowhere is this documented better than in the division's attempt to present its skills-content pedagogy in order to justify the need for separate discipline courses and to countermand the charges of duplication. Part of the problem, as will be seen in the following narrative, revolved around either the assumptions by some divisional faculty that outsiders understood the purpose and philosophy behind the pedagogy or, more importantly, because some members so passionately and clearly supported its centrality to teaching underprepared learners, they could not understand why the others could not comprehend or support its uniqueness. This often resulted in remarks like, "they just do not understand what we do," "we must make it clear," or "we are the only ones who really know how to do this, and their misunderstanding just belabors this point." What was clear, however, from a sociological perspective, was that the problematic nature of meanings endemic to interorganizational interactions resulted in members talking past one another and continued conflict over intent and purpose, fueled by the continuous presentation and interpretation of divisional ideology.

The aftermath of the meeting with the President marked the beginning of the planning for the academic year; one that both the director and faculty perceived as a crossroads in the division's future. In a meeting between the director and the chairperson of the Curriculum Committee, the major issues for the year were outlined:

1.   Integration: the problems of cross-registration out and integrating in were essential to the division's future. Meetings with the Freshman Studies Program were proposed to start the process of integrating in.

2.   Student Performance and Attrition and Divisional Response: the continued low performance of EOD students and the high attrition rate would become a central concern of both the Curriculum and CAP Committees.

3.   Divisional Curriculum and Pedagogy: the director suggested the systematic review of the division's curriculum and methods to explore "what works and what doesn't work for this population." The director cited two related reasons for his request: First, to provide solutions to the problems of student failure and attrition, and second, to back up the "rhetoric and ideology" of divisional presentation. He thought it ironic that although the division's members constantly presented a set of ideological and philosophical propositions about the special nature of the division, rarely were they backed up substantively. Moreover, he argued that the data on student performance could not support the evidence of any special formula. Although he did not deny that the faculty had developed a unique program over the past 12 years, he thought that the faculty needed to codify it in writing. Since the division used its educational philosophy and methods to defend its existence, more than rhetoric, according to the director, should have been available to support these arguments. He therefore asked the Curriculum

Committee to undertake the writing of a curriculum and methods document to present as its "documentation of expertise" and as a way of sharing the various successful and unsuccessful methods used with the population. If for no other reason, the process would pull the faculty together around its most important goal, the successful education of its students.

4.   Enrollments: the declining enrollments of the division, due to lower admissions, high attrition and increasing cross-registration threatened the division's very existence. In the numbers game, the division was losing. The director suggested a number of policies to address the problem: First, he would push for the clarification of admission policy for EOD students and demand administrative attention to the problem. Second, he promised to devote 40% of his time to recruiting. However, he noted that to spend so many hours on the road would administratively hurt the division. Third, to reduce attrition, he would sponsor a systematic evaluation of curriculum and methods. Fourth, the college had to recognize that when EOD students cross-register, the divisional numbers are reduced. Finally, the concept of integrating in could help to replace the lost FTE's.

5.   The transition to the junior year: the Curriculum chair and the director agreed that the transition to the junior year presented serious problems for EOD students. Up until 1980, one of the EOD counselors acted as a liaison to the other divisions and served former EOD students in their upper divisional careers. However, when he left the college, this role went unfilled; therefore, the EOD needed to rebuild this type of structure.

Having outlined the major problems facing the division, the director asked the faculty to consider them in the course of the year. Among the first issues raised in the 1981–82 academic year was the systematic review of curriculum and methods.

Curriculum Review and Presentation of Pedagogy

The chairperson of the Curriculum Committee proposed an evaluation of the EOD curriculum that addressed both pedagogy and curricular integration. The objectives of this enterprise were as follows:

1.   to improve the EOD success rate by analyzing which methods worked and which did not.

2.   to support the divisional claim of expertise; that is, if the EOD faculty were to continue to speak as experts and of special methods, it had to produce tangible evidence of these.

The chairperson and director suggested a series of written documents prepared by each faculty[2] member as well as oral presentations to the faculty. However, the majority of the faculty opposed the entire project as too time consuming and possibly an infringement of academic freedom. Some faculty feared that this was the first step in moving to a prescribed curriculum. The director of the EOD, however, stated that "if we are truly different and if our population is special, as we claim it is, we should be able to talk to these issues."

After a number of meetings devoted to the adoption of a workable mechanism for review, the faculty could not reach a consensus over the necessity for such a review or the process of implementation. The combination of continued budgetary concerns, persistent internal problems, and the general malaise that seemed to define the program, left the faculty unwilling to devote the time or energy to this process. The faculty already felt overworked, overburdened, and as one member stated, "burnt out", and this seemed to be asking too much. Toward the end of the fall semester, the Committee tabled the entire project until the spring, when the continuing college and state budget crisis would take center stage and remove the curricular review as an active project.

Movement Toward Integration: Articulation
with Freshman Studies

In the previous spring, the division established the path to integration on two counts. First, the EPC representative proposed the concept of integrating in by suggesting the expanded role the division could take. Second, preliminary discussions with the Associate Dean for Lower Division (director of the Freshman Studies Program) led to the decision to formally begin discussion in the fall. Although nothing concrete had emerged from these talks, the fact that the division was openly talking to other segments of the college, and that they were in fact welcoming the opportunity, represented an important first step in breaking down the imaginary and real walls that divided the college.

The Curriculum Committee decided to call a joint meeting to

discuss "Writing Problems" at State College as a way to rekindle the articulation with other campus constituencies. The selection of this issue for a collaborative effort reflected the centrality of writing to the division's future. More importantly, its selection pointed to the division's strategy to fill the skills void across the campus. While State College directed its programs at students with competent academic skills, many members of the campus community recognized the differences between the ideal State College student and the real student. Contrary to the image that State College had of itself, many faculty across the college believed that there was a considerable gap between expectations of the programs and the levels of incoming students. Moreover, a large segment of the faculty had complained about skills deficiencies of their students and their inability to write an acceptable college level paper, let alone a senior thesis. Combined with its extraordinarily high attrition rate and the realization that to meet enrollment projections the college would be attracting a large number of students with skills deficiencies, the value of the EOD faculty was apparent, at least within the EOD. Seizing this opportunity to expand its functions and using its presentation of expertise to support the process, the division moved to organize a discussion of the writing problems on campus with an eye toward solidifying its future.

The division selected the chairperson of the Curriculum Committee to organize a general meeting on writing. The meeting would include the EOD English faculty, the Associate Dean for Lower Division and the Freshman Studies faculty, the Dean of the Humanities, and a senior member of the Literature Board of Study, who had authored a writing proposal two years earlier.

The division's EPC representative prepared a written proposal for a structured freshman-sophomore year at State College. Continuing with the concept of integrating in developed in her earlier recommendations, this statement enlarged the place of the EOD on campus. This proposal utilized the skills-content synthesis of EOD courses to offer a multidimensional approach to writing problems. Arguing that writing problems cannot be solved by separate writing courses, the author stated that only by adopting a "writing across the disciplines" approach would the college be on the right track, and who better to lead the way than the experienced EOD faculty, with twelve years of concrete experience in this respect. The proposal, perhaps the most organized presentation of EOD educational philosophy and the place of the division on campus to date, included the following points:

> *The Goal*: The goal of Liberal Arts Education should be to
> give students an all around education as opposed to

specialized training. An educated person is someone with a basic fund of knowledge about the past background, attitudes, issues, ideas, and concerns of his culture... and he must also have the skills necessary to absorb new knowledge and relate it... *The Freshman and Sophomore years should lay a foundation of this general fund of knowledge and concentrate intensely on the development of the skills.*

Method: No college faculty can assume, as we did routinely in the past, that students enter college with the skills needed to do academic work. Students at State College come into the Freshman year with varying degrees of deficiencies, which should be addressed at different levels. On one level, students have severe problems with the English language-grammar problems. These should continue to be addressed in the EOD Sentence and Paragraph level workshops, which could be opened up to admit regularly admitted freshmen.

More complex is the development of the intellectual academic skills — reading with a purpose, listening intelligently, distinguishing between the general and the specific and between different levels of abstraction, recognizing bias, and generalizing and making relationships.

Since deficiencies in these skills become most apparent in student papers, the remedy is usually discussed in terms of providing the necessary "writing" courses. I submit that the problem is not a "writing" problem, but a matter of understanding/organizing/learning... We should not think in terms of "writing" courses and the "writing" problems, but in terms of ways in which we can best develop the intellectual skills and teach our discipline.

This can be done in two ways:

1. In courses which focus directly and exclusively on skills; English 101 and 102 in EOD and the first semester of Freshman Studies. None of these is in fact a "writing"

course. English 101 and Freshman Studies stress reading with a purpose and expressing your understanding of what you read in clear and well organized papers, although the EOD courses use essays, whereas Freshman Studies uses books... I believe that Freshman Studies would not be suitable for EOD Freshmen, because of the different requirements, and because of the length of the readings [READ AS: EOD Freshman cannot handle the material, although as we shall see, the author did not believe the Freshman Studies course was appropriate for *any* freshman population.] *The EOD faculty could, on the other hand, open its courses (English 101 and 102) to those freshman who could profit from them.*

Such courses, however, can address only part of the problem. They do nothing towards offering students the basic fund of knowledge they need, and the skills acquired there do not easily or automatically transfer to the other courses students take.

The experience of the EOD has shown — and this is supported by an increasing volume of research — that students must be taught to apply their skills in every course they take. Moreover, students will not understand and learn, if they are not required to work with, write about, the subject matter of a course, in an academic discipline.

2. I propose, therefore, that students in the skills courses be *required* to enroll simultaneously in courses in academic disciplines which are structured so as to make students learn by using and refining their skills. Such courses *already exist in the EOD* and are being discussed in the EPC for other divisions.

Form: Freshman and Sophomore courses can be offered in three different forms: non-disciplinary (skills courses), courses in the academic disciplines, and interdisciplinary courses... Disciplinary courses should precede interdisciplinary offerings. It seems to me that subject matter must be informed by disciplinary structure to promote learning at the Freshman and Sophomore levels. Substance without such a framework loses its meaning for the yet uneducated person. By the same token, a student can appreciate an interdisciplinary course much better *after* he has some idea of the concerns and outlooks of the individual discipline. (1982a:1–3)

In this well organized presentation of a program for all State College lower divisional students, the author accomplished a number of important points. Not only did she define the place and function of the EOD in the overall scheme, she defined what she considered the heart of the division's unique pedagogy and curriculum and simultaneously implied the fundamental differences between EOD and other programs including, but not particularly, Freshman Studies. Moreover, in retaining the traditional claim to difference in student population (i.e., Freshman Studies is not appropriate for EOD students) and reiterating the special experience methods of the EOD faculty, she introduced a new variation on divisional difference. Although the EOD had developed a unique program for underprepared students, its fundamental value was its ability to transcend its population. That is, what the EOD really had to offer was the best possible approach to undergraduate education for all students. It was not just a program for the underprepared, but a general model that could be applied to all populations. Moreover, as the skills levels of regularly admitted students continued to decline, she argued, the role of the EOD in constituting an essential part of a Freshman-Sophomore program was crystal clear.

The direction that had begun to take shape in only a vague form the previous spring had now blossomed into a concrete proposal. There was some opposition to the specifics, however, it concerned strategic implications ("we had better proceed carefully") rather than content. It is important to note, however, that although one of the major spokespersons for the division, this faculty member did not always speak for the division. Many did not share her unwavering commitment to the divisional philosophy and at times were skeptical of its actual existence.[3] Nonetheless, in all intra- and interdivisional interactions, she emerged as a spokesperson for the divisional identity and she, more than any other faculty member, became associated with the divisional ideology. Although this influence would diminish in the coming years, her role as the "presenter of organizational identity" was extremely important.

The points presented in her proposal need to be further analyzed, as they set up the conditions for ongoing negotiations about the role of the EOD and the future of the program. The proposals set up two opposing situations: First, a view of compatibility — that the EOD could integrate with other programs and, second, a view of dissimilarity — that the EOD was significantly different from other programs and superior in its ability to educate lower divisional students. Within this context a potential contradiction emerged: the dual identity of skills program and general education program. Although the document posited the division's fulfillment of both roles, the rest of the campus did not seem to understand the concepts in the same way. Therefore, they suggested that if the EOD was a general education program for all students, the EOD as a separate program should not have been necessary; or, if it was a skills program for underprepared students, then it cannot and should not teach other things. The problem that emerged is that in claiming two different but simultaneous identities and positing expertise in both (but not having the overall philosophy understood), the program left itself open to a double-edged assault. On the one hand, when the State College faculty proposed placing its weak students in EOD in response to the division's proposals, but rejected the idea of their students needing EOD discipline courses, the author of the proposal would angrily charge, "we are not just a skills program; we are not the dumping ground of State College; we have a package." On the other hand, when proposals for more complete integration emerged, she would defend the necessity of the skills component for underprepared students. Although the EOD faculty understood the reaction — that the special character of the program involved skill-content integration in all courses, thus making it more than a remedial program — it was never really understood by the outside faculty and administration who did not readily support the division's notion of uniqueness, nor believe that it had a monopoly on what it took to teach freshmen.

    With these tensions defining the negotiations between EOD and the rest of the college, the process of integration began to take shape. The text of the proposal for a Freshman-Sophomore program, although only in its infancy, provided the context for exploration. A number of key phrases may be extrapolated:

1.   *and concentrate intensely on the development of the skills*: all college level courses had to be skills intensive, thus extending the EOD philosophy to a college-wide curriculum and firmly stating the foundation for the value of the EOD.

2.   *No college faculty can assume, as we did routinely in the past, that students enter with the skills needed to do academic work...* therefore, the EOD could open its courses: the decline in skills was a college-wide phenomenon, reducing the difference between the

EOD and regular populations. What was needed, was not the extinction of the EOD, but its expanded role on the campus with all "needy" students enrolling in its courses. The concept of integrating in became justified.

3.   *The experience of the EOD has shown ...that students must be taught to apply their skills in every course they take...*: The use of the ideology of expertise and history to justify the division's *discipline* courses. Long the object of external pressure for their elimination (because of duplication), these courses were viewed as central and essential to solving problems.

4.   *...disciplinary courses should precede interdisciplinary offerings... Freshman Studies would not be suitable for EOD freshman*: Implicit to the proposal, although not a view supported by all of the EOD faculty, especially the radical-liberals, was a critique of Freshman Studies as inappropriate for any freshman. The author opposed the course on two grounds: first, she felt its scope and difficulty of material was indicative of State College elitism and not appropriate for college freshmen and, second, she felt its interdisciplinary content made it inappropriate for the skills-content synthesis and that this was a significant shortcoming of the program. Although many disagreed, especially with the second point, both issues would constantly re-emerge in the coming interactions.

Finally, the proposal raised a number of highly charged and politically sensitive problems. In a time of budgetary crisis, and when all programs were struggling to survive, the perception of EOD invading other people's turf could easily be charged. Although the administration clearly wanted integration and efficiency, and viewed all faculty lines as college lines, State College remained in the President's own words, "a feudal system with separate manors protecting their territorial rights." The politics of integration would not only revolve around educational and philosophical concerns, but maybe more importantly around the politics of organizational survival, with each program pushing or avoiding integration based on its own particular perception of its needs and vulnerability to administrative elimination. In this latter context, although the EOD and Freshman Studies often had fundamental differences in educational philosophy,[4] they both viewed themselves as particularly vulnerable from both the administration and the other divisions. Therefore, it was only logical that the initial movement toward integration would begin between these programs; both, in the words of the director of the Freshman Studies Program, at the bottom of the State College status hierarchy, and both struggling to keep afloat.

Like the meeting with the college President, the "Writing Problems" meeting required serious preparation and staging. Although the prospect for integration was the primary motivation for the EOD faculty, they could not be perceived as looking for FTE's. Therefore, the faculty decided to begin with a general discussion and then subtly move to the more sensitive issues under consideration.

The initial impetus for the meeting was the integration of writing courses in the EOD and Freshman Studies Program. The Freshman Studies Program, developed in the 1980–1981 academic year to alleviate the high college attrition rate through a common academic experience to all L&S freshman, offered a two semester "Great Books" course that integrated writing skills. Although some EOD faculty rejected its utility, the division felt that, given administrative concerns for further integration, it was the right time to discuss EOD responsibility for the freshman writing program. Therefore, the concept of integrating in began to take shape: "Why not let those faculty with the most experience in teaching writing take responsibility for all freshmen, thus expanding the EOD's role on campus." Although this new form of expansion received some enthusiastic support, the director warned of the sensitivity of such matters, the territoriality of each division, and cautioned against premature endeavors.

The meeting attracted a good turnout and in all respects supported a Goffmanesque picture of situational interaction. The first stage involved the presentation of individual and organizational self, with members of the EOD and the Freshman Studies program introducing their respective philosophy and pedagogy on writing. The EOD stressed the skills content synthesis, writing across the disciplines and the need for intensive application in all courses. The continued reference to "time tested methods" was an essential aspect of the presentation, as the EOD faculty invoked the ideology of expertise to support its position. Likewise, the Associate Dean of Lower Division (director of Freshman Studies) presented the ways in which faculty integrated writing into the freshman studies courses and how, in many ways, his courses were similar in pedagogy to those in EOD.

The final aspect of the first stage involved the "conflict over organizational definition." During this part, members of the EOD redefined the EOD methods in order to clarify its differences with Freshman Studies. The coordinator of the EOD disciplines, in particular, denied any similarity between the two programs and continued to defend the special character of the division.

The second phase of the meeting involved the "sharing of experiences," with each faculty member discussing personal problems and methods in teaching writing, as well as an overall evaluation of the extent and severity of the problems. Although it provided some interesting and valuable material and a plethora of perspectives of writing, this segment was long and individuals began to become uneasy with the length of the meeting.

The last stage of the meeting concerned pragmatic avenues for meeting the writing needs of State College students. At this point, the sensitive issues of the writing line, integration, and FTE's would be introduced. The Curriculum chairperson, sensitive to the conflicts that might develop, broached the subject with great care. However, the Associate Dean of the Lower Division, in a statement that produced both comic relief and the irony of the politics of interaction, said "its about time, I thought this is why we were here in the first place." Suggesting that it was time to get down to basics, he pulled out computer lists and proceeded to project that 10% of his students needed extra help in writing and he asked about the best way to provide this help.

The discussion of placing Freshman Studies students into EOD classes produced considerable tension and disagreements over the role of the EOD, and although no agreement was reached, the initial groundwork was placed into motion. The major point of controversy revolved around what some EOD faculty defined as the proper program for lower divisional students and their rejection of Freshman Studies as the appropriate vehicle. These faculty, especially the coordinator of the EOD disciplines, argued that "needy" students required the entire EOD skills-content package by enrolling in EOD writing and discipline courses. In contrast, the Associate Dean of Lower Division felt that tutoring by EOD writing faculty or enrollment of Freshman Studies students in EOD writing courses was the most he could support. At the heart of the matter were the differing conceptions of each division's methods held by the two programs.

The EOD faculty reacted to the meeting with mixed emotions. Some believed that the initial dialogue represented a step in the right direction and that the EOD and Freshman Studies programs had mutual interests. Others cautioned against being used and receiving nothing in return. Once again the coordinator of the disciplines cautioned against allowing the EOD to be viewed as the college "garbage can," where it could dump its problems and expect instant results. She urged that unless Freshman Studies students were placed in both EOD writing and discipline courses the value of the EOD program would be lost.

In the subsequent discussion it became clear that a compromise would have to be reached as the Associate Dean for Lower Division did not believe this complete package was necessary or possible. The negotiations ended with the agreement that "needy" Freshman Studies students would take EOD writing courses and in some cases possibly an EOD discipline course. The parties agreed that about 40 incoming freshman in Fall 1983, including some dance students,[5] would need to be placed in EOD writing courses and the next step would be to agree on placement procedures. Although no concrete plan emerged, the EOD moved closer to integrating in non-EOD students.

Looking Ahead: Toward Further Integration

The Fall 1981 semester ended with the EOD closer to integration than at any time in its history. The elimination of the attendance policy and the open cross registration policy that went into effect the previous year considerably opened the doors from the inside. Combined with the withering away of EOD courses offerings by continued budget cuts, EOD students were taking more regular courses, earlier in their careers, than ever before. In addition, the beginnings of a systematic policy for integrating in other students set the stage for further integration. Although this represented the culmination of three and one half years of gradual movements, affected both by internal (student and faculty) and external (faculty, administrative, budgetary) pressures, the division's direction did not please everyone. More importantly, most of the faculty felt a sense of caution and apprehension as it became apparent that integration could mean elimination.

By late in the Fall semester, the sense of uneasiness pervaded the program, as faculty perceived the possibility that the program's place on the campus was in question. Nonetheless, these were still only rumors, and after almost 13 years of living with crisis the faculty did not obsess about this; rather, it proceeded to plan its future by continuing to address the issue of integration and at the same time move to solve its continuing internal problems.

During the previous two years there had been a gradual breakdown in the division's isolation and attempts continued to break down the divisive barriers. However, there was little faculty sentiment to eliminate the program and, quite the contrary, its view of integration was based on the retention of a more effective and efficient divisional structure. Through increased campus wide communication and more effective mainstreaming mechanisms, the program would work to integrate its students into the college. In addition, through the opening of its doors to all students with need for its services, the EOD would serve a larger function on the campus. Both processes, the division hoped, would retain the strengths of the EOD while addressing the major problems of separation and isolation.

The Spring 1982 Budget Crisis:
The Beginning of the End

The Spring 1982 semester began with the most severe budget crisis of the previous three years. The Governor's proposed budget and the state university's reduction in funding meant the possible loss of 35 faculty positions at State College. In an emergency college wide address, the college's President outlined steps to coordinate a political strategy to convince the state legislature to increase funding levels. Combining apprehensiveness and realism, he proposed the construction of a catastrophe plan, so that the college could respond if no relief were forthcoming. He announced the creation of State College budget hearings, with every division coming to an administrative meeting to discuss and defend its current funding levels and to present alternative plans to incorporate the proposed cuts. The message came over loud and clear — no program was safe, and every program would have to justify its existence in order to survive.

The EOD felt particularly vulnerable. With its severe problems (including declining enrollments, admissions projections down, and the administration's already existing perception that many of its courses were duplicative) the faculty and director geared for what many believed might have been the last ditch effort to save the division. In addition, the beginnings of an anti-EOD sentiment began to emerge from some segments of the State College with some non-EOD faculty suggesting in both private conversations (according to some EOD and State College faculty) and public meetings what the EOD had always thought they felt — that the EOD was not special and did not deserve its unique protective canvas. The claim that circulated stated that the EOD was too expensive and unproductive, its faculty less "able" (the non-EOD faculty often used some of the EOD's faculty members' lack of the Ph.D. and failure to publish as the basis) and most importantly that any State College member could teach their population.

During the pre-budget hearing discussions, the EOD began to realize who its friends were and, conversely, which constituencies opposed its existence. The divisions that seemed most solidly in support of the program's retention were Freshman Studies and Social Sciences. The Natural Sciences and especially the Humanities seemed ready to offer the EOD as the State College sacrificial lamb. The pro-EOD divisions based their support on political and educational grounds, suggesting that compensatory programs were necessary to ensure quality programs for minority and working class students. The anti-EOD forces rejected the concept of compensatory higher education altogether. The program had been tolerated in times of fiscal abundance, but in a contracting economic situation it was a luxury the college could not afford.[6]

The central feature of the debate concerned the nature and accessibility of the overall State College curriculum. EOD and Freshman Studies argued that the lack of a structured curriculum, the preponderance of advanced, overspecialized courses, and the elitist tradition of graduate education (junior exams, senior thesis) all contributed to student dissatisfaction. The Humanities and Natural Sciences, from sometimes very different perspectives,[7] asserted that the paucity of major course offerings in their divisions led upper divisional students to move on for their final two years. While any analysis of attrition[8] would support both positions as, in part, valid, the budget crisis just fueled those conflicts and resentments that had been repressed or perhaps contained for years.

In preparation for the Budget Hearings, the President requested that all programs present a budgetary statement that would propose a minimum 10% cut in staff and funding. Insisting that a defense of the status-quo would not be accepted, he promised only to keep the overall needs of the college as his first priority. In addition, although he promised to do his best to honor contractual obligations, he would not rule out retrenchment. Since the university by-laws mandated retrenchment by program, not individuals,[9] the EOD perceived its elimination as one option the President could consider.

In an emergency meeting, the director and EOD senior faculty decided on a strategy to defend the EOD by stressing present moves toward integration and the elimination of duplication. Moreover, the division chose to respond angrily to the continued chipping away at its resources and to demand that the college live up to its commitment to minority students. Furthermore, the director would claim that further cuts would render the program unable to minimally achieve its goals.

The director realized that this strategy was a calculated risk. Although the college was required by law to have some type of educational opportunity program, it did not have to fund a separate division.[10] The college could retain a small remedial program and eliminate the EOD's discipline and elective courses and subsequently eliminate a number of faculty positions. The entire faculty perceived this as a possibility and viewed the budget hearings as a way to avoid this fate.

The director formulated a written response to the administration based on discussions in the emergency meeting. Although it was a lengthy document, some direct quotations from it illustrate the division's position as it prepared for its toughest battle to date:

First, framing the divisional attitude to the proposed cuts:

> A lengthy discussion by senior faculty and staff of the division produced the requested budget projections, but unfortunately, left the participants with a deep sense of futility and of the imminent demise of the division, attitudes that are altogether understandable, given the serious reductions in staffing and funding in previous years. For those who are unaware of the economic history of the division, this most recent request comes on top of cuts imposed upon the division by the college in each of the last four years... It is a fact that almost every division of the college has benefitted by the reductions in the EOD budget. This brief sketch of the division's fiscal history is a necessary backdrop to an understanding of the distress the division now feels. Nevertheless, the process was undertaken. (1981b:1)

Therefore, in a critical and "offensive" introduction, the director claimed that the division had suffered enough, that other constituencies had been the beneficiaries of its decline, and the faculty had reached a state of anguish, disenchantment and alienation. Nonetheless, he proceeded to propose a ten percent reduction through the elimination of all part-time faculty and the assistant to the director, a position mandated by state EOP law for programs with more than 100 students. Although the college, not the state EOP, funded this position, it was required; however, the director stated that he would rather violate the state education law than further reduce instructional positions. Moreover, he argued that despite its temptation, the division would not replace full-time untenured faculty with adjunct appointments, a practice beginning to define higher education's response to fiscal constraint (B. Scott, 1983). Although one full-time line generating six courses per academic year could be divided to create sixteen courses taught by adjuncts (minus the benefits paid to full-time faculty), the division deplored this as both unconscionable and detrimental to the division's educational mission. A part-time faculty, with no commitment to the students or methods of the division, would have unthinkable consequences (1981b:2).

On the effects of the proposed cuts he stated:

> The effect of these reductions would be sweeping, eliminating in each semester eight mathematics, two English, and its only two American History courses. It eliminates half of the mathematics offerings, forcing the division to double its student teacher ratio in mathematics to approximately 25:1. In addition to the effect on the curriculum, the impact on

the administrative functions would be extensive. Educational Opportunity Programs, with enrollments of 100 or more students should have, according to the *EOP Guidelines*, an Associate Director. The Educational Opportunity Program at State College, which should be distinguished from the EOD[11] has 182 students enrolled in the four year program. The Assistant to the Director, whose part-time position would be reduced by forty percent, carries out some of the responsibilities that should be assigned to an Associate Director, particularly those involving preparation of reports and other duties for the State Special Programs Office. In addition, she assists the director in a number of ways, which gives the flexibility so crucial in carrying out the myriad responsibilities of the director's office, including his implied duties of recruiting and counseling of candidates for admission to the division (1981b:2).

Therefore, to support his point that further cuts would devastate the division, the director documented the (in his words) disintegration of curricular and administrative responsibilities. These cuts would paralyze the program, and the implication (developed later in his statement) was that the program could not maintain itself at the proposed level.

The director proceeded to comment on the abolition of the EOD registrar's office by merging it with the State College registrar's office: this move had long been a point of debate, misunderstanding, and controversy. The office had come to represent symbolically, if not for some literally, the primary example of duplications of functions and was attacked always from the outside as the first place to apply the pruning shears. On this move he commented:

> The inference that other offices of the college could more efficiently assume the admissions and registrar functions of the EOD, continues to persist without resolution. The recent history of merger and redefinition with respect to EOD administrative functions,[12] does not support this inference. Where merger has been tried or reassignment of EOD personnel has taken place, the results from the EOD perspective have been less than satisfactory. Often, EOD has found itself delicately negotiating with the office with which the merger has taken place and even with its former employee. It should be said with equal haste, however, that

the difficulty of merging or redefining of functions cannot be assigned to any one person or to any one office; offices appear to be so understaffed that the effect of the merger or redefinition is lost, the reassigned employee turning his/her attention to the central needs of the office to which he/she has been recently assigned. This is said to convey the complexity of merger and redefinition, alternatives to be considered with caution and thoroughness (1981b:3).

Through an explicit defense of its separate registrar's office, the director raised two implicit points, one referring to the past and one to the future. First, previous redefinition and merger of separate EOD offices, like its separate financial aid office upon its arrival in 1978, turned out disastrously (according to the director) and robbed EOD students of vital services. In particular the EOD financial aid officer, once she moved to the overall State College financial aid office, became lost in its bureaucratic entrapments, and therefore was less accessible to EOD students. Moreover, her allegiance, if not the definition of her responsibilities, was to the entire campus, and often the special needs of the EOD population were less than adequately served. In an area as vital to the retention of economically disadvantaged students, this presented a perplexing situation one that, according to the director would be reproduced by the elimination of the EOD registrar's office. The claims were clear: the division by virtue of its special population required special offices to meet their special needs. Second, as the division moved closer to curricular integration, it should not lose sight of the consequences. That is, if the college chose to integrate or reassign faculty to other divisions with the belief that because they would be teaching courses that included EOD students the population would be served, its position did not rest on solid assumptions. The director implied that this probably would not be the case, with the overall needs of each division taking precedent over the needs of EOP students. As the classificatory boundaries framing the college disappeared, so too, he cautioned, would its commitment to the EOD population.

On the misplaced priorities of the college, the director focused on the high cost of the college summerfare:[13]

Summerfare has probably brought more people to the Campus than any of the college's other activities. As it has brought invaluable publicity to the campus, it has detracted financially from the college's academic functions, and if not checked, will erode further the college's budget. The puzzle to be solved is how can State College retain the benefits of Summerfare, and at the same time, prevent that event from altering and diminishing the scholarly endeavors of the college. The simple answer, it would appear, is to ask the private funders for more money. At a time when we are being told that the private sector will assume, given sufficient tax incentives, some of the responsibilities we have come to understand as governmental obligations we should not allow the reverse to occur (1981b:3).

Moreover, on the overall State College problems, the director summarized the division's position by defining the EOD as essential to reversing the college's decline and lumping it together with Freshman Studies as an antidote for what he saw as the traditional misguided elitism at the college:

The problems that have plagued the college, most notice-ably during the last five years, are insufficient enrollment, inaccessibility of its programs to a broader and less well-prepared student body than anticipated, and the retention of those students. In attempting to address these inabilities, the EOD was transferred to the campus, continuing education was recognized as an important and central operation of the college and Freshman Studies was created. It is important to keep in mind that none of these divisions would have been discussed had the college acquired its requisite enrollment, provided the kind of entry level accessibility essential to the engagement and retention of its regularly admitted students, as well as met its legal obliga-tion regarding poor and educationally disadvantaged students. Obviously, the establishment of these three divisions discloses at best a faculty inability, or worse, its disinclination to adjust to exigencies. There is no reason to believe that these attitudes do not continue to persist. Where these attitudes recede, they are replaced by a grudging practicality — a posture of let them in if we are going to save our jobs. Faced with serious budget cuts, some of the college's original divisions began to make noises about sharing the responsibility for the new constitu-encies. *It is a gift horse whose mouth deserves the closest scrutiny.* It is difficult to envision a State College thriving without Freshman Studies, the EOD, and a fully fleshed out Continuing Education program. Indeed, they are the divisions which have at least begun to address the problems of low enrollment, diversity of population, accessibility of discipline at the entry level and retention of students. They continue to be needed in their present form, and should not be reorganized, abolished or merged until there is a clear indication that the entire academic community is willing to assume, with generosity, their functions (1981b:4).

Thus, the director presented the Freshman Studies, EOD and Continuing Education alliance and defended all three programs. By choosing this collective strategy, he succeeded in systematically casting responsibility for the college's problems to the elitist programs on the campus, and placed the future health of the college in the recognition of more realistic educational strategies, of which the EOD was, in his view, a vital component.

Finally, on the division's needs and future direction he stated:

> The single most urgent need of the EOD is to acquire a recruiter or to have Admissions assume total responsibility for recruitment for the division, just as it has for other divisions of the college.... There has been some discussion within and outside the division of expanding the definition of the division's mission to include Arts as well as Letters and Science students, who academically are not substantially unlike students admitted to EOD. Though pedagogical as well as logistical problems have to be solved before any substantial movement towards this kind of integration could take place, the discussions should continue, and include the total of EOD offerings, rather than just a narrow discussion of the division providing only writing courses for students other than its own (1981b:5).

The director, therefore, spoke to the division's future by raising two points, both speaking in a very different way to the division's survival. Covering both flanks, he stressed the need for an improved admissions policy to guarantee EOD enrollments (strengthen the EOD from the inside) and also to enlarge the integration discussions to include all EOD courses (strengthening the program from the outside, and more importantly, saving the entire program, not just its skills component).

The Budget Hearings

The budget hearings were held over a week long period during which each division was allotted a two hour time period. All members of the scheduled division could attend; in addition, all members of the college community were invited as spectators and questioners. The administration team consisted of the President, the Academic Vice President, the Assistant Academic Vice President and the Vice President for finance.

The majority of the EOD faculty, its director, and assistant director represented the Division at the hearings. After its own emergency budget meeting, the public discussion of the director's budget statement, and numerous ad hoc planning sessions, the EOD contingent was prepared to defend its existence, while simultaneously offering possible avenues for savings, including integration. The strategy included three main points: First, to force the college to clarify its commitment to minority students; second, to present the current divisional structure as the best model for these students and third, to stress how the plans for integration would provide a more efficient and effective use of faculty.

The EOD meeting began with the President asking one simple (to his mind) question: "Why do you need an American historian, at $10,000 per year to teach in your division, when we have so many American historians on this campus. This is a prime example of the kind of duplication that we can no longer afford." The President's remarks translated into, "why can't any American historian on the campus teach your students," which hit directly at the heart of divisional difference.

After considerable debate about duplication, the reality of the situation echoed through the presidential chambers. Despite EOD claims that its special methods and skills-content synthesis made the charges of duplication unfounded and EOD discipline courses necessary, the President did not accept the argument. He did not philosophically support divisional separation, nor did he accept the proposition that State College faculty could not teach underprepared students. His overall message was that in times of budgetary constraints the college would not continue to fund what it considered costly and duplicative offerings. When pressed by one EOD professor about the college's commitment to minority students, the President replied somewhat angrily, "this college, as a public institution will by law and by morality uphold its commitment; however, the definition of commitment does not preclude change in the present program." At one time, he argued, the college's fiscal resources allowed for a separate EOD program with very small classes and duplication. Today, he continued, all of these things were not a given, but subject to scrutiny and change. The college would keep its commitment, but not necessarily in its present form.

Having failed to convince the President of the necessity for separate discipline courses, the EOD faculty attempted to present the division's recent attempts to become more efficient through integration. Pointing to the plans for accepting large numbers of non-EOD students into its skills courses and preliminary discussions to avoid duplication, they urged that viable solutions within the separate divisional structure were possible. While the President acknowledged that these types of reforms were vital, he would not commit himself to the long range support of a separate EOD.

The director of the EOD then responded to the entire discussion by reiterating the history of budgetary attack on the Division. Arguing that the program had been cut to the bone and could not function with continued assault, he fired a direct ultimatum at the college's administration:

> ...if it is your intention, as I have believed, to change the fundamental nature of the EOD, then I ask you to do it now. Please do not keep cutting at the edges, nibbling away, until we just wither away and die. You have a legal responsibility to support some type of EOP program. Therefore, either come up with a plan to change us, or stop gradually destroying us.

The President replied that at the present time he could not make promises, but hoped to continue the present process of retaining the division with integration. The director continued by pointing to admissions policy. For three years, he stated, he had attempted to reach an understanding with the College Admissions Office about their responsibility to the EOD. It seemed that a systematic process of decline defined the college's attitude. That is, the college took away the EOD recruiter, did not mandate admissions to recruit, and therefore left the EOD on its own with its director doing the major part of recruiting. In a metropolitan area so heavily populated by minority students, to systematically ignore this population, in his words, was a disgrace. The college, he charged, viewed the EOD as fulfilling the college's legal mandate, but would not assist the division, or so it seemed, in assuring its enrollment through healthy admissions. What better way to kill a program, he inferred, than by having it fold due to lack of students. The director reiterated his concern for a clarified admissions policy and suggested that this, more than any other single issue, was the key to the program's health.

The President replied that no conspiracy existed, and he would attempt to develop a clearer admissions policy for the division. As time was getting late, and the next divisional hearing was about to convene, the President thanked the faculty, director, and staff for their concern, ideas, and participation. Commenting that the EOD attendance was the largest of all divisions as of yet, he praised the division, stating that such an experienced and dedicated faculty was vital to the college, and he promised to explore all his options. However, at no time did he promise to retain the division in its separate form.

The Post Budget Meeting Debates

The aftermath of the Budget Hearing involved the attempt to interpret what actually occurred. Although most faculty and staff felt the division presented its case and defended itself well, members were uncertain about its success. Many felt the President had made up his mind, and that if the budget crisis did not resolve itself in the legislature, the division could be the victim of the numbers game. At the same time, the faculty proceeded to debate possible directions for the future.

In the week after the Budget Hearing, the President announced a "worst case" proposal. Arguing that he was impressed with the presentations of all programs, he would stick to a 10% reduction across the board, rather than eliminate divisions. Nonetheless, he stated that with the budget crisis a fact of life in coming years, he would reevaluate all programs, and reorganization was a distinct possibility in the future. The one exception to this was the Urban Studies Board of Study that, as rumored, would be eliminated by the end of the following year. This administrative decision evoked outrage in the Social Sciences and did not make the EOD feel secure about its future. It had temporarily escaped and been granted a reprieve, but this certainly did not indicate any administrative support for the future. Moreover, the President announced the formation of a budget committee to advise him on the cuts and future budgetary planning.

At the next faculty meeting the division weighed its options. Two conflicting perspectives emerged: a coalition of liberal and radical-liberal faculty claimed that the division had to take responsibility for its future and make a proposal to the administration concerning its place on campus. The conservative faculty opposed any immediate moves and suggested that the division sit tight, wait for, and then react, to any administrative proposals. The former position was supported by two key points. The first pointed to Urban Studies as a symbol of administrative actions and that, without taking immediate action, the EOD could be next. The second was based on the presiding officer of the EOD faculty's remark that, "the President had off the record commented to her that, in a year, the EOD would not exist in its present form." As the divisional representative and chair of the newly formed Budget Committee, she cautioned that passivity would surely mean demise and that the faculty had to propose a plan to save its jobs, even if it meant losing some divisional autonomy. Although no one wanted this, to wait, she argued, was foolhardy.

The coordinator of the EOD English program prepared a statement concerning the division's options and presented it at the EOD faculty meeting. Agreeing with the presiding officer, she began:

> Rumor has it we may be merged, absorbed, disbanded, (you name it). If there is to be a change in our status, it would seem sensible to have some say in the matter, rather than letting whatever it is, just happen. In order to arrive at what is acceptable to us, we need to focus on specifics. I am presenting the following scenario simply for purposes of discussion (1982c:1).

The proposal included an explicit development of previous recommendations for integration:

1.   If the regular admissions standards are lowered (as was suggested at the Budget meetings), there is a need for a developmental program. The core of this program (which would continue to consist in good measure of EOP students) would address problems in reading, writing, quantitative skills and might eventually offer computer courses.

2.   Articulation with this core program and staffed by ex-EOD faculty and other interested (and suitably equipped) faculty would be skills intensive entry level (and possibly second level) courses in social science, language, natural science and humanities. These courses would be listed in the catalogue under the appropriate Board of Study and would simply be labeled "skills intensive."

3.   Ex-EOD faculty would be attached to the appropriate Board of Study and would divide their time between the core program, the skills intensive discipline courses, and more advanced courses which they are qualified to teach (1982c:1-2).

The core of the proposal recommended the elimination of the present Educational Opportunity Division and in its place a small developmental program with remedial courses in basic skills areas and counseling complemented by the introduction of skills intensive courses in the discipline. The recommendation would create an integrative EOP program similar to those at all other state colleges, with one major exception. By incorporating the present EOD faculty into each Board of Study but having them continue to teach (as the major aspect of their course load) skills intensive lower divisional courses, the philosophy of skills content synthesis would, in theory and hopefully, in practice, be maintained. Moreover, this arrangement would end duplication, provide services for the entire campus, and eliminate the isolation and lower status of both EOD students and faculty. Although the proposal was still in its infancy, it did represent the next logical progression of the division's decline as an autonomous program.

The proposal evoked considerable controversy within the EOD, as it became apparent to everyone that it called for the elimination of the division. The conservative faculty strongly opposed any plan calling for the EOD's elimination, citing that it was the best and most rational program on the campus.[14] One faculty member argued that to submit such a proposal was politically unwise, and he accused the EOD faculty of really not believing in the program. He asserted that a complete defense of separation and a commitment to strengthening enrollments was the most productive course. Nevertheless, the majority of the EOD faculty did not agree with this perspective and felt that a defense of separation was impossible since the President seemingly was against a separate division. These faculty believed that some type of integrative proposal from the EOD would be the only solution.

After considerable debate, the faculty appointed an ad hoc committee to develop a specific proposal from the skeletal outline presented at this meeting. The division charged the committee with incorporating the spirit of these recommendations with the needs of the EOD population in mind. No one had to say that the faculty were included in the population. For the original EOD faculty this was a most difficult time as the program they worked so hard to build appeared to be slowly withering away. Now they chose to take an active role in its reorganization.

The Proposal for a Unified Lower Division

Within two weeks the committee presented its report to the faculty. Entitled "Proposal for a College Wide Lower Division," it recommended the merger of the EOD with the Freshman Studies Program to form a unified Lower

Division. Based upon the logical development of its year long deliberations on integration, the proposal represented an attempt to retain the strengths of the EOD, as perceived by the committee, within an integrative framework. Moreover, in recommending a unification of the two present lower divisional programs, the document spoke to the end of isolation for minority students. Finally, the concept of a lower division itself reflected the division's concern with the educational program at State College and its graduate level curriculum; and, by uniting with Freshman Studies, the division attempted to formalize the alliance that had been in the making for the past year.

The proposal began with a statement of intent and stressed the notion that the reorganization would require no additional funding:[15]

> This is a preliminary proposal for the establishment of an integrated college-wide Lower Division at State College. The proposal suggests that such a division have a General Education distributional requirement for all students. It outlines a pedagogical approach tailored to a wide range of student proficiencies. And, finally, it offers a way in which this program can be staffed with present resources (1982-d:1).

The document then moved to justify the proposal and trace factors leading to its evolution. In a section entitled the "Need for a Lower Division," the authors stated:

> Pressure to modify the approach to the Freshman and Sophomore years is building from several directions. It is increasingly acknowledged that Freshman and Sophomores must have a more coherent and soundly advised academic experience. The EPC is now moving towards the construction of a core curriculum. There is a sense on campus that the barriers surrounding EOD, Freshman Studies, and Continuing Education must be lowered. And, finally, all contemplated moves are now subject to the urgency engendered by diminishing resources. A well conceived Lower Division program could alleviate areas of present stress and provide a stable academic and social environment for entering students (1982d:1).

The authors framed the section on justification around two related areas: first, the lack of coherence and the problems of isolation in the present lower divisional programs and second, the need for efficiency mandated by continuing budget crises. The proposal attempted to carefully suggest that college needs, both educational and fiscal, rather than the realities of self-interest and survival produced these ideas. Whereas the proposal's timing certainly could evoke charges of such singular concerns, the authors stressed that the recommendations were the culmination of over two years of debate on integration.

The next sections discussed the educational requirements and pedagogical approach of this new division. Relying heavily on the educational philosophy of the EOD, the proposal stated:

On Requirements:

A core curriculum for the Lower Division might make the following demands on Freshman and Sophomores: All students will have the same General Education distribution requirements: fine arts, humanities, social science, natural science, and physical education. All students will take a semester of writing and will attain an agreed upon proficiency in mathematics (1982d:1).

On Pedagogy:

The EPC is presently beginning to evolve a core curriculum for all students. Of necessity, courses in such a curriculum given by the Upper Divisions would have large enrollment and would be lecture courses with little, if any, student involvement. This proposal establishes in addition, a complementary curriculum for students who are not able to follow a lecture and absorb assigned reading without help... Since students come to college with a wide range of capabilities, a flexible program which encompasses skills needs as well as academic interests is essential. Thus, the academic program will include three types of courses. First, there will be entry level courses taught by the various boards of study. Capable students who require little or no support can go directly into these. Second, there will be a group of skills intensive courses in the various disciplines. Less proficient students will take these courses which have a narrower focus and smaller class size than do the large lecture courses, and which require student participation in terms of papers, in-class writing, and frequent testing... Finally, for the weakest students, English and mathematics skills sequences will be available. Entering freshmen will be tested and placed according to their abilities:

—students who test in the middle and upper range in reading and writing will go into the second level of a two-semester English sequence. They may choose their other courses from the entry level courses in the various disciplines, according to their interests and the dictates of the distribution requirement, but one of them should be a skills intensive course.

—students who test in the middle and upper range in mathematics will go directly into the appropriate Natural Sciences, mathematics or science courses.

—students who test low in reading and writing will be placed in the first level of the two-semester English sequence, with reading and lab support, if necessary. Concurrently, these students will choose at least one skills intensive course in humanities, social sciences, or natural sciences.

—students who test low in quantitative skills will be placed in a three-semester mathematics sequence at the appropriate level. (Again, these classes are small and there are frequent homework assignments and tests) (1982d:1–3).

The section on requirements and pedagogy, in actuality, only eliminated the EOD name. The proposal applied the EOD educational philosophy and its requirements to all entering students and created an elaborate testing and tracking system to determine appropriate placement. Working from the perspective that EOD students were different from regular admits only in degree, not in kind, and that a considerable skills overlap existed,[16] the EOD committee recommended expanding its program to all students. Therefore, the proposal managed to justify all present faculty in one way or another in the reorganized Lower Division. The section on staffing dealt directly with this issue:

The Lower Division academic program will be staffed by

faculty from the various Boards of Study who are teaching entry level courses, by the Freshman Studies faculty and by the EOD faculty. Members from the first of these three groups will take turns teaching the Freshman and Sophomore courses (as they do now). The second two groups will make up a permanent Lower Division core faculty composed of individuals who are practiced in instructing entry level students with a broad range of skills. (With the exception of Economics, this faculty — as it stands, without further depletion — can cover all academic areas.) Although the larger proportion of the skills-intensive courses will be taught by the permanent core faculty, the boundaries will not be hard and fast, there will be exchanges between the groups. All faculty teaching Lower Division courses will meet at regular intervals (1982d:3).

Thus, the proposal for a reorganized Lower Division included all present faculty members in all programs and placed the EOD and Freshman Studies faculty into a unified lower division. In closing, the committee recognized the problems ahead, on a campus with strong differences about higher education and with sometimes rigid divisional affiliations, and called for an atmosphere of collegial deliberation:

Clearly, much discussion and refinement is needed before a plan such as this can be put into effect. It has been composed under pressure and in a climate of crisis. In particular, the applicability to the arts students needs further definition.... However, several distinct advantages to the plan must be obvious. It offers a stable, yet flexible, core curriculum. It ensures a centralized, coherent experience to all Letters and Science Freshmen (such as has been begun by Freshman Studies) and to Letters and Science sophomores (who are now in limbo). It eliminates the sense of separation experienced by EOD students and faculty. And, finally, it makes full use of an experienced faculty and thus is conservative of resources. Assuredly, there is a trying period of metamorphosis ahead. However, if this proposal can be approached in a spirit of compromise, it might lead to an innovative venture which could be exciting and rewarding for all concerned (1982d:4).

The proposal thus represented the culmination of two years of discussion and, for the first time, a coherent statement of integration emerged out of the EOD. Although the proposal eliminated the separate divisional structure, it also integrated the major components of the program into a new Lower Division. The faculty now had to proceed with a debate of the proposal and, if accepted, the development of a strategy for its implementation and presentation to the entire campus.

The central issue in the ensuing debate concerned the practicality of initiating the action. Although most of the EOD faculty supported the recommendations in principle, they did so reluctantly. That is, the proposal represented the best solution to a bad situation: complete elimination. However, the majority still supported the concept of a separate division and would have preferred a policy that retained it.

As with the preliminary discussions, two opposing positions emerged, the first in support of the proposal and in favor of immediately moving with it and, the second, in favor of defending the divisional structure and placing maximum effort into recruiting a large freshman class. At this point, the director stated that admissions projections were not encouraging and without more assistance from the Admissions Office the division could not even expect to meet its numbers.

Essentially, the debate centered on the EOD's role in its own demise. Some faculty felt that sending the proposal would be premature and that the division should await an administrative proposal before acting. The majority, however, of the EOD faculty believed that the decision to eliminate the separate EOD was a fait accompli and therefore supported the integrative proposal. After a lengthy and emotional debate, the faculty voted to send the proposal to the entire college community.

Upon completion of the final draft, the director issued his support. Calling it a creative and bold statement, he promised to defend it. At the same time, he indicated a certain sadness that factors had conspired to make this a necessary step. He hoped the faculty realized that, if accepted, the division would no longer exist in its present form. Nonetheless, he argued that he knew when the division arrived in 1978 that the separate structure would become the focus of attention and even then he feared for its survival. He praised the division for forcing the college to recognize its obligation to underprepared and minority students and commented that, to survive, the college would have to deal with the reality of its population. This proposal, he stated, made the EOD a vital part in a new path to meeting the college's students "where they are not where the faculty thinks they should be."

Having accepted the proposal for a Lower Division and sent it through proper channels, the division could only wait for a response. In the meantime, the semester continued and the educational problems of the division needed attention. Moreover, given the college's history concerning important decisions, one could not expect quick results. However, a problem concerning direction existed — should the division proceed as if it would exist the following year or plan a gradual phase out? The faculty agreed that until any decisions were finalized, it would continue to pursue ad hoc avenues of integration as it had before the proposal and begin to initiate within the present structure some of the proposal's recommendations. Despite this conviction, the division faced a difficult dilemma. The atmosphere of resignation and decline continued to permeate its walls and not knowing its fate left the faculty disheartened and disenchanted. Nonetheless, it proceeded on its course and awaited word on its fate.

The End of the Academic Year:
Toward an Uncertain Future

The remainder of the Spring semester saw a partial return to normalcy at State College. The Budget Crisis never really was resolved as the governor and legislature battled;[17] but the campus had temporarily put it out of the everyday discussions. The Budget Committee continued to meet and optimism defined the situation. Although no formal response emerged to the EOD proposal, indications of some support and some opposition developed. Moreover, the director stated that the administration was taking the proposal under consideration, but no action would be taken until the 1982–83 academic year. Therefore, the division would exist, at least for one more year.

The faculty reacted with realistic skepticism. Most felt that the next year would be a phasing out period, and that the division should proceed with its integrative proposals. At the same time, the reality of student performance began to hit home. The shift from H-P-NC to letter grades that began in Fall 1981 at State College affected EOD students more than others. As many in the faculty feared, a larger number of grades that formerly appeared as P's were now D's, and EOD student grade point averages were extremely low. The probation and dismissal rate continued to grow and, most importantly, the complete loosening of cross registration requirements resulted in dismal performances by EOD students in regular courses. Moreover, so many students had been cross registering that divisional FTE's were extremely low. All in all, the division faced numerous problems. Its walls had come down, and with its uncertain future and its students barely keeping their heads above water, the EOD began to face a series of difficult paths. Furthermore, the continued uncertainty over divisional identity led to an interesting pattern. The division began to simultaneously proceed as a division, making policies for its students, etc., while also moving to integrate completely. Often the two paths were contradictory; more often it seemed foolish to plan for a program that seemed doomed. As one faculty member exasperatingly commented, "we fiddle and Rome burns."

Two major areas dominated EOD business for the rest of the semester. First, continued discussions with Freshman Studies about the placement of their students and second, the reaction to newly emerging student claims about EOD; claims that were both ironic and encouraging to the division's future.

The news of the division's uncertain future reached the EOD students, who reacted angrily. Although the students had been instrumental in breaking down the walls, although they had often claimed the division was racist and that separation isolated and degraded them, they apparently did not want the division eliminated. Although no formal protests emerged, at a Town Meeting, students defended the division's existence. Although they admitted the program had problems, they also spoke eloquently to its necessity.

A number of factors contributed to this reaction. First, the division for the most part represented the minority students on campus and, despite student criticisms, the EOD students felt part of a unit. They perceived the threat to the division as another example of institutional racism, with the college taking away a program for minority students. Second, the reality of cross registration had sunk in and the value of the EOD became more obvious. As the director had hoped in his proposal to loosen up all structures, "the kids [metaphorically] were returning home from the cruel world with a greater appreciation of their family." They began to appreciate the patience, commitment, and availability of the EOD faculty and, although still supporting further integration, felt the retention of the program in some form was vital. Third, a pattern of support from EOD upperclassmen began to emerge. Looking back, the early negative claims came mostly from freshmen and sophomores anxious to get out of their perceived imprisonment; now, with many students out of the division at the junior level, they began publicly to defend the division. These students called for a better transitional period, noting the extreme differences between EOD and junior level courses, but arguing in favor of retaining some separate divisional structure.

The student reaction initiated a re-emergence of the debate over separation within the EOD faculty. Some members felt that maybe the Lower Divisional proposal was premature, and that a defense of the division should become the new strategy. Student stories confirmed the inability of the State College faculty to meet their needs, and this demonstrated the need for a separate EOD. Others argued that a return to separatism solved nothing and that the division should continue on two fronts, integrating in, that is, retaining the strengths of the division as long as it existed and opening the division to all needy students, and developing a coherent transitional program both administratively and in the curriculum. They argued that the division needed to better prepare its students for the realities of State College.

While the student defense of the program resulted in a newly found optimism, it did not deter the faculty from continuing to pursue avenues of integration. The faculty rejected a return to the past, and immediately initiated discussion with Freshman Studies about integrating in. Once again, the coordinator of the disciplines opposed integrating in Freshman Studies students into EOD writing courses without also enrolling them into EOD discipline courses. Her position, although never publicly stated at a meeting with the Freshman Studies members, is best summed up in a memo she authored prior to these discussions:

> It is my understanding that the Freshman Studies Program both historically and philosophically has always been structured along non-disciplinary lines. It has been our experience over the 13 years we have been working in this area, that students who are lacking or are weak in academic skills need more structure than this kind of course provides. They have difficulty in understanding abstract concepts and in seeing the relationships between them; they also lack the educational background and information necessary to give meaning to this material they are expected to absorb and discuss. This tends to result in grandiose but superficial verbosity or in attempts to memorize and repeat what they read and hear. They do much better if they are given a framework within which new ideas must be discussed (a discipline).

Her demands for a "total package" were rejected by both EOD and Freshman Studies faculty. The meetings concluded with the agreement for EOD to enroll between thirty and fifty Freshman Studies students in the English 101 courses the following Fall. Thus, the division, by integrating in, moved one step closer to expanding its role on the campus.

In the aftermath of these meetings and the Proposal for a Lower Division, the EOD continued to move in an expansionist mode and attempt to legitimate its place at State College. The presiding officer of the faculty and the coordinator of the English department proposed a college wide writing program as the next logical step.

The end of the Spring semester left the EOD faculty looking ahead to the 1982-1983 academic year with apprehension. Although the division had apparently survived the budget crisis (and with the state legislature enacting additional funds, the crisis temporarily was averted), they viewed the coming year as a final crossroads. Some of the faculty thought that perhaps the Lower Division proposal should not have been sent because the administration had been considering a merger plan and would use the next year to gradually implement it.

Toward the end of the Spring semester, one particular issue seemed to define future considerations, and although it did not create any serious controversy, it did suggest a pattern for future integration. The Division of the Social Sciences asked a member of the EOD faculty to teach one of their courses each semester for the next year. In the past, EOD faculty had taught non-EOD courses, but a reimbursement had always been included.[18] However, the past Fall, two EOD faculty taught courses outside of the division and the question of reimbursement had never been settled. Some EOD faculty felt none would be forthcoming, and the request for another of its instructors was perceived by some as raiding. However, the Division of Social Sciences stated that the instructor in question would be teaching the same course in EOD, and that since the Social Sciences had no reimbursement funds, and because this course was crucial to its lower divisional offerings, an obvious solution would be offering their course to both sets of students.[19]

This issue raised a number of serious concerns regarding integration. From the administration and Social Science's point of view, the offering of two somewhat identical courses to different sets of students was expensive and unnecessary. However, to the EOD, placing underprepared students in a large (70+ students) non-developmental course was educationally unsound. Many EOD faculty opposed integration of this kind and argued that this solution indicated the college's continued misunderstanding of the division's methods.

The EOD Curriculum Committee debated the consequences of offering one course to both Social Science and EOD students. First, the large class size, some EOD faculty argued, would make skills intensive work impossible. Second, the two day meeting schedule for regular division courses raised a serious dilemma, as the EOD director felt that without the third day the EOD students would suffer. More importantly, the third day symbolized a major difference between EOD faculty and other instructors, and its elimination suggested that there were no real differences.

In addition to the educational question, this issue raised the thorny issue of academic status and credentialism. The third day represented an increased teaching load to EOD faculty and had always been used to justify their different criteria for EOD reviews (no need to publish, primary emphasis on teaching). According to many EOD faculty, to eliminate the differences would only raise the questions of teaching versus research and the status of EOD faculty. The EOD faculty for a long time believed that they had lower status at State College; more importantly, to eliminate the differences between the EOD and regular divisions spoke to the larger issue of the need for a separate EOD faculty. If there were no differences then any State College faculty could teach EOD students in any class setting. Clearly, this issue could threaten the job security of the EOD faculty, and this became a major concern throughout the deliberations.

After considerable debate, the committee proposed the concept of transitional EOD courses taught by EOD instructors to the entire college population. This social sciences course would be an example of such a course whose purpose was to integrate EOD students into the college mainstream. The director insisted, however, that EOD students be required to attend a special workshop on a third day. This resulted in a "double listing" of the same course under two numbers in two different sections of the college class schedule. In the Social Science it was listed in the following manner: SOC.201, Monday/Thursday, 3-4:20, 4 credits, and in the EOD schedule, XSO.201, Monday/Thursday, 3-4:20, 4 credits and Wednesday, 3-4:20 (workshop), no credit.

Thus, one course had two different numbers, in two different sections of the schedule. Moreover, the EOD section included a separate discussion on a third day, whereas the Social Sciences section did not. In attempting to defend its educational philosophy, the EOD increased the level of confusion, especially with the third day. EOD students demanded to know why they and not others had to attend a discussion group. To avoid the re-emergence of claims against stigmatization, and because the instructor was against any special designation for EOD students, the instructor posted a notice at registration stating that the discussion would be optional and open to all students, not just EOD students.

The debate over the Social Sciences course convinced the EOD faculty that its separate discipline courses would be in serious trouble in the coming years. The college did not seem to accept the EOD's definition of divisional difference and rejected the idea that separate EOD discipline courses were necessary. Therefore, the EOD believed that its skills courses were the key to its expansion and survival. A committee of EOD English faculty began work on a proposal for a college-wide writing program, to be completed over the summer. Its authors envisioned that it would fill a great void at State College and place EOD instructors (or at least its writing instructors) at the center of the solution. At a later date, a similar proposal for a college-wide mathematics program could be developed.

The 1981–82 academic year ended with a sense of anxiety, confusion, and apprehension. This year represented the beginning of the integration and merger process and witnessed the final rejection of divisional separation by its own faculty. Although the "Lower Divisional Proposal" emerged in order to salvage the program and protect its faculty, and most EOD members only reluctantly supported a plan to eliminate its separatism, the wheels, nevertheless, had been placed in motion. An important transition in the EOD's claims to institutional legitimacy had occurred, with the original *defense of difference* in its population and methods used to justify its separation changed into the *defense of its expertise* as vital to the entire campus, and therefore to its full integration into the State College mainstream. In the coming year these issues would become central and the process of integration would shape the EOD's future.

NOTES

1. He stressed the psychological and attitudinal differences and related them to cultural differences. Thus, since the EOD's student population was culturally different, the EOD was necessary.

2. Faculty under review were required to present a written statement of objectives, methods, and philosophy.

3. A growing skepticism over the effectiveness of the EOD philosophy was emerging within the division with a small minority viewing it as ideology without substance.

4. The major difference, from the EOD's perspective, concerned the non-disciplinary nature of the Freshman Studies curriculum.

5. According to the Associate Dean, the Arts students (at this point, only the Dance Division participated in Freshman Studies) often had severe writing weaknesses, as there were no academic requirements for admissions to the School of Arts, only portfolio or audition requirements.

6. Although this had not yet been explicitly stated, it appeared to be a growing sentiment at State College.

7. The Natural Sciences had a very structured curriculum; the Humanities departments did not.

8. The State College Office of Institutional Research report on attrition supports both reasons.

9. Individuals could only be terminated on the basis of seniority. However, the administration could eliminate *departments* completely and thus bypass seniority.

10. And since faculty lines are allocated to the college, not to a division, the college could shift lines from division to division.

11. The Educational Opportunity Program included all designated educational opportunity students both in the EOD and outside it (Upperclassmen and Arts students). The Educational Opportunity Division included all designated underprepared students at the lower divisional level, and this includes *EOP* and *non-EOP* students.

12. The EOD financial aid office was integrated into the State College financial aid office in 1979 and in this statement the Director referred to this merger.

13. A complete analysis of the problems addressed here is provided in Sadovnik (1983:Chapter 8).

14. The EOD never adopted the short term and supported the adoption of the letter grading policy, and these faculty saw the EOD curriculum as the only structured program at the College.

15. While it is clear that the aims of the proposal were to save all existing jobs, in an extreme budget situation requiring actual layoffs the plan would have to be altered. However, the committee recognized that this proposal would, if adopted, possibly lead to other kinds of savings.

16. This idea originated in the accreditation report and now became the basis for the claim that underpreparation was a college-wide problem.

17. The final resolution did not come until after the end of the Spring semester.

18. This was either by direct payment or in kind, with a non-EOD faculty member teaching an EOD course. Since the EOD did not have an anthropologist or economist, the social science division often traded a faculty member.

19. With the EOD instructors teaching the course.

6

THE POLITICS OF DECLINE: THE FINAL DEMISE OF THE EDUCATIONAL OPPORTUNITY DIVISION (1982-1983)

The End is Near or Is It?

Although the previous spring ended with guarded optimism, the entire faculty knew that the 1982-1983 academic year could be the division's last, but no one had any clear understanding of what the college administration was planning. The beginning of the new term saw a number of critical issues appear:

1. the presentation of the completed Writing Proposal;
2. the monitoring of the Freshman Studies students in EOD English courses;
3. clarification of the division's future and the status of the Lower Divisional Proposal; and
4. the poor enrollment in the EOD: high attrition, due to student withdrawal and dismissal combined with its smallest freshman class since its arrival at State College (N=45), placed the division in an extremely precarious position. Small class size across the board meant trouble, and the division clearly understood the possible ramifications.

The Writing Proposal

The EOD English faculty committee returned from the summer break with a completed proposal for a "College Wide Writing Program." Beginning where the "Proposal for a Lower Division" left off, they recommended the development of an overall writing program for all State College students, with the EOD writing faculty a central part of the newly established program. Referring to its first proposal, the authors began:

> During the 1981–82 academic year, the EOD submitted a preliminary proposal for a college-wide lower division. The proposal envisioned a curriculum which explicitly addresses student skills as well as academic interests. Last year's proposal was general in nature and did not discuss means. The present proposal expands on a part of the previous one and offers in rough outline an approach to constructing a writing program framework for the four years at State College (1982e:1).

This proposal, as the last, began with a justification of need. Clearly, to define a new place for itself on campus, the EOD had to define skills problems as college-wide. Thus, in Spector and Kitsuse's language, the division was making claims about the skills problems, and in doing so defining these as serious educational problems, with the division in a position to offer its expertise as a solution. Thus the proposal stated:

> There is a widespread feeling at State College that something must be done to improve the quality of writing. Public schools have not been preparing students properly in the skills areas since the 60s, for reasons too complex to enumerate here. In recent years, the national average in verbal SAT scores has dropped 42 points, from 466 in 1967 to 424 in 1980. When one adds that a poor economic climate along with a lower birth rate had led to a constantly shrinking pool of college applicants, two things become obvious: first, the often bewildering variety and degree of language skills problems from which too many of our students suffer is part of a national phenomenon. Second, we can expect that the percentage of students who enter State College with these problems will increase throughout the remainder of this decade (1982e:1).

Thus, the divisional claims were supported by the definition of writing deficiencies as a central educational problem, not particular to State College, but rather of a much more encompassing nature. Moreover, the statement that it would continue to worsen given demographic conditions, opened the door for elaboration of the centrality of the EOD to the college's future. Consistent with Spector and Kitsuse's analysis of one type of claims making,[1] the authors used empirical evidence and expertise to legitimate their points. Continuing with their presentation, the authors moved from a statement of the problem to an analysis of its causes and solutions:

Before we reach in and attempt to solve these problems by applying one of a number of standardized approaches; perhaps we might pause to consider the relationship between reading, writing and analytic thinking. Poor writing, more often than not, is the result of incompletely realized thought. A student who responds to an assignment with an inadequate piece of work may have had difficulty in understanding ideas in lectures and reading, may have had trouble selecting or analyzing material appropriate to the assignment, or may have had difficulty organizing a coherent and unified body of thought, or structuring clear, grammatical sentences. All three types of difficulty appear as 'writing problems' (1982e:1–2).

The document began with an identification of different writing problems, but what is significant is it reflected the overall framework of the EOD Writing Program. Certainly this is not unusual, as the authors' presentation of a campus-wide program began with the EOD foundation and then expanded upon it. Continuing in this direction, the authors argued:

Traditionally, at the college level, there are two ways that students acquire and improve language skills. The first is by taking basic writing courses in what is commonly known as a 'writing program.' The second, and by far *the most effective*, occurs within the context of a course in a traditional discipline; written assignments related to coursework provide an active type of learning which both enhances mastery of content and sharpens language skills; the writing clarifies thought by requiring focus and rendering feedback. It cannot be emphasized strongly enough that to be successful both of these means must be used (1982e:2).

Once again, as we have seen repeatedly, the introduction of the skills-content synthesis, and the complementary nature of discipline courses was the central aspect of the EOD philosophy and permeated all claims making activities.

Upon introducing the methodology on which the writing program rested, and suggesting that examples could be found at State College both in EOD and Freshman Studies, the authors cited the need for a more expansive and integrated program and proceeded to introduce their model.

Arguing against a stop-gap or one year program, the Writing Proposal suggested a complete four year integrated curriculum combining special writing classes with designated writing intensive discipline classes from the freshman to senior levels. Stating that the State College senior thesis requirement made the proposal central to student needs, the authors defended the all-encompassing nature of the program. State College could not continue to assume, as it had done in the past, that students reach the senior level prepared to write a competent thesis; quite the contrary, without a rational and structured program most students would arrive at the task woefully unprepared. Speaking to this issue, the authors stated:

> It is obvious that for a writing program to work at State College, it must require students at each level of learning, from the freshman to senior year, to complete specific coursework, along with a senior thesis, in fulfillment of a writing requirement. Thus, the program itself must be extended horizontally as well as vertically across the disciplines, affecting all divisions on campus and involving as many faculty as possible. At the same time, because writing skills vary markedly from student to student, the program must be flexible enough to permit an incoming freshman with severe weaknesses or whose progress is slow to spend more time meeting the writing requirement, without academic penalty, than one whose writing is clear and well organized or whose progress is rapid (1982e:4)

Therefore, in addition to preparing a writing program of massive scope, involving a large number of faculty over a four-year period, the document included this protection clause for EOD and other underprepared students. While it is clear that the EOD was expanding its functions, its faculty still were acutely aware of the division's original mission and, more importantly, their role as advocates of EOD student needs. Therefore, they carefully avoided any integrative proposal that lost sight of EOD students.

This Writing Proposal continued the process initiated with Freshman Studies in the Fall of 1982. Over 25 non-EOD students from the Freshman Studies program were placed in EOD English courses based on admissions reading and writing placement examinations. This proposal recommended the institutionalization of these testing procedures and a tracking system to place incoming students at an appropriate level in the writing sequence.[2]

The proposal recommended that all students at State College be placed in writing courses on the basis of placement examinations. Modeled after both EOD writing courses and the Freshman Studies sequence, the writing program would require proficiency in reading, essay writing, and the research paper. Furthermore, integrating the EOD skills-content synthesis, the committee proposed a series of writing intensive discipline courses taught by EOD discipline faculty. Finally, the authors recommended a Learning Center attached to the Lower Division to provide intensive tutorial assistance to students with skills problems.

In closing, the authors re-emphasized the points concerning integration introduced in the Lower Division proposal:

> We do believe that this proposal will address the problems related to writing as well as effectively utilize faculty in a more extensive and economical way than the present system allows. The alteration of monolithic, isolated divisions such as EOD and Freshman Studies should encourage growth in enrollment and limit attrition. The integration necessary to unifying State College as a college will be addressed (1982c:11).

Therefore, as in the lower division proposal, the EOD faculty called for its own integration and the subsequent demise of the division. These two proposals represented a final shift in perspective away from divisional isolation to full integration. Although there was certainly no unanimity on this direction, it clearly symbolized the evolution in thinking from 1978-19-82, and although the factors leading to the change were multifaceted and complex, it was now apparent that the division was actively participating in its integration, rather than only responding to external pressure. The key to the entire process continued to revolve around the changing nature of divisional claims. In the early period at State College, the division's existence depended on its presentation of difference, one that stressed its different student population and therefore the need for a separate division with special methods. At this point, the divisional claims stressed the similarities in student populations (or at least the overlap) and its existence (in integrated form) depended on the presentation of its expertise to this wider constituency. In fact, this process was marked by the divisional efforts to define "the declining skills of all students" as an educational problem and in so doing attempted to cement its place at the college.

The faculty approved "The Writing Proposal" and forwarded it to the administration, EPC, division heads, and the new Letter and Science Dean.[3] Since the college community had not as yet responded to the "Proposal for a College Wide Lower Division," the faculty was concerned about overall interest. It seemed that in times of budget crisis the EOD became an easy target, but when things calmed down the college returned to business as usual. To some of the EOD faculty, the message indicated that other divisions did not want integration, but rather were satisfied with a separate, isolated EOD as long as the budget permitted. If, however, fiscal constraints actually forced the elimination of positions, they would rather those cuts came at EOD expense, than to support any integration scheme. The implication seemed obvious to certain EOD faculty: the college viewed the EOD as a remedial program, not a complete academic division, and it would not support EOD faculty doing "real" academic teaching. While others did not see this pattern, the presentation of the second proposal would begin to clarify things. If this too did not receive attention or the State College faculty bitterly opposed it, then the concept of integration would be in trouble.

Searching for Direction

By the beginning of the Fall semester, the entire EOD faculty was confused and concerned. The lack of response to its lower divisional proposal, its extremely low enrollments (due especially to a very small freshman class of 45), and a pattern of administrative recommendations for reappointment of EOD faculty contributed to a sense that the division was under considerable scrutiny. The problem, however, also concerned its inability to set clear goals or plans, for the division did not have any sense of its future. To plan for a merger or significant integration would require moving in one direction, however, if the division were to retain its separate structure, alternative plans would have to be implemented. To teach the EOD population was difficult enough, but to constantly live with uncertainty made the task impossible. Thus, it asked for a special meeting with the Academic Vice-President to clarify its position. Since the new Dean of Letters and Sciences was meeting with every division, he decided to invite the Academic Vice President to the meeting.

The special meeting exacerbated the uncertainty, as both the dean and Academic Vice-President would not divulge any concrete plans. The year, according to the Vice-President, would be used as a transitional period; however, he would not definitely state what this meant. The only certainty he would divulge was that duplication would be eliminated and EOD faculty would be utilized in other Boards of Study, where needed. In sum, the meeting consisted of EOD members asking for a clear answer to the uncertainty of the future, and the Dean and Academic Vice-President refusing to indicate that any decision to disband the EOD had been reached. The administration denied any pattern of phase out and responded angrily to the director's charges that the division was being systematically ignored and allowed to die a slow death.

The director continued his "offensive" strategy by demanding the college renew its commitment to minority students. Stressing that declining enrollments were due to the elimination of college support for recruiting, he once again demanded a full time recruiter. The Vice-President, while saying that no conspiracy existed, stated that the college did not have a budget for a recruiter. Moreover, in a response that squarely placed the responsibility on the EOD, he argued that low enrollments were caused as much by internal problems like attrition and dismissal, and the EOD had to improve its own retention rates.

The faculty and staff responded by claiming the division's problems were in fact college problems. First, the EOD admissions staff stated that the division needed its own recruiter because regular admissions did not want to recruit EOD students. Arguing that regular admissions was committed to the profile of the typical State College student and that its staff did not feel comfortable with minority students, they pressed either for an EOD recruiter or a minority recruiter in the admissions office. Second, a number of EOD faculty stated that the high attrition rate was consistent with the State College rates and that the latter might just as easily explain the former, rather than placing the responsibility on "internal problems." Moreover, since EOD students left in greatest numbers as they approached the junior year (that is, when they became more integrated into State College), perhaps the separate divisional structure was a strength, not a weakness. The faculty implied that perhaps the problem was State College rather than the EOD.

At this point, one faculty member stated that the uncertainty made working conditions and planning impossible: "How do we plan a curriculum, how do we set policy, if we do not know if we will exist. Many of the faculty feel this is the last year, so they are playing out the string, waiting to find out if they will be excluded in an integrative plan. It is very difficult to commit yourself to divisional needs when deep down you associate this with a dying program." Moving from the general appeal for clarification to administrative decisions over the summer, the faculty member asked if review decisions did not indeed mean that the administration really had made up its mind. The faculty member stated to the Vice-President:

> Over the summer, three junior faculty reviews were ignored by your office and the President. In one, the divisional review committee recommended a continuing appointment and a three year contract and the administration granted a continuing one year contract; in another, the review committee recommended a continuing appointment

186 Equity and Excellence in Higher Education

and promotion and a three year contract, and the administration granted a one year appointment and denied the
promotion; and third, the review committee recommended
a promotion and a three year contract and the administration took the instructor off tenure track and placed her on
a temporary appointment. In all three cases, for somewhat
similar reasons the administration cited credentials and
denied lengthy contracts or promotions, and in complete
opposition to the EOD guidelines that emphasize teaching,
advisement and community service, the administration
invoked State College guidelines. In two cases, where the
instructors taught skills courses, the administration pointed
to the terminal master's degree and demanded further
graduate education. In the other, where the instructor
taught a discipline (and is a Ph.D. candidate), the administration demanded the completion of the doctorate for
promotion and retention. While some of the faculty do not
necessarily disagree with this, in theory, you have, by
rejecting the EOD guidelines changed the game in the
middle and in doing so seem to be inferring that the
division's future is questionable. Did the college take other
faculty off tenure track or just in this division?

The Academic Vice-President did not wish to publicly discuss personnel
decisions other than to say the college had stayed away from long-term
contractual obligations because of continued budgetary pressures. Further,
he suggested that the EOD guidelines were not binding on the administration
and, in the future, EOD faculty would be subject to the State College
guidelines, then in the process of being rewritten.

A senior member of the EOD faculty responded to these statements
by pointing to divisional differences. Historically, the EOD guidelines
recognized the importance of teaching and advisement to the success of its
program. Therefore, the division placed its major emphasis on excellence
in these areas. Moreover, the division required far more of a time commitment from its faculty in terms of contact hours and workload. It was always
understood that these differences were essential to the division's mission and
the divisional guidelines legitimated them. It was also understood that while
State College faculty were required to use their time for research and
publication, the EOD faculty were not required to publish or perish, as their
major time commitment was to teaching, tutorials, and advisement. In
conclusion, the senior faculty member stated that if the college wanted the
EOD faculty to be the same as all other faculty and demanded publications,

the timely completion of the doctorate, etc., then the EOD faculty should have the same schedules, course loads, etc. To do otherwise, was to create a double standard. He concluded by stating, "In applying the same review standards to our faculty you are denying our special mission; and at the least we would like some straight answers about our obligations."

The Academic Vice-President did not agree with the charges and stated that while teaching would always be the major criteria for EOD faculty, he believed that steady progress toward the doctorate was necessary for all State College faculty, most of whom were appointed with Ph.D.'s in hand, and that the EOD faculty, as self-proclaimed experts on compensatory higher education, should be encouraged to publish their methods, theories, etc. Although the parties did not reach a consensus, the debate defined a number of fundamental issues concerning divisional identity and separation, including credentialism, teaching versus research, and workloads, issues that would surely re-emerge as integration proceeded.

On the whole, the faculty left the meeting with no clearer indications about its future than before. The Academic Vice-President implied that duplication would be eliminated and forms of integration would continue, but beyond that he would not reveal his cards. The division felt it was left with only one choice: to proceed in two directions, one as if the division would be retained and the other with a constant eye toward integration and possible merger or elimination.

The EOD, although still clinging to its divisional existence, was not the same program as in 1978. In addition to its adoption of a semi-integrative philosophy, the cohesive unit that defined its transition to State College had gradually eroded. As evidence of this, the EOD faculty, by the Fall 1982, looked less and less like the original, as increasingly the original faculty disappeared from the scene. The coordinator of the Math-Science faculty, due to a serious illness, still was not back on a full-time basis. Another original faculty member left to take another position; two others were granted sabbatical leaves. Only a small core of the original Coop College faculty remained and, more importantly, continued budget cuts had reduced the faculty to a point where it could barely offer a viable program. Moreover, in the second week of the semester, the director, the program's administrative leader since its inception, announced that he would be leaving as of October 1 to take an administrative position in the State Office of Special Programs. Although the division's members were happy for his ascendancy to state-wide administrative office, they also feared the effect this would have on the division's ability to survive. In a year that promised to be critical, the transition to a new director might prove disastrous.

Nonetheless, the division proceeded to choose an acting director from its ranks. The director selected a senior faculty member, who was jointly appointed as a counselor. Feeling that his rapport with students, his understanding of the instructional and counseling components of the program, and his long tenure with the division made him an appropriate candidate, the director recommended him to the EOD faculty and the State College administration. In a remarkably smooth transition, the new director received unanimous support from the EOD faculty and met with the administration's approval. By the first week in October, the original director moved upward, and the new director began the difficult task of regenerating the enthusiasm of a badly demoralized faculty and dealing with the significant problems ahead. To many, the original director's move only symbolized the division's certain demise, with remarks like "he is leaving a sinking ship" expressing a common feeling.

The new director called a special faculty meeting to outline his plans for the year. In a presentation defined by a cautious optimism, he called for the reconstruction of divisional strength by recapturing its original goals and mission. Suggesting that elimination was not a fait accompli, he called for a careful exploration of divisional goals and the solution of its problems. Adding that the program should proceed on the assumption that it would continue to exist, the director called for a redefinition of community. The program, in his estimation, had disintegrated under external pressures toward integration and, in capitulating, had lost touch with its population. In trying to become acceptable to the rest of the campus, he stated, "we have forgotten the need to be different."

While stressing the need for divisional identity, he indicated that the division could never return to isolation. The administration would never allow duplication and the plans for forms of integration would have to continue. Moreover, the division remained in an extremely vulnerable position because of its low enrollments; so all attempts to integrate in non-EOD students were essential. The question of enrollments, both in terms of admissions and retention, were the central problems the division would face in the coming year.

On admissions, the new director pledged to push for greater involvement by the regular admissions office. However, he cautioned that history had demonstrated the futility of such expectations, and to rely on them would spell certain disaster. Rather, he promised to initiate a forceful recruitment campaign involving the entire registrar's office, counseling office, and his own office. Moreover, he felt that if the division could attract 100 new students the next fall, the pressure toward total integration would diminish. The college would be all too happy in his estimation to continue to support the division as long as it supported itself.

Although attracting students was an important concern, retaining them would prove to be the central issue of his administration. He suggested that the sources of attrition were both internal and external, and that although the division could do little to change the attitudes and methods of State College programs, it could deal effectively with EOD students during their time in the division. Referring to the continued poor performance of EOD students, especially in cross registered classes, he asked the faculty to reconsider its loosening of divisional rules, such as the liberalized cross registration policy, and the abolition of an attendance policy. In conclusion, he pointed to the problem of bringing minority students to State College:

> Sometimes I want to tell them to go elsewhere, that this isn't the place for them. For example, in good conscience, I can't promise them a solid economics program (and so many are interested in economics) when the division doesn't have an economist, and the economics board of study is inaccessible to our students. On the other hand, we can offer them two years of solid education that will prepare them for a college degree. If they leave after two years to a more accessible college, then we've done our job.

For the first time, the director publicly stated what the faculty had felt for a long time — that the problem was State College and its graduate type programs, and perhaps EOD students should not be expected to finish at the college, but could be encouraged to transfer to other branches of the system. The State College faculty, now receiving many EOD students at the junior level, had begun to insinuate that the program did not work. The EOD faculty were aware that many of their students moved to the junior level still with severe educational problems, and that the State College faculty seemed non-responsive to their needs. The EOD faculty defended the program by saying all faculty had to be involved in remediation and that often two or three years were not enough to make up for twelve years of deprivation; nonetheless, most State College faculty felt that this was the division's responsibility and reacted unfavorably to the presence of underprepared students in their classes. While the degree of their dissatisfaction wavered between understanding and contempt, the problem was a critical one. The division would have to more carefully monitor student progress and deal more effectively with skills problems, although most faculty were at a loss for how to do this. As one faculty member stated:

> This is a serious problem. We cannot continue to speak as experts and use our expertise to justify our proposals for integration, while many of our students move on unpre-

pared. While we realize the difficulties, other faculty measure us by our students' performance. Last spring, I was the second reader of two senior theses (by former EOD students), and quite frankly they were terrible; certainly no more than mediocre research papers, not at all minimally acceptable as theses. Now it is clear that their advisors spent little time with them, and did not give them the structure and attention they needed; however, we receive the blame. Then they are passed through out of a most insidious form of paternalism; how can we tell them the truth now. We might want to address the entire senior thesis requirement as problematic, however, as long as it exists we cannot continue to send our students up unprepared (conversation with EOD faculty member).

Thus, what began with the director's plans for the year developed into an overall discussion of the problems facing the division. The path seemed clear: internally, the division would have to deal with continuing problems of attrition, attendance, and performance. Externally, the division would have to continue to pursue integration by avoiding duplication and integrating in.

The division's policies and plans for the coming year were somewhat confused as the director and faculty did not really know in which of the two directions to move. Therefore, the division went in both directions simultaneously, although at times this would lead to inevitable contradictions. On the one hand, the EOD continued to negotiate plans for integration, both by allowing non-EOD students into its classes and by offering its discipline courses to the entire college. On the other hand, the new director's charge to the faculty required a re-evaluation of the division as a separate division, and attempts to strengthen the EOD were sought. Although the director spoke optimistically about the possibility of bringing in 100 new students in the next fall semester, many faculty expressed concern that there might not be a division to bring them to. While rumors of its demise continued to flourish, nobody in an official capacity would verify or refute these claims. The director commented:

If we can get 100 students, we may be safe, but how can we recruit them for a separate division only to bring them in without one. It is very difficult to tell prospective students that they should come here. All of this uncertainty is extremely difficult.

The Path to Total Integration: Cross Listing
and Interdivisional Conflicts

It became obvious to everyone that the Division was in an extremely vulnerable position. The Dean of Letters and Science commented on the small enrollments in many EOD courses and decided that steps should be taken to strengthen the offerings for the Spring semester. In a meeting with the director and the chairperson of the Curriculum Committee he requested that most EOD disciplines courses be offered to all students, and that none duplicate any other offerings on campus.

The Curriculum Committee attempted to develop its Spring offerings in consultation with the various divisions. The concept of cross-listed EOD courses emerged, with these formally listed in both the EOD and the divisional schedules. As with the solution developed the previous semester, two different numbers would be assigned to allow equitable distribution of FTE's.

While the concept of cross listing EOD courses seemed a viable solution to enrollment problems, the questions of class size and meeting schedules continued to pose difficult problems. The Curriculum Committee's debates revolved around the tension between educational philosophy and organizational survival. Educationally, the committee believed that small class size and three meetings per week were essential to EOD student needs. Politically, to remove size restrictions and meet two days would eliminate any differences in EOD classes and place EOD discipline faculty in a precarious position. On the one hand, if their courses were exactly the same as all others, then any number of a board of study could teach them and the possible implications were obvious to all. On the other hand, the declining enrollments in the EOD made separate EOD courses impossible to justify and the Dean would not permit such separation to continue.

The Committee adopted a compromise solution that they believed to be both educationally and politically sound. Although the Committee was extremely sensitive to the political aspects of these negotiations and was certainly motivated by the desire to maintain their positions on campus, the issues of educational effectiveness and student needs were also central areas of concern.

The Curriculum Committee suggested that a distinction be drawn between cross listed and cross registered EOD courses. The latter, courses in other divisions taught by EOD instructors and open to EOD students, would be subject to the class size restrictions and meeting schedule of the particular board of study. These courses, although open to EOD students, were not really EOD courses and EOD students should be subject to the same cross registration requirements as any other non-EOD course. The only advantage seemed to be that if EOD students enrolled in very large classes, it would be better if they had an EOD instructor. Cross listed courses, however, would be EOD discipline courses offered to the entire college and, as such, subject to EOD rules and requirements. In a compromise, the division distinguished between writing intensive EOD courses and transitional EOD courses. The former would be all 100 level and some 200 level courses with intensive skills orientation. These would meet three days per week and be limited to 25 students (with priority to EOD students). The latter would be most 200 level EOD discipline courses and would also meet three days but have enrollment up to 40. These courses would serve EOD students in preparing them for junior level work, in both atmosphere and requirements, and be open to an integrated population.[4]

The compromise seemed to meet with the concerns of most committee members. As with previous discussions of integration, the majority of the faculty sought to defend the divisional philosophies and practices. The question of EOD students' needs always were the first concern, with questions of self-interest and survival sometimes beneath the surface. To some faculty members, the politics of integration remained somewhat ironic. As one stated:

> It is somewhat curious that we keep talking about the sanctity of EOD methods with our terrific record. Our student performance continues to decline, our attrition continues to rise, our students perform very poorly in the regular divisions, even after finishing our program, and we continue to invoke a brand of pedagogical superiority. At some point we will be challenged and I'm afraid we cannot support the effectiveness of our claims. In addition, it is a little amusing to watch us, dealing out of a position of extreme weakness, make demands as if we were in a position of extreme strength.

Most perceptively, this faculty member articulated two very important points defining the politics of integration. First, in continuing to invoke its educational philosophy and more importantly an ideology of expertise, the EOD left itself open to charges that the reality did not support the claims. That is, the data on EOD student performance did not support any hypothesis of difference. Although the reasons for this were too complex for the instructor to pin down, and although he did not attribute these to any programmatic deficiencies, the EOD placed itself in a vulnerable position by continuing to take an intractable stand on its methods. It could only do this if student performance under these special conditions indicated significant differences from students under other conditions. Evidence was beginning to emerge to the contrary,[5] and this instructor felt the division stood on very thin ice. Second, since the division's enrollments made it extremely vulnerable, the instructor implied that its "stubborn" posture betrayed this vulnerability. He added:

> Given our present position we'd be better to compromise and survive, then to go down with the ship. It is ironic that we criticize some State College faculty for refusing to bend some of their methods and requirements (for example, a senior thesis) to increase accessibility, but we do the same thing. I am not saying the three day schedule and class size are unimportant, I think we all agree they are. But at some point, we must be pragmatic.

Despite some of the differences on the Curriculum Committee, the Committee voted to adopt the proposed guidelines for cross listed courses, dividing them into writing intensive and transitional courses. With support of the Dean, the chairperson of the EOD Curriculum Committee implemented negotiations with the other boards of study to put the cross-listing into motion.

The integrative process seemed to go smoothly, and an integrative program was approved by the Dean. To many EOD faculty this meant that the integration process that began over two years before was beginning to take shape. Moreover, by broadening the scope of its discipline courses and expanding the clientele of its skills courses by integrating in, the EOD had possibly managed to integrate and simultaneously retain its separate divisional structure.

Things, however, proceeded too smoothly and in an event characteristic of the miscommunication that often defined State College politics, the Humanities Division raised serious objections to the cross listing procedure. Stating that EOD courses were not approved for Humanities credit, the Humanities faculty issued a memo to the entire campus stating that EOD courses would not receive such credit and demanding that the EOD courses be removed from the Humanities listing. The sending of the memo angered the EOD faculty and students and, in a special meeting, the division considered the appropriate response.

First, the committee assessed the damages. The Humanities memo resulted in the cancellation of the EOD cross listed courses from the Humanities schedule, leaving them as EOD courses. This would mean that the chances that non-EOD students would enroll in these courses would be significantly diminished. In addition, during the registration week a sign noting the cancellation of all four courses was posted at registration, and it did not state that the courses were still open under EOD numbers. This only deepened the numbers problem. More importantly, EOD students began to react angrily and negatively to what they considered the public display of degradation toward their division and its instructors. Many demanded to know why EOD teachers could not teach regular students and why they (EOD students) could be integrated in regular classes, but the reverse was not the case. Although, in the past, many EOD students had been critical of divisional separation, their reaction to this incident pointed to a most important aspect of their claims. EOD students had always challenged the negative labels associated with the division and claimed that the label EOD student was degrading and stigmatizing; however, now it became apparent that their claims were aimed more at the reactions of outsiders to the EOD than the quality of teaching inside it. While certainly many students had made claims against certain instructional and pedagogical aspects of the EOD, the student reaction in this case could not support a hypothesis that state EOD students disliked the division. Rather, they reacted defensively and argued that their instructors should teach to the entire community. As one disheartened student stated:

> I don't understand this. I have had excellent teachers in
> EOD and many are better than those in the upper division.
> If they can't teach regular division courses what does this
> say about my first two years here?

A small number of students wanted the EOD faculty to take immediate action and one wished to organize student protests. On the advice of an EOD faculty member, the student agreed to wait until the EOD faculty decided on a course of action.

Although the Humanities memo clearly caused damage both in terms of EOD enrollments and its effect on EOD students, the underlying message behind it became the major focus of EOD faculty interest. As one faculty member stated: "the important thing is not its literal meaning, but its intended meaning and what the memo actually symbolizes." Most EOD faculty felt the memo represented the public display of the private sentiments of the Humanities faculty and their action just supported what many in EOD had always believed, that the Humanities faculty perceived the EOD and its faculty as inferior and tolerated them as long as they were separate and silent, but given the opportunity to accept them as academic equals, they rejected any such notion. To one EOD faculty member the action symbolized the larger issues of racism and elitism: "It is ironic that a program for minority students receives the same kind of treatment that minorities in

American society receive: as long as the Division stays in the basement and keeps its mouth shut it is patronizingly tolerated."

Although the faculty reacted emotionally, most could also understand a legitimate basis for the Humanities faculty's feelings. As one senior member stated:

> Every board of study has the right to approve all courses listed under its heading. If a division wanted us to cross list one of their courses we would ask them to come before our curriculum committee, submit a course description and outline and discuss their understanding of EOD student needs. The fact that time constraints did not permit such a process, and because the boards of study did not approve the courses gives some legitimacy to their objections. However, their tactics were deplorable and their real meanings much more insidious.

At this point, the Curriculum chairperson attempted to clarify the negotiation process:

> To some extent this was a big misunderstanding and for that I have to take responsibility as I handled the negotiations. However, everything was handled through channels. I talked with the Humanities chairperson and she approved the cross listing. The Dean's office oversaw the entire process. I assumed the Humanities chair would inform her faculty, obviously she didn't. I don't think we realized the delicate nature of cross listing. I assumed that they would understand that the cross listed courses were EOD courses open to everyone. I never realized they would view these as intrusions on their curriculum.

Moreover, a senior faculty member spoke to the heart of the matter:

> For thirteen years we have granted college credit for our courses. Now the Humanities faculty is publicly stating that our courses do not deserve college credit. First of all, the registrar does not grant credit for majors, just credits. The board of study sets credit requirements to fulfill a major. In the past all of our discipline courses received full credit as electives or in some cases fulfilled board of study requirements. This memo questions our credibility as a

division. We cannot allow this to stand unnoticed.

Finally, in a sarcastic comment one professor, noting the "structured" requirements of the Literature board of study, stated:

> Isn't it ironic that a department that has no formal require-ments, no sequence of courses, practically no lower divisional offerings defends the sanctity of its major from EOD offerings. It really defines the differences between our divisions.

And in a remark linked to the mission of EOD, the instructor of one of the questionable courses (Black Drama) asserted:

> A department that cannot and doesn't offer relevant courses for black students resists such a course in its schedule. This certainly says something to our students, none of it complimentary.

The Humanities memo had certainly resulted in extreme tension, but nothing else defined its effects more than the reaction of one junior EOD literature instructor. He was scheduled to teach an EOD cross listed literature course and a writing course for the Humanities Division in the Spring semester. The assignment to the Humanities Division had caused some tension a few weeks before this incident, as the EOD felt his services were needed within the division. The Dean, however, overruled the EOD by arguing that divisional enrollments did not warrant it, and a greater need existed elsewhere. (Once again, the college administration defined college needs above divisional boundaries; more importantly, the EOD clearly understood that its low enrollments would continue to make it vulnerable to what it considered "divisional raiding.") The instructor took the Humanities memo very personally and threatened to refuse to teach the Humanities course and instead offer an additional EOD course, open only to EOD students. At the Curriculum Committee meeting he stated:

> I am really fed up. This public statement is degrading and a vulgar comment on all our capabilities. After publicly stating they don't want us, that we are inferior, and that our courses are not worthy of credit, there is no way I want to teach a course for them. I don't know what you plan to do as a committee, but right now I just don't think I want anything to do with them.

At this point, the Curriculum chair attempted to depersonalize the intent of the memo:

> You have every right to be furious, but I think it was directed at the entire division rather than any one individual. In fact, although it may be of little solace, the fact that they have no problems with you teaching the Writing course, supports this view. Moreover, at least in your case it is not a credentials issue, as you have the credentials.

After considerable debate the committee reached a number of conclusions about the memo:

1. Giving the Humanities faculty the benefit of the doubt, the committee agreed that it was possible that their major motivation was procedural and their main objection was the failure to approve each course.

2. Although the committee believed this to be a legitimate claim, it also strongly believed the memo symbolized more central conflicts between the two divisions, and its "hidden agenda" was far more destructive.

3. The hidden agenda centered on a number of related issues, all indicating future problems in any negotiations about integration, at least with the Humanities Division. Among the hypotheses considered:

a. The Humanities Division had always resented the EOD and never supported its existence, and this situation represented a public statement of what had been private sentiment.

b. The Humanities Division did not respect the quality of EOD faculty, with credentialism a significant aspect of this.

c. The Humanities Division did not recognize EOD courses as college level and therefore would not approve them for its own students. EOD courses from this perspective were tolerated as long as they were separate. More importantly, it either misunderstood or rejected the skill-content synthesis and viewed courses as either remedial or substantive. Therefore, it viewed EOD discipline courses as remedial and denied that one could do both skills and content at the college level. From this perspective, all EOD faculty were perceived as skills teachers, and skills courses should not be treated the same as substantive college courses.

d.   The Humanities Division wanted to have autonomy over the use of lines assigned to its courses. Many EOD faculty believed that this could have been the bottom line — the Humanities Division might have been saying, we'll take the line and hire our own faculty, but we do not want EOD faculty teaching in our division. At a time when joint appointment or the reassignment of EOD discipline faculty to Boards of Study was definitely a possibility, this reaction could prove a serious obstacle.

Although the meeting began with angry calls for action and public defense of EOD integrity, by its conclusion cooler heads prevailed. Most EOD faculty were still furious. However, they decided that the division did not need a full scale airing of the incident, nor did they want to risk a public presentation of the possible "hidden agenda", as a public degradation ceremony would not help the division in its struggle to survive. Yet, because of its severity, the situation could not be ignored. Therefore, the committee charged its chairperson to raise its objections to the Dean and draft a letter to the college community in response to the memo. The committee agreed that the tone should not be vitriolic, but rather begin by supporting the Humanities' right to divisional and curricular autonomy, explain that proper channels had been followed, apologize that a misunderstanding had evidently occurred, but condemn the propriety and timing of the memo. In addition, the letter would point to the detrimental effects, intentional or not, on the integrity of the EOD and, more importantly, on the self-concepts of its students.

Toward Clarification: The Dean's Meeting on the Future of EOD

In the weeks immediately following the "Humanities Memo," things began to move quickly. The Dean of Letters and Science called a special Dean's Meeting to discuss the future of the EOD and announced a preliminary proposal to eliminate the EOD as a separate division and replace it with a small integrative educational opportunity program (that would offer only remedial courses, with opportunity students mainstreamed at the outset into discipline courses).

The Dean then began to present the reasons behind the possible change. First, he cited the extreme budgetary pressures facing the college and suggested that an integrative EOP program would allow for the more efficient and effective use of faculty. Second, pointing to the isolation and separation characteristic of all State College programs, he pledged to begin to remove the barriers; integrating the EOD would be a step in the right direction, as the college could not support the continued separation of its minority students. Third, the division's own Lower Division proposal suggested similar integration strategies. Fourth, citing a report written by one of the EOD faculty that concluded that little significant difference existed between the EOD and other integrative state EOP programs on two measures of educational performance, the Dean concluded that, given the division's expense, it could not be defended as a separate entity if it did not produce significantly superior results.[6]

The Dean indicated that the needs of disadvantaged students would be protected in his plan. As he envisioned it, the college would retain a small integrative EOP program providing remedial courses in writing, reading and mathematics. The skills faculty presently in the EOD would comprise the core faculty. In addition, the present administrative and counseling staff, as mandated by law, would continue to serve the EOP population. Moreover, a Learning Center would be permanently attached to the program and serve all students, including EOP students. All other EOD faculty would be assigned to boards of study, with their primary responsibility to offer lower divisional courses, some of which would be writing intensive. The Dean noted that this seemed consistent with the intent of the EOD Lower Divisional Proposal, but he did not indicate that a separate lower division would be formed. Rather, he preferred eliminating all restrictive classificatory systems by simply integrating EOD faculty into boards of study. He added that a similar proposal could emerge for the Freshman Studies Program, with its faculty continuing to have primary responsibilities to the Freshman sequence, but also appointed to specific boards of study.

Despite the EOD director's concerns over the extent to which the new program would meet the needs of educational opportunity students, including whether they would enroll in Freshman Studies[7] and the status of non-EOP students,[8] the Dean insisted that the problems could be resolved. Moreover, he added that his proposal was based upon the EOD's own "Lower Divisional Proposal" and would place all incoming State College students into appropriate skills courses and eliminate all duplication in the discipline areas.

After a brief discussion, the meeting turned from debating the question of change to the politics of implementation. This would prove far more difficult and, although this meeting was informal and not binding, the problems discussed suggested the difficult road ahead. Two related issues emerged: first, the autonomy of boards of study and the needs of their programs and second, the protection of EOD faculty in a reorganization.

These issues surfaced when the EOD director pointed to the recent Humanities memo as an indication of the potential problems. He stated:

> Our two proposals assumed the college wanted greater integration; however, the recent unfortunate incident with the Humanities Boards of Study made us feel that some members of the college do not want integration. They either want to leave things alone, which would have been fine with us two or three years ago, but the external pressure did not allow it, or they want our lines, but not our faculty.

The Humanities representative replied that indeed the incident was unfortunate and handled poorly from all sides. However, the primary issue had been their divisional autonomy and the proposed mergers would create similar problems. Addressing the issue of particular boards of study accepting former EOD discipline faculty, she pointed out the following sensitive issues:

1.   Some EOD faculty members did not have what her division considered adequate credentials. While the number was small, the idea that the college administration could dictate to a division that it must accept faculty from disbanded programs could prove highly problematic.

2.   Although many EOD faculty were eminently qualified, they often did not meet the needs of a board of study in strengthening its major. For example, the last thing the History board needed was another American Historian; the last thing the Literature board needed was another American literature faculty member; both programs needed European specialists or other areas, and this merger would not eliminate duplication. Moreover, if the Freshman Studies faculty were included, it would mean three more American historians to be integrated into a board already oversaturated with American historians.

Her two points defined a major conflict in undergraduate education and one that would certainly become a controversial issue in any on-going discussions. The tension between upper divisional curriculum organized around viable majors and a structured lower divisional program was emerging as an essential roadblock to merger. Although the EOD faculty and director did not see this as a major problem, to the other boards of study it certainly posed a serious dilemma. For example, one EOD faculty member observed:

> While I understand the problem of curricular needs, and certainly this could only be solved by letting EOD faculty go and replace them with specialists in your area of need; the strengthening of majors could be accomplished without this. For example, by EOD and Freshman Studies faculty teaching lower divisional courses, and to a large degree introductory sections (which most State faculty do not want to teach), your faculty would be free to teach more upper divisional electives and thus strengthen the major.

To this, the Associate Dean for Lower Division added:

> This is so characteristic of State College. We lose over 40% of our Freshmen by the junior year, before they even select a major, in part because we have no structured lower divisional curriculum. At least this proposal speaks to strengthening these offerings and now you want to place emphasis on the upper divisional curriculum. While I agree you have needs, we have to start at the first two years.

The Humanities representative replied:

> We also lose students because we cannot offer substantial offerings in major areas. Many students transfer to colleges with greater variety and diversity in their offerings. This is a very serious problem.

At this point, both the Dean and the Social Sciences chairperson indicated that the first priority in all subsequent divisions should be "that every State College faculty member be retained within budgetary realities and replacing EOD faculty with specialists should not be an issue." The entire committee agreed unanimously to this, with the Humanities representative indicating that her objections were theoretical and in no way suggested any desire to retrench the EOD faculty. Nonetheless, she hoped that she made her point concerning the need to insure viable upper divisional offerings.

This discussion directly led to the issue of protection. An EOD faculty member raised the issue:

> Before any merger would be approved by our faculty some assurances are necessary. Technically, in order to reorganize the EOD, you would first have to eliminate the Division. In theory, before any reassignment would occur, the program would no longer exist. Under the state guidelines, the college could then retrench the entire faculty, break tenure and contracts and reorganize lines minus the faculty now holding them. While your plan precludes this, and the spirit of this meeting substantiates this, nonetheless we would want certain assurances that we would be protected.

The Dean responded by saying this would not happen (retrenchment), but nonetheless he would seek necessary protection.

The problem of protection did not suggest EOD paranoia, but did indicate the faculty's perception of extreme vulnerability. The previous discussion of majors versus lower division and the low enrollments in many tenured EOD faculty courses did nothing to eliminate these fears. The same faculty member, continuing in the same line of questioning, posed the following hypothetical situation to the chairperson of the Social Sciences:

> Nothing will stop a division from taking junior EOD faculty for the remainder of their contract, then because their area of specialization is not suitable, terminate them at the end of the contract, and then search the position.

The chairperson acknowledged the tenuous position of junior faculty and indicated that although divisional needs would be a long term priority, she would hope the commitment to former EOD faculty would be taken very seriously.

Toward the end of the meeting, the Dean attempted to envision the actual direction the merger might take. He indicated that except in a few areas, he believed all EOD faculty would "find homes." The skills faculty would remain in the new EOP program and, in addition, teach writing and mathematics courses in boards of study. The social science and natural science faculty seemed to be acceptable to their respective boards; however, some problems remained in the Humanities, especially in the Foreign Languages, where a pedagogical conflict existed between the EOD and the Language Board of Study. The latter used the "silent method," the former did not, and bridging the gap would be difficult. Although all argued that the politics of integration would be difficult, most believed it could work.

At the very end of the meeting, however, the actual difficulties facing the division became very clear. The chair of Natural Sciences, commenting on the lower divisional-majors controversy and the protection of EOD faculty, stated:

> We will gladly take your Biologist and Chemist. Both can support our programs. However, we will not promise to offer developmental courses at the expense of other courses.

This led to a heated discussion of the needs of EOD and other underprepared students. In response to the EOD's director's claims that EOD type science courses were fundamental to the success of disadvantaged students and that the Natural Science chair's comments supported all of his worst fears, the Natural Science chairperson replied:

> In times of budgetary abundance one can support these types of programs. However, given present fiscal realities they are luxuries we can no longer offer. I am publicly on record that both the EOD and Freshman Studies be eliminated.

Casting a sobering view on the meeting, his comments pointed out the serious negotiations ahead. Although the Dean promised to begin work immediately on a substantive proposal, the EOD representatives left with more questions than answers. One thing was certain: the elimination or, at least, major alteration of the program was beginning.

Looking Backward and Planning for the Future: The Reconstruction of the Past and the Reality of Elimination

At the first EOD faculty meeting following the special Dean's meeting, the EOD representatives to that gathering informed the entire faculty of the events. Although the Dean introduced a number of ideas for integration, he stopped short of making actual proposals, and although he indicated that a formal recommendation would be developed, it was not clear when this would happen. By this time, the EOD faculty seemed drained by the continuous uncertainty and crisis setting. A small minority wanted to defend the division, others seemed resigned to its imminent demise, and yet others wanted to wait for a concrete proposal and then react. Despite the fact that those who attended the Dean's meeting insisted that the decision to disband the division had already been made, the majority of the faculty did not seem ready to accept this fate. There was some discussion about job protection and the division's union representative agreed to get definitive answers about retrenchment and breaking tenure in the event of the division's alteration. Overall, the faculty appeared resigned to a major change in the division's status, and although most did not particularly support the moves, they seemed ready to capitulate.[9]

During the final month of the Fall semester, the EOD continued to operate within two distinct contexts. On the one hand, the faculty proceeded as if nothing would happen and the division would be maintained. On the other hand, the Curriculum Committee, in consultation with the Dean, planned an integrative two-year curriculum, which to a large degree would pave the road for integration or merger.

The reintroduction of these issues, at a time when many felt the division would not survive was rather ironic, and pointed out the continuing ambivalence most of the faculty felt over the possible integration. While some faculty satirically commented on these events as rather ludicrous given future plans, the fact that the majority of the division, despite its disheartened state, continued to proceed in a status quo manner suggests a number of possible interpretations:

1. The faculty did not want to face reality; hence they regressed into a period when divisional autonomy was more solid and issues of EOD student performance dominated divisional concerns.

2. The faculty changed its mind on integration, and attempted to solidify the division even at this late date. Although there is some evidence to support this view, overall the faculty still seemed resigned to some form of integration; however, it appears they attempted to point out, especially with a new limited cross registration policy, the problems an integrative program would face.

3. The faculty was aware of the severity of its situation, but decided that as long as the division remained, the faculty would concern itself with its responsibilities. In this respect, the division attempted to avoid a "syndrome of decline" where members, realizing their positions are being eliminated, or in this case, that the division would no longer exist, begin to go through the motions. It would be incorrect to suggest that no evidence of this process existed, as it

certainly did (many faculty stated how difficult it was to work and be motivated under these conditions), but the discussion of issues central only to a separate division suggested an attempt to avoid the deleterious effects of this particular collective psychology.

Whatever the main reason for these events, and all three have some validity, the division began to act as if it would continue to maintain its separate identity. In a cyclical pattern, old issues re-emerged and the division acted to strengthen its divisional boundaries. In fact, as a final reaction to its decline, the EOD appeared to be undoing what two years of semi-integration had accomplished.

While the division engaged in the "politics of reaction," the movement toward total integration continued. In his statement to the Dean concerning "catastrophe planning" for the following year, the director, like his predecessor, chastised the administration for its continual uncertainty concerning the division's future. Arguing that the EOD could not continue to move schizophrenically in two separate directions, he demanded an end to continual piecemeal cuts and either a firm commitment to a separate division or a structured plan for merger. To support his argument, the director invoked "the special mission" of the program and the extraordinary efforts necessary to fulfill this. The statement of differences, always used to defend the division's existence, now (as by the past director) was used to demand the treatment vital to its existence or a change in organization. He concluded his remarks by stating:

> To summarize, the EOD program cannot function in its present divisional structure with any more staff cuts. Further faculty cuts will make the present structure unable to deliver to EOP students the extra support mandated to help them succeed at State College. It is necessary for the college to take a long hard look at how it wants to fulfill its commitment to disadvantaged students. Whittling away the resources of the present division is not serving anybody well. It is shortchanging students and creating an atmosphere that is detrimental to their entire campus (1982f:5).

As in the last budget statement, the director challenged the administration to take a firm stand. While the new director seemed to support a retention of the separate divisional structure, he was pragmatic enough to realize that poor enrollments would mitigate against this. Although he publicly hoped the division could attract new students and retain more than were presently enrolled, he privately expressed some doubts. His challenge to the administration then, should not be viewed as an abandonment of the division, but rather like his predecessor, as the realistic understanding that the division could not continue to operate.

The director's statement indicated the futility of operating the EOD as he had been required to over the year. In addition to continual assault on a budgetary level, the administration's failure to either support or merge the program resulted in a disheartening uncertainty, according to most faculty. Moreover, the development of a "policy schizophrenia," with the division moving simultaneously in two different directions was evidenced during this period. While the faculty recreated divisional autonomy through policies intended to restructure the program's walls, the Curriculum Committee worked with the Dean and the EOD director to develop an integrative curriculum. The college administration requested a proposed two-year curriculum, and for the EOD this posed a difficult problem. As the Curriculum chairperson stated in a meeting with the Dean:

> How can we draw up a two-year plan if we don't know what we're planning. Either we plan for a separate division, or we plan for integration. Our committee will not proceed as if the division will exist, if it is not going to.

The Dean responded that he was in the process of writing an integrative proposal, and therefore the Curriculum Committee should develop an integrative curriculum by avoiding all duplication. The negotiations that began earlier in the Fall on cross listing EOD courses into boards of study would continue, so that when the integrative proposal appeared, the wheels would already be in motion.

The EOD Curriculum Committee began to develop the integrative curriculum. Once again, the tensions between educational philosophy (class size, writing intensive courses, three-day schedule) and survival defined the proceedings. However, where past deliberations focused on organizational survival, these discussions emphasized individual or departmental survival. With some type of merger of the division a certainty, the committee attempted to create a plan that would simultaneously protect all EOD faculty members, and the interests of EOD students.

The Curriculum Committee began negotiations with the various boards of study in order to develop an integrative curriculum. The goal of the curriculum was to avoid all duplication by placing EOD discipline faculty into appropriate boards. Within the EOD a number of conservative faculty still opposed active planning and believed the division should be strengthened internally and that "integrating in" was a better solution. Other faculty members, although supporting the concept of integration, insisted

that the integrity and intent of the EOD skills-content synthesis be pre-
served.

Overall, the negotiations faced a number of internal and external
problems:

1.   Board of study autonomy: on two levels, the personal and program-
      matic, the sensitive question of divisional and departmental control
      would have to be gently handled. Although some members of the
      college, as stated in the Dean's EOD meeting, supported the protec-
      tion of jobs concept, others did not necessarily share this view. To
      some, individual EOD faculty may not have fit into their programs
      (for personal or programmatic reasons), and the division should not
      have been compelled to take these faculty.

2.   College-wide budget concerns and faculty uncertainty: The possible
      movement of senior (tenured) EOD faculty to other programs
      created tensions for junior faculty in these boards. For example, the
      transition of the tenured EOD political scientist posed an under-
      standable threat to the politics board of study's junior political
      scientists. One, at this time up for tenure, (and with similar areas
      of specialization) envisioned a draconian scenario. Although he did
      not oppose her integration, he demanded that the EOD faculty
      member not teach in his general specialty, but only in her particular
      area of expertise not overlapping with his. As he stated:

      The idea of integration is fine if it's mutually beneficial and
      this means we have to have our needs taken care of. She
      should teach courses in Soviet and East European politics,
      which we cannot offer, but I retain introduction to compar-
      ative politics and all other comparative courses.

Continuing by shifting from programmatic needs to personal threat he
added:

      I can see the administration arguing at my tenure decision
      that we have the EOD political scientist to teach compara-
      tive politics, so why give me tenure.

This junior faculty's reaction underscored the situation of junior faculty
nationwide, with increasing administrative decisions against tenure and
toward a rotating junior faculty, or perhaps an adjunct faculty.[10] Moreover, the politics department had recently absorbed the senior member of the

Urban Studies Department because of its closing, and felt somewhat infringed upon. Nonetheless, they seemed amenable to integration.

3.   Contrasting views of EOD courses: the major roadblock revolved around what EOD faculty considered the misunderstanding of EOD discipline courses. Although the EOD maintained the skills-content synthesis in a three day schedule allowed for a substantive college course, many faculty either did not understand the EOD's philosophy (in the same way it was intended by the EOD) or rejected it. According to them, courses were either skills or regular college courses, and they considered EOD discipline courses the former and therefore rejected them as inappropriate to their curriculum.

4.   Integration in versus integration by merger: Although the entire EOD faculty understood that some form of integration would occur, most opposed a merger and instead favored the retention of the division in some form. Some wanted to retain all courses as EOD courses and allow non-EOD students to register in, thus maintaining divisional separation but increasing enrollment. A larger number supported the retention of the division in a lower division (as in the Lower Divisional proposal) with EOD faculty jointly appointed to boards of study (with 100 level courses taught out of the lower division and 200 level courses out of the boards of study). While few supported a third possibility, some believed the Dean would propose complete merger, with only a small remedial EOP program and complete integration of all other EOD discipline faculty into boards of study. Although the Curricular chair suggested that the complete merger was a strong possibility and that it represented the Dean's apparent direction, most EOD faculty did not seem to agree with this assessment or perhaps did not want to think about it.

By the final week of the fall semester, the Curriculum Committee worked out agreements with all boards of study except the Humanities (meetings were scheduled for the spring) and a tentative two-year curriculum was sent to the Dean. The proposal retained EOD skills courses in reading, writing, and mathematics but opened them to the entire college population. It also integrated EOD discipline faculty into appropriate boards of study where their courses would open to the entire campus. Moreover, the document specified that a significant number of these courses be labeled "writing intensive," with class size limited to 25.

In the final week of the semester, the Curriculum chairperson submitted a tentative two-year plan to the committee and the director.

Because all negotiations had not been completed, the proposal remained somewhat incomplete. Nonetheless, the committee forwarded it to the director, and he sent it to the Dean. The document represented the EOD's integrative proposal, and technically it could be implemented by either retaining the division (joint appointments) or merging it.[11]

Immediately following this, the Dean of Letters and Science called a meeting to address the future of the EOD. He announced that he was in the process of completing an integrative proposal for the EOD for inclusion in his 1983–1984 budget recommendations, and he stated that the basics of the recommendations should be revealed immediately. The Dean's proposal was consistent with his earlier statements at the special Dean's Meeting on EOD, and would do the following by the Fall of 1983:

1.   Eliminate the EOD as a separate division.

2.   Replace it with a smaller integrative EOP program, staffed by the director and counseling office and funded by State EOP funds.

3.   Expand the present Lower Division to include Freshman Studies, a writing program, a newly created Learning Center, and some former EOD members.

4.   Appoint most EOD discipline faculty directly to their appropriate boards of study if agreements could be reached (where they could not be, the faculty would be attached to the Lower Division and have joint Lower Divisional responsibility). Likewise, all Freshman Studies faculty would be jointly appointed to their board of study and, in addition to their lower divisional responsibilities, teach occasional upper divisional electives in their specialty.

5.   In accordance with the EOD Lower Divisional Proposal former EOD discipline faculty would primarily teach introductory and writing intensive courses, and EOP students would be encouraged to enroll in these during their freshman and sophomore year.

6.   Former EOD faculty (now Lower Divisional faculty) would be responsible for EOP student advisement.

7.   The Lower Division and the new EOP program would meet regularly to discuss the needs of all lower divisional students and to place special emphasis on the needs of EOP students.

Arguing that his plan retained the EOD's special commitment to disadvantaged students and at the same time ended the indefensible isolation of minority students in a separate division, the Dean asked for support. Although his presentation did not address some of the difficult problems of implementation, he promised to have a written document before the entire EOD faculty by the beginning of the Spring semester.

Two major oppositional processes emerged at an emergency meeting of the EOD to discuss the Dean's proposal. First, the "politics of nostalgia" and second, "the politics of defense." In regard to the first, some faculty began to invoke the history of the program to incite a newly charged spirit. For example, one member stated:

> We have faced crises before and are still in existence. Remember at Coop... when we needed more students to survive, and we all went out and recruited.

Statements like this incited a string of sentimental and nostalgic remembrances all functioning to recreate a divisional solidarity.

In respect to the second process, some faculty suggested the division be retained and the college lower its regular admissions standards, thus increasing EOD's available pool both from the inside (EOP students) and the outside (Freshman Studies). One faculty member stated:

> I just don't think we should give up without a fight. This division is the best on campus. We have been leaders in moving the college toward a more accessible curriculum. We took the lead on the grading issue, on the calendar. We have something vital to offer and we must convince the college of this.

While both the politics of nostalgia and defense created some movement against the merger, the majority of the faculty either felt resigned or supported the Dean's proposal. The director stated that any plan had to first be approved by the State Office of Special Programs, and he would immediately consult with the Division's former director (now the director of the office) for his reactions. Finally, the faculty asked its presiding officer to call another meeting with the Dean on the last day before the winter recess.

The EOD faculty and staff met with the Dean to discuss his proposal. The Dean presented his seven-point plan (as he had at the English department meeting), and asked for the division's reaction. Surprisingly, there was very little opposition; only one senior EOD faculty member, who always defended the separate divisional structure, voiced his strategies for defense and, in closing, he asked for an open meeting in the Spring to debate the issues. The Dean assured him that such public debate would occur.

The rest of the division seemed anesthetized. Either because it was the last day of class, or because they accepted the finality of its demise, the divisional members seemed resigned to a merger. For some, the ending of years of uncertainty presented a small comfort. Most members agreed to await a formal proposal and then begin discussions toward a smooth transition. The director concluded by insisting that EOD student needs be protected under any future proposals and the Dean agreed.

Policy Schizophrenia: Re-establishing Divisional Regulations in a Time of Final Decline

The beginning of the Spring semester was defined by the continuation of the EOD's policy schizophrenia. Despite the Dean's public acknowledgement of the division's merger, the faculty did not seem ready for a transition. Rather, as in the Fall, the early faculty meetings were dominated by business that only had meaning if the separate division would continue to exist. The faculty voted to approve new CAP guidelines for retention and dismissal and to adopt a new restrictive attendance policy. While both issues recreated a number of old debates and their outcomes strengthened the divisional structure by defining specific rules for its students, as one faculty member noted, it was "like rearranging the deck chairs on the Titanic."

After considerable debate in which many of the past controversies over the psychology of student adjustment, the effectiveness of punitive measures, and the treatment of symptoms versus causes, the EOD faculty voted to adopt the CAP guidelines on retention and dismissal and to reinstitute the compulsory attendance policy. It was quite interesting that a division almost certain that it would be merged out of its present form would continue to operate as if no such plans existed. As proposed above, a number of factors seem to explain this process including the following:

1.   Using Kübler-Ross'(1979) analysis of responses to death as an analogy,[12] many were in a stage of denial and did not yet accept the realities of the division's transformation.

2.   Others awaited an official proposal before deciding on the proper strategy, and until then they would proceed as usual.

3.   Many wanted to avoid the "psychology of decline" and as long as the division existed, they planned to work for its needs and fulfill their responsibilities.

The Annual Budget Crisis

The concern with divisional issues did not last long, as the budget crisis of Spring 1983 took center stage. As in the previous four years, the governor's budget mandated reductions in the state university system, and this time State College would be seriously threatened. If the proposed budget was not altered, State College would lose 18 faculty lines and 72 staff and non-teaching professional lines. For two weeks the entire college mobilized around a concern over how the administration would solve the crisis, as the State University central office requested a contingency plan in the event no budgetary relief emerged in the legislative process. The State College President prepared a "hit list" of potentially terminated positions, but for one week no one knew if the basis for his decisions was seniority or programmatic.

In mid-February, the President released his decisions to the deans and directors of programs so they could inform their affected constituencies. The President recommended (as the major part of the academic proposal) that if no budget relief developed, the complete elimination of the Freshman Studies Program (and the retrenchment of their entire faculty, all junior and without tenure) and the complete retrenchment of the junior faculty of the EOD (including six full time and two part time junior faculty members). While the eight tenured members of the division would be retained, for all intents and purposes this meant the total elimination of EOD, as no program could be mounted. The tenured faculty would apparently be merged into the boards of study.

Essentially, the President had responded to the challenges of both EOD budget statements in the last two years suggesting he either stop cutting piecemeal or take more drastic action. Neither the director nor his predecessor expected he would take the challenge, and certainly all indications from the Dean suggested the merger plan would not eliminate most of the EOD faculty. While the President felt compelled by budgetary constraints to act in what he would term, "the best interests of the entire college," the EOD faculty and students did not share his views but rather saw his actions as an assault on them. Moreover, the inclusion of Freshman Studies in the retrenchment only supported what some EOD faculty viewed as the return to elitism at State College. The two programs concerned with lower divisional students and with skills and writing problems had been attacked, while the President left all other "degree granting" (defined upper division) programs untouched. The entire integrative plan would now be impossible, as the entire Lower Division would be eliminated.

On a political note, one EOD faculty member suggested the effectiveness of the President's action:

> In singling out the two divisions on campus that have always received only marginal support from the entire faculty, or in fact have been the subject of significant faculty opposition,[13] the President minimized the public outcry. For most State College faculty it will be back to business as usual, as the majority are in no way directly affected.

In the week following the President's announcement, the State College community reacted to the decisions. EOD students were outraged by what they perceived as the systematic assault on their program. Most EOD faculty bemoaned the elimination of their junior colleague's positions and understood that for all intents and purposes the division would no longer exist in its separate form. However, the reaction of the State College faculty was mixed, with some criticizing the abolition of the two lower divisional programs, other accepting the decisions as unfortunate responses to the budget crisis, and still others praising the decision as the most reasonable course of action available to the President. Overall, except for the angry responses of EOD students and faculty, the State College community did not seem overly concerned with the demise of EOD and Freshman Studies; in fact, after the announcements a collective sigh of relief seemed to engulf the campus.

The reaction of those outside EOD suggested a number of important points about its place on the State College campus. As one Social Sciences professor (non-EOD) suggested:

> For many faculty here, this decision is not a problem at all, in fact, many think it is about time. There is a great deal of insidious racism on this campus, most of it beneath the surface, but nonetheless it exists. The college liked and supported the program when it was off-campus; a symbol of the college's benign commitment to minorities, but not close enough to offend or disrupt people's sensibilities. The trouble began when the program moved on campus; I think many faculty and students were threatened by all those black faces and never really supported the concept. Now, as good "liberals" they could not come out and say it, so

often it became disguised in pseudo-academic justifications, like the defense of standards and from students as the critique of EOD students' work habits or motivation, but at the root was the feeling that the program and its students did not belong here.

One senior EOD faculty member added:

> It's funny, but as the support for the program grew in some quarters, the opposition began to publicly grow in others. When we were separate and off-campus, we were tolerated. When we moved to the campus and were separate, seen but not heard, we were also tolerated, but never really accepted. However, as we began to integrate into the college's mainstream the public opposition mounted. You know, the President's decision is supported by many faculty; the Budget Committee almost recommended our elimination, as well as the elimination of Freshman Studies, but we managed to stop it. I hear one of the Deans is applauding the decision.

If the State College faculty's response was less than completely supportive, the non-EOD students reacted in a similar manner. EOD students had always insisted that racism was a major problem at State College, and that non-EOD students had always seemed to resent their presence on campus. EOD students often complained about being labeled and stigmatized, with the concept of a "free ride" a central point of controversy. It seemed that many State College students, reacting from their own "meritocratic" ideologies, resented the financial assistance given to EOD students. In fact, as one EOD student stated:

> They (non-EOD students) never really talk about the educational mission, rather they always talk about this division in terms of financial assistance. They don't even understand that many non-EOP students in EOD don't get checks; they treat us as if we were welfare cheats.

Likewise, an EOD faculty member supported these contentions:

> After the decisions were announced I began to talk to students, both EOD and non-EOD. If anything defined the reactions of many non-EOD students it was either a

misunderstanding or complete ignorance of the division. Although it does not surprise me, it is ironic that after five years here, many students have not heard of EOD. One student typified the non-EOD student response when she stated, 'I really can't get upset about it [the elimination of EOD]. I was here when the program moved up. Never has the campus been so dirty, so noisy... graffiti all over the dorms. I can't believe it, this is a campus, not Brooklyn. Most of them don't study, party all the time, spend their book money on clothing... and I can't afford to take a full load, I have to work 30 hours per week, it just doesn't seem fair. Now don't get me wrong, two of my ex-roommates were EOD students, they worked real hard and did real well, but I'm afraid they are the exceptions. The program had good intentions but was abused; it should only be for the truly motivated.'

Although this student's remarks did not appear to represent a majority of non-EOD students, from discussions with many students it is fair to say they symbolized a sizeable minority. The perception of EOD students as "privileged abusers" of public educational assistance and the claims that non-minority students were getting the short end was indeed a common, if not public, sentiment. The extent to which these private feelings represented overall public hostility had never been clear to EOD faculty and administration, but it certainly represented a concern for the division.

Despite the anti-EOD sentiments on the part of some students, a good deal of support from non-EOD students emerged during the crisis. At the emergency EOD Town Meeting called four days after the President's announcements, a sizeable number of non-EOD students attended to show support and solidarity. At this meeting, EOD students and faculty revealed their outrage.

The meeting began with the EOD director stating the extent of the budget cuts and announcing that the Division would continue to serve its population, but in all honesty he could not promise how it would do this. Moreover, he realistically stated that the Division would have to be merged into a regular EOP program, as the cuts threatened the existence of a separate EOD. He stated, "With eight faculty left, we cannot run the same program."

Throughout the entire meeting, students expressed outrage at the assault on their program. Many did not understand why it was singled out, and some expressed the feeling that institutional racism was at the core of the actions. The students felt betrayed, angry and wanted some advice on possible actions they might initiate to change the outcomes.

The racial angle, certainly a visible and useful tool in the defense of the division, received mixed reactions from the faculty. One retrenched faculty member (the only black faculty member left at State College) asked:

> I hope you realize that this decision means that there will
> be no black faculty at State College next year. I thought, as
> a public institution, the college had to have an affirmative
> action plan.

Although to some her remarks seemed a little self-serving, they did symbolize the significance of racism as the larger issue of the EOD. Despite the many problems that EOD students had with the division over the years, despite their own charges of racism aimed at its separateness and isolation, the EOD represented the institutional "home" for minority students, a place, in the words of an EOD counselor, "where you have a family, where you can feel safe." For many students, the assault on EOD was a direct assault on them as minorities, and it indeed became a racial issue.

For some EOD faculty, the issue of racism was less clear. Although they realized the decisions reflected the existence of latent institutional racism, they also understood the broader educational meanings of the actions. The complete elimination of the Freshman Studies program meant that a more multidimensional explanation of the decisions was needed. One faculty member stated:

> I understand your anger about the EOD and I also see
> racial implicatiojs. Let's understand the educational mean-
> ings. The decision to eliminate EOD and Freshman Studies
> represents a return to the State College that existed upon
> our arrival: a return to elitism. By removing the entire
> lower division, and leaving the other programs basically
> untouched, the college has ignored the needs of large
> numbers of incoming students, in terms of writing and
> skills problems. Some administrators will argue that the
> merger of the division had already been planned and this
> just continued the trend; this will be a complete distortion.
> Having worked intimately on the proposed integration of
> EOD, it was premised on three important contingencies that
> no longer exist. First, the integration of its entire discipline
> faculty into boards of study where they would continue to
> teach EOD students in small, writing intensive courses.
> Second, their continuation as faculty advisors to EOD

students and third, the retention of the Freshman Studies program where EOD students, at some point in their freshman or sophomore years, would be enrolled. Furthermore, none of the plans vital to integration, such as the Writing Program or the Learning Center seem possible given these cuts. Let's face it, the college has decided that the needs of its incoming students do not really matter. They have returned to a view of the typical State College students as those who decide not to go to Yale; it was not so in 1978, and it certainly is not true in 1983.

After a number of faculty and staff joined in the condemnation of State College's failure to consider the needs of EOD and all freshman students, a senior member of the EOD faculty, in an emotional and well reasoned statement, summarized this particular point:

> State College is a body with no legs. It has no lower division, except EOD and these actions all but eliminate it as a Division; the College of Letters and Science has three other divisions, none of which have lower divisional programs. Students begin at the junior year, but receive little if any preparation. I want to ask the college, now, with the destruction of EOD and Freshman Studies, the only two programs at least attempting to meet students where they enter, not where we want them to be, who is going to fill the void?

Upon completing her passionate response to the administration, the entire audience gave her a loud ovation, and most students declared the desire to "turn things around."

The discussion of the dismantling of the lower division led to focusing on the needs of EOD students and how they would be met under a restructured program. One counselor rhetorically pondered:

> Let's imagine the cuts stand. How are you (the EOD students) going to handle regular division courses; how are you going to survive in large lecture classes; how are you going to get quality advising? From what you have told me, the regular faculty, for the most part, is inaccessible, not sensitive to your needs... I am afraid that many of you will not survive.

Then, in what many EOD faculty felt was out of place and a classic case of "blaming the victim," the counselor added:

> You need to ask yourself what you can do to survive. Some of you, even with the best teachers and advising, by some of the teachers you now are so upset about, did not care enough to take your work seriously, to attend classes, to fulfill your contract to the division. Now it may be too late.

The counselor appeared to be both chastising EOD students for not appreciating what they had until it was threatened and, more importantly, seemed to imply that if they had done their job (received high grades, etc.), the administration could not have attacked the EOD. Although many faculty saw some degree of truth in his words, most felt it missed the point; that the attack of the EOD was more complex and moreover, to blame the students missed the essential mission of the program. That is, high risk students will not perform, at least early in their careers, as well as regularly admitted students. If they could, the EOD and other compensatory higher education programs would not be necessary.

The meeting ended with students planning their next moves in hopes of saving the division. Although many faculty were pleased to see their response as an indication that for most EOD students the division did indeed matter, the majority were not hopeful. While many hoped the jobs of the junior faculty in EOD and Freshman Studies would be restored, most felt that even if this occurred, it would not be in the EOD. The prevailing attitude was that the administration had always intended to eliminate the EOD, either through gradual integration and eventual demise, or given extreme budgetary contingencies, through immediate retrenchment. As one senior faculty stated:

> The President told me last year that we would not exist as a separate division for more than a year. I guess he really meant it.

A Social Sciences faculty member also remarked:

> Quite frankly, I am little surprised he did not close the entire division and retrench its tenured faculty. I thought he might have really contemplated this. However, I guess he believed that breaking tenure would have hit too close to home for the majority of State College faculty, and to do

this might have caused too much support for EOD.

Thus, the majority of the EOD faculty and staff perceived these decisions as marking the division's final demise. While the senior faculty spoke of carrying on, they privately revealed their own despair. State College would have an EOP program for next year, but it would not be the EOD; it would be like all other state EOP programs, without its own instructional faculty. Moreover, given the budgetary constraints most feared, the new program would be very small and woefully inadequate.

The Spring 1983 semester would come to represent the end of an experiment begun fourteen years before in a small converted church building at Coop College. After fourteen years of battles, crises, experiments, successes and failures, the concept of a separate compensatory higher education program at State College appeared to be over. As one EOD faculty member aptly stated:

> Let's not allow the excuse of budgetary crises and fiscal
> exigencies to confuse the issues. The administration can
> defend its action as its only available course, it can also say
> the overall needs of State College were defended; or that
> what they term, "unproductive and duplicative" programs
> eliminated. The fact is, the decision to eliminate the
> program, one way or another, either gradually or all at
> once, had been made early in the President's first year
> [1981]. The ignoring of EOD guidelines, the refusal to
> honor EOD review committee recommendations, the
> granting of one-year contracts to junior faculty and above
> all the complete lack of recruiting support contradict any
> other conclusion than that the division was systematically
> allowed to die.

The Final Demise: Budget Solution and Merger

In the weeks immediately following the President's budget announcement, the future of the EOD began to take shape. Although the state university central administration developed a plan to save faculty positions leading to the reinstatement of the Freshman Studies Program and four EOD faculty positions, the proposed merger of EOD still occurred. For those who incorrectly believed that the budget crisis was the major factor, the administrative and faculty decisions during this period certainly proved otherwise. This should not have come as a surprise and to most EOD faculty and staff it did not. The plan to merge the EOD had been discussed throughout the year and when the crisis hit, the Dean's proposal had been delayed. While many used the budget decisions to make politically charged statements about the death of EOD, its demise had been charted over a three-year period. Although it was true that a majority of the EOD members would have favored the retention of the division with sincere administrative support, the fact that such support had systematically eroded led the EOD to actively pursue a merger. The important question at this point concerned the direction the merger would take and the degree to which the needs of underprepared students would be met.

At a meeting with the EOD faculty, the Dean of Letters and Science informed the division that as of Fall 1983 it would be merged into a unified lower division. He stated that due to continued difficulties with the Humanities Boards of Study, the concept of placing all EOD faculty into their appropriate departments would be difficult. Under the merger plan, some EOD faculty would go directly into their boards, others would be appointed to the Lower Division and teach remedial and/or writing courses.

At this point, the divisional faculty did not seriously object to the plan nor, with one exception, attempt to defend the separate division. In legitimating his decision, the Dean focused on two related issues. First, he stated the college would no longer support the separate placement of disadvantaged students, citing the stigmatizing effects of such isolation. Second, he argued that the college wanted to move toward further integration (for example, some integration of the Arts and Letters and Sciences programs were in the works), and the unification of the Lower Division would be the first step. Stressing that his proposal was based upon the EOD's own "Lower Divisional" proposal, the EOD could not effectively challenge his position. However, many were skeptical about the degree to which he understood or would actually follow these recommendations.

Finally, the EOD director posed the most important question concerning the needs of present and future EOP students. He asked what would the college do about the non-EOP students that EOD admitted every year as educationally, but not economically, disadvantaged. This was an important point, because the separate EOD program had allowed the college to admit approximately thirty underprepared students each year, who under a regular EOP program could not be admitted (as they did not meet economic criteria), but nonetheless demonstrated the potential to complete college. Without the EOD, the director wondered if the college would return to its regular admissions standards for all non-EOP students, thus further limiting access.

The director's remarks on admissions went directly to the heart of the egalitarian educational philosophy of EOD. He implied that the merger would not only eliminate access to underprepared non-EOP students, but the decision as well, to eliminate the EOP registrar would continue to diminish the minority and disadvantaged population at State College. Although the Dean reasserted his commitment to the EOP population, he stated that the admission of underprepared non-EOP students would be a college admissions question. [14]

At this point, the director charged the college with an ambiguous direction for disadvantaged students and stated that the college needed to develop an acceptable alternative EOP program for the Fall. Otherwise, all state EOP funds would be withheld from State College if the campus did not meet its legal obligations, and no freshman EOP class would be admitted until a plan had been submitted and accepted.

This meeting ended with some confusion and apprehension. While the Dean continued to pledge his commitment to both EOD faculty and to disadvantaged students, the unanimous feeling was that the college's overall needs would take precedence. The events of the following week did nothing to remove this perception.

Since the Fall curriculum schedule was needed within two weeks for Spring preregistration, the college moved quickly to implement the merger. A joint faculty EPC-Curriculum Committee unanimously approved the integration of the Freshman Studies Program and the Educational Opportunity Division into a unified Lower Division of the College of Letters and Science and, in spirit, approved faculty appointments (or joint appointments) to their appropriate boards of study. The Dean, without the consultation with the EOD faculty, made the decision to place all EOD Natural Science faculty into the Natural Science boards of study; retain all EOD writing teachers for composition courses and tutorial work in the newly proposed Learning Center; place the EOD Social Sciences faculty joined in boards of study and in writing and/or Freshman Studies assignments; and assign the EOD language instructor (with a Ph.D in philosophy) to Freshman Studies. Math and Science instructors explicitly were committed to teaching remedial and developmental math courses, and the writing instructors would continue to focus on verbal and written skills, but the skills-content synthesis of the EOD discipline courses was almost completely ignored. The EOD proposal to have its instructors teach small writing intensive introductory discipline courses was not included in this plan; rather, EOD discipline faculty were assigned to teach Freshman Studies or courses needed by the boards of study (sometimes at the upper divisional level). It became increasingly clear to many EOD faculty that integration and merger meant placing EOD faculty where the college perceived needs; not necessarily where the EOD felt it best served its population. A good example of this is the assignment of EOD faculty to teach Freshman Studies, a course that incoming EOP students would not take until their sophomore year. Because the college decided to integrate all arts students into this program, twice as many sections would be needed. Therefore, the college's needs appeared to determine faculty assignments.

The failure to incorporate EOD discipline type courses into the plan indicated serious differences between EOD and other segments of the college on this issue. Although the EOD faculty believed that placing incoming EOP students into large introductory sections without any direct attention to skills would be a regressive step, the Dean and other constituencies did not agree. They still believed that courses are either skills or content, but not both, and the Dean believed that through the continuation of writing and developmental mathematics courses the EOP students would be served.

It began to be clear to some EOD faculty that the needs and interests of particular boards of study were most important in understanding the negotiations. Every board began to negotiate for its needs, emphasizing their major as the essential aspect of the curriculum. Moreover, while EOD faculty were told what they would teach without any choice, other State College faculty were asked to volunteer for Freshman Studies. The EOD political scientist, when told she would teach two writing courses and one political science course each semester, angrily commented:

> I am a political scientist, who also teaches writing because our students need it and we have been understaffed. However, I resent the fact that after 14 years I am told I am an English teacher, when not one member of the Literature Board of Study is willing to teach English composition.

Her comments certainly suggested an interesting phenomenon at State College that supported EOD charges of its elitist-graduate type programs. At a time when the majority of literature Ph.D.'s were struggling for employment and were usually willingly teaching English composition to survive, the State College literature faculty saw itself as a graduate faculty and refused to teach English composition to anyone. It seemed rather a convincing indictment of the college's lack of commitment to undergraduate education (never mind, underprepared students) that its largest board of study was Literature, and yet it could not mount a much needed writing program. The concern that EOD faculty voiced for years about State College faculty refusing to acknowledge or meet the needs of underprepared students was a credible one, and the division's concern for its students after the merger a reasonable one.

Despite the glaring problems with the merger, it did appear that the college administration and faculty were concerned with developing a more structured experience for all its students, especially at the lower division. The EPC began to discuss a core curriculum, and the development of a unified lower division was presented as a step toward curricular rationality. The coming years would prove significant both for State College and its EOP students and one could only hope the merger would not be an excuse to return the college to its elitist roots, although there is some evidence to suggest that this has happened.

One thing was clear at this point: the existence of the EOD as a unique and separate educational opportunity program had ended. The State College President in an interview with the student newspaper commented on the events leading to the decision:

> For a moment, let's forget this budget crisis, and let's look at it as it would have normally, peacefully evolved. In my judgment the institution was evolving towards the integration of the lower division, or the general education component of the college, into the entire curricqlum. In time, there would have been a proposal which included what we now do in Freshman Studies and EOD with separate curricula. Now, I believe in that. And as I said in the Town Meeting, that is not any way a negative judgment about the importance of what EOD or Freshman Studies provide. They provide excellent programs, but they're expensive programs, and they are separate programs. And I don't believe in separate programs. I believe in a college curriculum, in which the teaching of freshmen and the teaching of educationally disadvantaged students is as much the responsibility of full professors, associate professors, and assistant professors, as much the responsibility of one division as another. I believe in that, I always have. There was a plan being evolved which would have integrated the whole EOD with the College of Letters and Science. That was happening, before the budget crisis.

Thus, the President suggested the two essential reasons for the merger were economic (the division was too expensive) and educational (the college would not support continued separation). However, in indicating a distaste for rigid classificatory systems, he promised to support the integration of EOD functions into the entire campus. That this would occur was unclear; perhaps, rather than a victory for loosened boundaries, the elimination of

EOD meant the strengthening of other divisional boundaries and a victory for divisions with more elite conceptions of higher education. The answer to this question would have to be found in the history of State College in the coming years.

Speaking to the confusion over the direction the college would take for disadvantaged students, the President commented on the future of the college's educational opportunity program. When asked what it would look like in the Fall 1983, he stated:

> We don't know the answer to that yet. We will in a few weeks. And that is a matter, essentially, for faculty decision, for academic decision, which I can influence with questions or suggestions, but which I neither can nor should dictate...

Finally, responding to the question of integration and the end of the EOD as a unique compensatory higher education program, he added:

> I think that integration is inevitable and desirable because it is a segregated program. And I don't believe in segregated programs.

After the Elimination: Educational Opportunity Students at State College

In the 1983–1984 academic year, State College had a new, integrative EOP program, which offered only tutorial and counseling services. EOP students now were mainstreamed into all of their courses. Although the participant observation upon which this study was based ended in 1982–1983, the year the elimination of EOD was announced, based on interviews with faculty and students in 1983–1984 and follow-up visits to State College and interviews with former EOD faculty and the director of its EOP program (still the former EOD director) in 1992 and 1993 a number of statements about the education of EOP students at State College may be made. First, in the years following the elimination of EOD, the new, integrative EOP program continued to struggle with many of the issues outlined above. Second, the number of EOP students admitted each year declined with the EOP program admitting about half of the students it admitted as a separate division. Third, former EOD faculty, although they continued to be advocates for EOP students, over the years became less connected to the EOP and far more connected to their new institutional homes. Fourth, retention and graduation data indicate some differences for EOP students under the new, integrative program.[15] That is, the fears that EOP students would fare far less well without the EOD have been partially substantiated. Fifth, that State College continued to have among the lowest retention and graduation rates for EOP students in the state suggests that EOD claims that State College had been a high risk institution for high risk students had some validity.

This study is not, however, concerned with the years after the EOD's elimination. Rather it is concerned with the rise and fall of a particular compensatory higher education program. The fourteen years of this unique compensatory higher education program were filled with all of the conflicts, problems, and complexities that define compensatory higher education. Moreover, they represented the continuous change and evolution of a program to meet internal and external pressures. Although this narrative history has provided indications and examples of these issues, nevertheless, the task of sociological analysis remains. First, the evolution of the EOD must be explored within the context of educational change; that is, how we can understand the factors resulting in its evolution and eventual demise. Second, the development of the program must be analyzed from the perspective of organizational sociology; that is, what interorganizational and intradivisional interactions defined the workings of the EOD and how did they relate to its evolution and demise?

NOTES

1. For example, the use of expertise as a claims making process. See Spector and Kitsuse (1977:142–158).

2. The college would now track all underprepared students, not just EOD students, into writing remediation courses.

3. The college had failed to appoint a new dean during the previous year's search and therefore appointed a senior Natural Sciences professor as Acting Dean for the 1982–1983 year.

4. The committee agreed to test the three-day schedule in the Spring. If it proved a deterrent to non-EOD enrollment, then it would adopt a two-day schedule for these transitional courses in the Fall. In addition, if it adopted a two-day schedule, then the committee would recommend an optional third-day discussion session for all students (but implemented to ensure meeting of EOD student needs).

5. Office of Institutional Research data could not support this position.

6. The Dean had requested a copy of this report prior to this meeting.

7. The EOD faculty did not support this proposal.

8. The distinction between EOP and non-EOP students had always posed a problem since EOP funds could only be used to serve EOP students.

9. The irony of this is the Dean's proposal was very similar to their own "Proposal for a Unified Lower Division."

10. See for example, B. Scott (1983) and Zwerman (1983) for a discussion of crises in higher education.

11. The two-year proposal was written as if the separate division would be retained.

12. The original faculty viewed the division in parental terms and took its demise very personally and with an extreme sense of loss.

13. According to one member of the Budget Committee, the co-chair of that committee proposed the elimination of both EOD and Freshman Studies for inclusion in the report to the President. Only the strenuous objections of those divisions' representatives overruled these recommendations. Likewise, the chairperson of the Natural Sciences made similar proposals at the Dean's Meeting on EOD.

14. He implied that these students would be admitted based on the college's enrollment needs.

15. State Office of Special Programs Data, 1982–1990.

7

THE RISE AND FALL OF THE EOD:
A SOCIOLOGICAL ANALYSIS

The history of the Educational Opportunity Division at State College represented the emergence, development, and decline of a liberal educational reform program. Originating as an off-campus educational opportunity program in 1969, it represented the response to demands for increased access to higher education that defined the period. After nine years at Coop College, due to fiscal crisis, budgetary constraints, declining enrollments, and affirmative action concerns at the main campus, the program moved to the main campus of State College, becoming the only separate educational opportunity program (with its own faculty and curriculum) in the state system. In 1983, after five years at State College which were defined by continual struggles over its separate model of compensatory higher education, the college administration, in part, as a response to severe budgetary constraints, recommended the integration of EOD into the overall college program. Although the college maintained a smaller educational opportunity (with counseling and tutorial services), the elimination of the EOD symbolized the demise of a unique type of liberal educational reform.

The history of both the EOD program and of State College provide interesting evidence on the decline of educational reform, but not its death. State College originated in the educational upheavals of the 1960s and symbolized some of its "radical impulses" (Grant and Riesman, 1978:179--354). Combining the elitism of selective private colleges with "radical educational innovations," such as individualized programs, tutorial systems, an unstructured curriculum, a pass-no credit grading system, and a unique academic calendar (with two short terms for special courses), the college entered the 1970s with the public image of an alternative institution. Although State College reflected a particular type of educational reform somewhat symbolic of the "free school movement" at a college level and in many ways characteristic of the high schools Swidler describes in *Organization Without Authority* (1979), it certainly did not emerge from what Grant and Riesman label "meritocratic discontent" (1978:197–217): that is, as an explicit critique of privilege and instead representative of a more egalitarian ideology of higher education.

Whereas the radical innovations of State College represented one part of 1960s educational reform, egalitarian ideology symbolized another significant trend. Programs, and entire colleges,[1] developed to ameliorate educational inequality and to open access to groups historically denied admission to colleges due to economic or educational disadvantage. Compensatory higher education programs whose purpose was to provide access and educational opportunities to disadvantaged and underprepared students reflected this type of reform. It was within this context that the Educational Opportunity Division emerged and developed.

Both State College and the EOD support the decline of educational reform, but not its complete demise. By 1983, State College eliminated its honor/pass/no credit grading policy in favor of traditional grades, abolished the short term for a traditional academic calendar, in some departments eliminated the junior comprehensive examinations, and initiated discussions about a core curriculum and the implementation of sequencing and requirements. Nevertheless, despite these obvious retreats from innovation, State College retained an experimental spirit as its curricular deliberations revealed. For example, a large segment of the faculty still resisted curricular structure and, when pressed for a core curriculum, resisted traditional disciplinary boundaries and instead proposed interdisciplinary or non-disciplinary thematic courses. Likewise, by 1983 the EOD had declined to a point that complete integration with the rest of the college occurred. However, despite the fact that its separate and unique identity disappeared, the college retained a compensatory higher education program.

The coexistence of two differing types of educational reform on the campus provides an interesting vantage point for understanding the evolution of the EOD. As the historical narrative documented, the development of the EOD at State College needs to be in part understood through its interdivisional relationships, and often those relationships were marked by tensions between the differing educational visions of each program. To some extent then, just as the decline of the EOD as a separate division must be explained in terms of external State College pressures, the decline of State College as a radical experiment may also be viewed in terms of the influence of the EOD.

The History of EOD: A Sociological Analysis[2]

As discussed in Chapter 2, Spector and Kitsuse (1977) proposed a model for the analysis of the emergence and definition of social problems. Drawing upon the previous work of Fuller and Myers (1941) and Lemert (1951), they proposed a four stage theory. To briefly review, they proposed the following:

> Stage 1: The Process of Claims Making: in this stage, "groups attempt to assert the existence of some condition, define it as offensive, harmful or otherwise undesirable, publicize these assertions, stimulate controversy, and create a public or political issue over the matter." In this context, a social problem is defined by these claims making activities and of those making counterclaims.

> Stage 2: The Process of Official Recognition: in this stage, the social problem is officially recognized by an official group or institution and therefore its legitimacy as a problem is acknowledged.

> Stage 3: Re-emergence of Claims or Counterclaims: in this stage, either the original claims making group restates the charges or demands and in turn expresses dissatisfaction with the official responses and/or solutions.

> Stage 4: Rejection of Institutional Response and Development of Alternatives: sometimes the claimant group, dissatisfied with the official institutional response, develops "alternative, parallel or counter-institutions as responses to established procedure" (Spector and Kitsuse, 1977:142).

In Chapter 2, this model was used to provide an understanding of the development of liberal educational reforms in general and compensatory higher education in particular. That is, in Stage 1, claimants charging that higher education did not provide equal access to the disadvantaged, politically organized to demand an institutional response. Demonstrations, articles, protests at colleges, such as the City College of New York, contributed to the definition of educational inequality and inaccessibility to higher education as a social problem. In Stage 2, the state and institutions of higher education responded by developing particular programs to ameliorate these problems. It is within this context that the emergence of Coop College may be understood. In Stage 3, both the original claimants and new counter-claimants began to express dissatisfaction with the programs representing the official response. On the one hand, many members criticized the liberal reform program as inadequate, or merely another form of the original problem of educational inequality. On the other hand, others criticized the programs as a debasement of higher education and meritocracy and pushed for the return to standards. Within this context, as the programmatic solutions developed, the continual redefinitions of the social problem (educational reform programs) had become the subject of new claims and therefore the newly constructed problem.

Although this natural history model of social problems helps in our understanding of the definitional processes leading to the development of educational reform programs, it does not directly apply to the analysis of the programs themselves. This, in part, is due to the relativistic perspective of Spector and Kitsuse's approach which, in their own terms, is more concerned with the subjective processes leading to definition of problems than to the etiological analysis of the conditions themselves (Spector and Kitsuse, 1977:Chapter 3). Nonetheless, this model is especially useful in understanding the evolution of EOD as a solution to an educational problem, as it provides a thematic framework in which to place the various conflicts that define the program's development. That is, if the emergence of Coop College represented an official response (Stage 2) to the claims making of the 1960s (Stage 1), then the development of the Educational Opportunity Division may likewise be understood within the context of claims making, counterclaims and official resolution. However, in this framework, the division itself represented the institutional network and its members represented the claims making agents. Once entrenched on the State College Campus, the network of organizational relationship became more complex, with both intradivisional and interorganizational claims an intricate part of the division's development. Therefore, the evolution of the EOD will be examined as a series of claims, counterclaims and resolutions with each signifying a series of crucial issues in the history of educational reform.

Whereas the national history approach (Fullers and Myers, 1941; Lemert, 1951; Spector and Kitsuse, 1977) was specifically designed for the analysis of social problems and their evolutionary development, the delineation of a *stage theory* may also be applied to the analysis of organizations. In the following section, the history of the Educational Opportunity Division is examined as a progression of steps, each leading to its eventual decline as a liberal educational reform. From this vantage point, it is possible to trace the emergence, development, and decline of the program and apply concepts of claims making, counterclaims, and resolution to a series of events in the division's history. Likewise, through the delineation of the major factors in the program's evolution, the themes central to a conflict approach to organizations may be discerned.

The history of the EOD is analyzed in the following stages:

Stage 1: Emergence and Initial Development

The first stage represented the Coop College period in which the educational opportunity program emerged as a liberal educational reform. As it has already been noted, its emergence coincided with the educational establishment's response to legitimation crisis (Wolfe, 1977) and represented an example of the state's official solution to the problems of educational inequality and unequal access to higher education. Once established, the educational opportunity program symbolized the legitimation of these problems as social problems (that is, the definitional process that resulted in the development of institutional solutions had in fact, defined the problems as real), and the program began to implement educational solutions. At this point, the educational opportunity program became not only the response to claims making, but had to engage in the definition of problems and the construction of solutions.

It is within this context that both an objectivist and subjectivist approach to social problems are applicable.[3] From an objectivist perspective, the division accepted the educational problems associated with underpreparation as the essential nature of its purpose, and proceeded to develop specific approaches to them. That is, once in existence, the division's members engaged in an analysis of the problems of underpreparation in search of specific remedies. From a subjectivist perspective, the division's members continually defined and redefined specific problems in the context of their work. For example, in the process of examining the etiology of student underpreparation or low student performance members constantly made claims about the "problems" associated with these situations, such as family background, societal inequality, racial discrimination, individual deficiencies, etc. Although these analyses were part of the division's examinations, they also represented subjective constructions of members and the definition of "problems" to explain the organization's major problem. Throughout its development, the Educational Opportunity Division engaged in this type of social construction, as often this process was essential to the division's identity.

In the first stage, essential definitional concepts emerged concerning the central mission of Coop College. The first, defining the central problem as social, viewed the main objective of the division as the amelioration of educational inequality as a means of addressing the overall problem of social inequality. From this perspective, the mission of Coop College transcended the educational and was concerned with the social, political, and economic meanings of educational reform. Although usually couched in a liberal analysis of social problems,[4] the division's goals linked the educational to the social, with the reduction of minority inequality through education its central assumption. The second approach concerned the definition of underpreparation and its solution as ends in themselves; that is, the view of the division's mission as essentially educational became a second definitional characteristic. Although the latter view always was implicitly connected to the former (that is, the purpose of the educational mission was to increase occupational (social) opportunities), it sometimes became its major motivation and was perceived outside of the social context. In fact, one of the major evolutionary processes that emerged at Coop College was the subtle transformation of the division's mission from an explicitly social to an essentially educational one.

This evolution from the social to the educational was an important aspect of the division's definition of its identity. Growing out of the 1960s civil rights movement, the early years were framed by the on-going reflection of social and racial issues with the concept of social justice an essential definitional activity. As the program developed at Coop College, the attention to the educational gradually became the dominant characteristic, with the legitimacy of its existence becoming engulfed in its construction of an institutional purpose; and by the time the division moved to State College that purpose had become explicitly educational. Within this context, the program developed an overall vision of the educational problem of underpreparation and began to claim a certain expertise in dealing with it. Although the implicit social mission never disappeared (and would continue to emerge as an important defense mechanism when the division was threatened) and was most often enumerated by the program's director, the overall theme became the amelioration of an educational problem.

If the transition from a social to an educational framework defined the Coop years, the development of a legitimate organizational identity was central to this process. Within this context, the Educational Opportunity Division sought to define itself as a legitimate educational enterprise and not as a temporal educational reform destined like so many others to disappear as quickly as it emerged. In order to successfully defend its existence, the program's members defined educational disadvantage and underpreparation as significant educational problems and attempted to present themselves as experts in dealing with its complexities. During this first stage, then, the ideology of expertise became an important claims making activity in the justification of the program's existence; and in order for this claim to have any real meaning, the division first had to successfully define underpreparation as a significant educational problem. There is no doubt that the notions of social justice and racial equality were central to the acceptance of educational underpreparation as an important problem. However, once accepted, the extra-educational justifications became less explicitly offered, except in times of threat.

As the division evolved at Coop College, the tensions between organizational survival and educational mission began to emerge. As Collins (1979) suggested, the realm of organizational life is defined by both political and productive labor, the latter concerning the organization's actual response to its goals and the former concerning the organization's mediation of organizational conflict. Political labor, according to Collins (1979:50–53), concerns the efforts of members to defend the organization's legitimacy and in times of crisis to ensure organizational survival. Within this context, the use of organizational ideology (Swidler, 1979) is essential to successful political labor, as the ideology often becomes the essential foundation for claims making. Although the concepts of political labor and organizational ideology became most useful for understanding the State College years, it is during this stage that the ingredients were formulated. A good example of these processes was described by an EOD faculty member who began at Coop College in 1976 and witnessed the transition to State College. According to his account, when the division began to see a move to the main campus as a distinct possibility, the primary concern of the program became political rather than educational. Although the everyday educational practices such as teaching, counseling and tutoring did not diminish, the major concern of the faculty was the production of a governance document. In his own words:

> The entire year was devoted to producing the governance document. All other issues were for all intents and purposes tabled until the document became complete. It was essential to the faculty to develop a document that not only defined its purpose and mission, but protected each individual in the event of a transition. As State College faculty, they understood the implications of a transition to the main campus, and chose to define themselves as EOD faculty members; that is, as distinct from other State College faculty.

The production of a governance document was an example of political labor, and suggested some possible tensions between political and productive labor. Although this faculty member clearly did not suggest that education suffered, the preoccupation with this organizational identity and survival are central to our understanding of the division. Moreover, the creation of an official document that recognized the educational opportunity program as a legitimate and separate program of the college was the first step in establishing autonomy and credibility within the college.

The governance document that emerged from the Coop College faculty and that was accepted by the State College administration defined the

Educational Opportunity Division as a separate and autonomous program within State College with its own guidelines for review, promotion, tenure, etc. Integrating its educational mission and its special population into the document, the authors cited these special circumstances as justification for a different set of review criteria. Arguing that the needs of its student population and the labor intensive teaching experience required for success mandated a preoccupation with the instructional aspects of the educational experience, the document rejected traditional criteria for appointment, promotion, and tenure. For example, the Master's Degree was considered the appropriate terminal degree for appointment and promotion to Assistant Professor and tenure at Associate Professor was possible without a Ph.D. Moreover, the criteria for evaluation heavily emphasized teaching excellence and community service, with little if any emphasis on scholarship or publications.

Although it is possible to defend the idea that scholarship may be unrelated to success in a compensatory higher education program, and that credentials may be unrelated to the qualities vital to teaching in this environment, or that teaching excellence is the most important aspect of faculty contribution, the essential sociological point is not the defensibility of the division's claims, but the nature of the claims themselves and their meaning in the context of organizational analysis. While the faculty based the legitimacy of their program and consequently their own positions on the needs of the student population, they also defined the division as unique and separate, both in terms of its educational goals and its evaluation of its program. More importantly, the document legitimated not only the differences between Coop College and State College, but justified the different credentials of many Coop College faculty. While these criteria would re-emerge in subsequent stages as significant areas of conflict, at this stage the division had successfully defined itself as an integral part of State College, but had retained a separate identity.

By the time the negotiations with State College over its transition to the main campus were underway, the major processes defining this first stage had emerged. The division moved from an explicitly social mission to an educational one and in doing so defined itself as a legitimate institutional response to an educational problem replete with its own theories and methods. Moreover, through its official governance document it successfully defined itself as a unique, different, and autonomous organization. Furthermore, over its first nine years it developed a series of methods to deal with its unique population, and they became the foundation of its educational philosophy and, therefore, its organizational ideology.

The end of this first stage was marked by the transition to the main campus. During the year long debate over the move, the issues of the educational needs of EOD students and the political ramifications of moving to State College emerged as central areas of concern. In the first area, the division's members expressed skepticism over the ability of the program to integrate successfully into the State College program and indicated a cynicism over the campus' concern for underprepared students. At this point, the conflicts between the "egalitarian" goals of the compensatory program and what the EOD faculty perceived as the elite ideology of State College began to emerge as significant tensions. Regarding the second area, many faculty feared that the autonomy of the program, not an essential problem as an off-campus program, would become threatened in an on-campus situation. Therefore, stage one ended with the development of the central conflicts that would define the coming years.

Despite the EOD's concern over the move to State College, the external and internal pressures supporting the transition resulted in the transfer of the educational opportunity program. Internally, continued low enrollments and high budgetary costs made a separate off-campus program difficult to maintain or defend. Externally, State College's problems concerning affirmative action and its lack of an on-campus educational opportunity program made the decision to move Coop College to the main campus a sensible response to bureaucratic pressures.

In conclusion, the first stage included the years at Coop College and represented the program's emergence, development, and initial decline. Despite its problems of low enrollments and budgetary constraints, it re-emerged as a separate division of State College.

Stage 2: The Transition Years at State College: Student Claims and Divisional Response

Although the autonomy and official legitimacy of the division was enhanced by the move to State College (as a separate division on the campus with a specific educational mission, the EOD had re-emerged with perhaps more status than it had as an off-campus program), the first two years were defined by its adjustment to the special problems posed by the campus.

The major feature of the Educational Opportunity Division during this transitional period was its definition of itself as separate and unique. Based upon a common history and set of methods, the division's members legitimized their experience at State College by alluding to its historical purpose, its special population, and its treatment of a special educational problem. Most importantly, it stressed the necessity of a separate division in meeting its mission.

This period may be analyzed in terms of a series of claims making and responding activities. During the first two years at State College the basic conflicts were intradivisional, with EOD students challenging the structure and policies of the division. Charging that the entire college was institutionally racist and that the division represented a form of institutional labeling, many students questioned the efficacy of a separate divisional structure. Many EOD students claimed they were unaware of the separate divisional structure when they accepted admission to State College and asserted that only during the first week of classes did they begin to understand the meaning of EOD student; and according to many students, the implications did not please them. Within this context, students argued that the division cut them off from the academic and social mainstream, required different courses than other programs and, most destructively, identified all minority students as underprepared, thus creating an institutionalized stigma.

The initial student claims making placed the issue of separate placement of the underprepared student immediately at the center of divisional politics. As Goffman (1963) pointed out, the stigmatized individual has a number of alternatives for the management of spoiled identity. First, he/she can accept the label and convert it into a positive force; for example, the woman suffering from cerebral palsy who ran the New York City Marathon, from this perspective, was publicly acknowledging her difference but publicly rejecting the stigma associated with it. Second, the labeled individual can attempt to pass as normal in order to avoid the social and psychological effects of labeling. Third, the stigmatized individual can accept the negative labels and become constrained by the structural and psychological constraints defined by them. In educational research, the concept of a self-fulfilling prophecy of failure has been proposed to describe the negative consequences of institutional labeling.[5] The EOD students, from the moment they arrived at State College, strongly reacted against their perception of institutional labeling and often characterized all three of Goffman's defense mechanisms. Some students publicly rejected the label of different and proceeded to pass as "regular" college students. For these students, the EOD label made this extremely difficult. Others, realizing the negative connotation associated with EOD by non-EOD students, defined themselves as different but equal; that is, "because of unequal education I need extra help, but that does not mean I am inferior." Finally, some students, despite their efforts to avoid negative feelings, expressed doubts about their academic ability and seemed to accept the damaging definitions sometimes associated with EOD membership. Although EOD students reacted differently to divisional separation, the vocal segment of the student population consistently pressed claims challenging what they termed divisional isolation and separatism and demanded greater access to mainstream programs.

The dilemma of divisional separatism was compounded by the racial composition of the student population. Although the question of separate educational placement of the underprepared student is a difficult and perplexing one, the fact that the majority of students labeled as underprepared at State College were blacks and Latinos added to the problem. In fact, for many constituencies at State College, the EOD became synonymous with minority students, and although a small percentage of EOD students were white and, likewise, a small percentage of regularly admitted students were black and Latino, the labeling of all minority students as underprepared defined the perceptions of most State College members. Combined with the difficulties that many minority students experienced in adjusting to life on a predominantly white college campus, the issue of racial conflict became a central problem for the EOD which, for all intents and purposes, emerged as the institutional advocate for minorities at State College.

The problems faced by minority students at white colleges have been documented in the sociology of education research.[6] Willie and McCord (1972) suggested in their study of three colleges that institutional racism was a major barrier to the educational success of black students. Moreover, they pointed out that the problem of cultural conflict and assimilation posed a particular difficulty for minority students. In their study of black students in the late 1960s and early 1970s, they described black separatism as one process that students used to avoid the problems of assimilation and to promote a collective image of solidarity. On the contrary, at State College, minority students with their own institutional form of separation did not easily accept isolation nor turn it into a form of institutional solidarity. Rather, they often rebelled against its imprisoning nature and its negative definitions about minority students. It appears that while the students in the Willie study formed separatist groupings and demanded separate programs (i.e., black studies) as a response to perceived institutional racism, the EOD students perceived the institutionally defined separatism as examples of institutional racism. Moreover, by 1978 the black separatist and nationalist movements had waned and EOD students reflected a less militant and more integrative posture than those studied by Willie. Despite the differences in the reactions, the EOD students reflected the sensitivity to discrimination and racism described by Willie and their claims against divisional separation reflected these concerns.

Finally, the last part of student claims reflected the challenge to the EOD curriculum. EOD students argued that the EOD requirements were restrictive, much more prescribed than other segments of the college, and often repetitive of their high school courses. A few vocal spokespersons linked the attack on the curriculum to the notion of institutional constraint and argued that contrary to the EOD's mission, it actually diminished rather than enhanced equal educational opportunity. Thus, in addition to challenges to the system of labeling and tracking and charges of racism, student claims making questioned the efficacy of the curriculum.

During this period of adjustment, the faculty strongly defended the separate divisional structure and, in Spector and Kitsuse's language, made counterclaims to the student challenges. These counterclaims essentially defended the separate divisional structure and, while not rejecting student claims, attempted to socialize EOD students to the positive aspects and necessity of the division. Thus, at this point, the student claims, although officially recognized by the division, did not lead to immediate policy changes. Rather, during this period the faculty used a series of town meetings to defend the program and its curriculum by presenting a "you are different, but not inferior, in fact, you are better because your division is better" ideology to its students. At these meetings, the faculty presented what they considered a realistic appraisal of its students by defining them as "educationally disadvantaged" and "underprepared." "If you met State College admissions requirements, you would not be here." Therefore, the counterclaims relied upon the public definition of educational deficit and the imputation of the EOD as essential to ameliorating the deficiencies. To counteract some of the negative aspects of this definitional realism, the faculty attempted to create a divisional solidarity by suggesting that EOD students had the best program on campus and that the students should be proud, not ashamed to be in the division. Within this context, second and third year students, especially those from Coop College, became spokespersons for the separate divisional structure and reflected on the difficulties of regular divisional coursework and the insensitivity of regular division faculty to the needs of disadvantaged students.

Throughout this stage, the majority of the faculty defended the separate divisional structure and legitimated the program's existence through a definition of difference. Most faculty argued that the division's survival depended on its claims to uniqueness, and that only through a continued public invocation of these differences would the division remain a viable enterprise. Therefore, while students pressed for changes in the separate divisional structure, the faculty strongly supported it for two essential and related reasons, one educational and the other political. From an educational perspective, most faculty at this point fervently believed that a separate divisional structure was essential to educating its population; from a political approach, the division believed that only by presenting itself as unique and different, that is, that others on campus could not duplicate their duties or expertise, would the division avoid external threats to its existence.[7]

In conclusion, the second stage was marked by consistent student claims making against some aspects of the separate divisional structure, and although they did not call for its elimination they did demand reforms. Using Spector and Kitsuse's perspective, this stage defined the separate divisional structure as a social problem. However, although the division officially recognized the sincerity of the claims, it did not respond by loosening the barriers. For the most part, the official divisional response defended the separate divisional structure, while seeking to ameliorate the racial tensions on campus. Moreover, the division attempted to turn the separation issue into a positive advantage by socializing EOD students to their special but equal position on campus.

The defense of divisional separation defined the period. However, the seeds of discontent had been planted. During this period a number of heated debates on the attendance policy, the honors grade and cross registration all revealed significant differences within the EOD faculty. Whereas the majority still defended divisional separation, a small minority began to seriously consider the student claims as valid. Although this stage ended with no serious threat to divisional autonomy, the student claims initiated here would prove instrumental in the division's future policies.

Stage 3: The Loosening of Divisional Boundaries

Stage three was a critical period in the evolution of the Educational Opportunity Division as it represented the turning point in its existence as a separate division. Although Stage two ended with the divisional boundaries intact and the majority of the faculty strongly supporting the separate divisional model, the seeds of discontent had been planted by student claims making. Moreover, the political and philosophical differences within the division carried over into this stage, with the questions of student performance and separation becoming significant concerns.

At this point in the division's history, the major conflicts were intradivisional. Where in the second stage the division offered counterclaims to the student challenges, during this period the EOD began to not only officially recognize the claims, but to legitimate them through policy reform. In the context of Spector and Kitsuse's natural history approach, this period represented the second stage (official recognition and response).

As the historical narrative indicated, the loosening of the divisional boundaries involved considerable controversy. During this period the major concerns revolved around educational issues, with the efficacy of the separate divisional structure for underprepared students the central aspect of debate. Where initially divisional counterclaims defended the division as the best model for educational success, at this point a small but growing skepticism began to emerge within the faculty. The combination of continued student dissatisfaction with aspects of the program and the reality of EOD student performance (high attrition and failure rate) resulted in a period of continuous soul searching for possible solutions.

Although a major part of divisional discussions revolved around the issue of student performance and the faculty was divided along philosophical grounds about the epidemiology of the problem, the undercurrent of all debates was still the effects of divisional separation. When the director of the EOD reluctantly recommended a complete loosening of the divisional boundaries through a liberalized cross registration policy and the abolition of the attendance policy, the movement toward integration began to take shape. At this point, the director's action was a defensive one, as he thought continued student pressure would destroy the EOD from the inside, but it certainly did not represent a rejection of the EOD's structure. However, it did symbolize the division's recognition that the program developed at Coop College would have to change to meet the difficulties faced at State College. Although the faculty did not heartily support this major reform, it reluctantly loosened the divisional structure and in doing so set a course from which it would never turn back, toward more total integration into the State College mainstream.

It is significant to note that this stage, perhaps more than any other, demonstrated the evolutionary process of organizational change. The application of a stage theory or natural history approach allows for the understanding that organizational change proceeds along a fairly systematic course and, despite the sometimes idiosyncratic events of any particular period, sociologists can trace the roots of one period back into another. As Giddens (1981, Chapter 1) pointed out, a key aspect of the sociological imagination is the development of a historical sensibility with which one views the present as the product of the past. In this case, this stage is crucial in linking the periods in the EOD together in an understandable manner, as it represented a crucial turning point. Up until this period, the conflicts that defined the division were centered within its walls and the defense of the separate model was a taken for granted assumption for most members; the end of stage three, however, marked an important shift in direction with the loosening of divisional boundaries, only the prelude to the decline of the EOD as a separate model of compensatory higher education. Moreover, although the overall impetus toward this major educational change may be understood both from internal and external factors, up until the end of this period it was clearly the internal pressures and conflicts (within the division) that proved far more instrumental in explaining the changes than the external factors (interdivisional conflict, administrative pressure, and budgetary constraint). Finally, up to this point the most important factor affecting divisional change clearly was educational, with the needs of EOD students and the response to their claims the central explanatory variable.

Stage 4: The Politics of Integration and Decline

The final stage in the history of the Educational Opportunity Division witnessed the integration of the division into the mainstream State College programs and culminated in its merger with programs in the College of Letters and Science. Although State College retained a small integrative educational opportunity program (with counseling and tutoring), the end of this stage symbolized the demise of a unique compensatory higher education program.

From a sociological perspective this stage provided an important look at the complexities of organizational life and educational change and suggested that a multidimensional theory of change[8] is required to understand and explain the events. For example, a number of factors (internal and external) and interest groups (divisional, extra-divisional) contributed to the final outcome, and no one group or factor may be said to have caused the division's decline. Rather, a series of interdivisional and intradivisional interests and conflicts interacted to force a final resolution in favor of total integration.

If the previous stage loosened the boundaries, this stage broke them down completely. However, where the impetus toward integration began from internal conflicts and student claims and for the most part were motivated by educational issues, the factors leading to integration were both educational and organizational. Once the boundaries became unfastened, the movement away from divisional separation became more easily approached and, although considerable internal disagreement over the efficacy of integration continued until the end, the direction initiated in the previous stage would continue.

From an educational perspective, the needs of the EOD population remained a central organizational concern. Internally, up until the very end of the program, the division agonized, debated and initiated policy to deal with the educational problems of its student population. Moreover, all discussions of integration were framed by the question of EOD student needs. Although the historical evidence certainly suggests that the EOD faculty placed its students high on its list of priorities, the factors leading to change were also organizational.

As Scott (1981) pointed out, a major concern of all organizations is survival and the threat of elimination became a major factor during this period. The continual budgetary constraints, state fiscal crises and administrative skepticism about the necessity of the separate divisional structure made the EOD a very vulnerable part of State College, and the EOD faculty recognized the need to shape their destiny. While major disagreements over integration existed in the division, the majority of faculty embraced an integrative course as the best chance for survival. Therefore, at this point, the movement toward greater integration was initiated by the EOD as a response to external pressure and resulted in a series of significant intra-divisional and interorganizational conflicts and debates.

This stage represented a significant shift in the division's definition and presentation of self. Where in the first three stages the division legitimated itself through an *ideology of difference*, that is the division's existence depended on its claims of a unique student population and its special methods and structure, it now developed an *ideology of overlapping functions*. That is, the division as a claims making agent defined educational underpreparation as an overall college educational problem and posited its expertise as vital to the entire campus. Reacting to charges of duplication and the administrative demands for efficiency, the EOD relinquished its total defense of programmatic separation and defined itself as necessary to a large State College constituency. In doing this, the division banked on its survival as an integrative part of State College, and recognized that as a separate compensatory division its existence was problematic at best. Within this context, the division proposed its "Lower Divisional" and "Writing Proposal" recommendations in which it integrated the ideology of expertise into the overall State College curriculum. Although the division itself never really understood if it wanted to integrate in (retain the divisional structure but open all EOD courses to all "needy" students) or integrate out (eliminate the divisional structure altogether and offer lower divisional courses to the entire campus), the fact remains that the EOD itself was a prime mover toward integration and played an active role in its own decline as a separate division. A careful analysis of the historical documents suggests that while most EOD members would have preferred *integrating in*, the administrative opposition to a separate divisional structure and continued budgetary constraints made *integrating out* the direction the college would take.

Throughout this period, the politics of negotiation defined the movement toward integration. Within this context, the EOD attempted to legitimate its claims for greater involvement in college curriculum and at the same time avoid accusations of self-interest and survival. The textures of interdivisional conflicts revolved around the differing definitions of EOD courses and its skills-content synthesis. After years of defining its courses as different and as requiring a unique faculty and methodology, the EOD's attempt to claim widespread acceptability was often met with skepticism. Many State College faculty did not share the division's argument that skills and content could be combined into a substantive college course and there-fore, their counterclaims suggested that a course was either remedial or college level, but not both. Within this context, the EOD faced a serious organizational dilemma: having made the decision to pursue integration as a means of survival, the ideology of difference no longer applied; however, if EOD courses and faculty were not special and its faculty like all other faculty, then not only the program, but the faculty could be viewed as unnecessary.

The key to solving this organizational problem revolved around the concept of underpreparation as an educational problem. At this point, the EOD as a claims making agent sought to define academic underpreparation as an ubiquitous educational problem not particular to the EOD student population, but applicable to a widespread segment of the State College student population. Beginning with its articulation statement in the self-study accreditation report which stated that EOD students were different in degree, not kind, from other regularly admitted students, and continuing with its "Proposal for a Unified Lower Division" and the "Writing Proposal," the EOD defined underpreparation as a significant problem and offered its expertise in providing solutions.

The reactions to these claims varied within the college, but the proposed integration of EOD into the college mainstream produced a series of interdivisional conflicts revolving around elite versus egalitarian visions of higher education. Some members of the academic community rejected the EOD claims, either from a skepticism over the validity of its definitions or a rejection of its methods. Others did not support the concept of compensatory higher education and while tolerant of EOD as a separate division did not want "remedial type" programs expanded to the entire college. In response to these attitudes, the EOD claims centered on a critique of the State College curriculum and its graduate type programs and continually pushed for an accessible structured lower division as an antidote to what it perceived as exaggerated emphasis on the upper divisional major at State College.

In addition to ideological conflicts, the politics of integration centered on the issues of status competition and organizational autonomy. According to Collins (1975:Chapter 4), a major basis for organizational conflict is the struggle over cultural meanings and definitions of prestige. He pointed out (1975:Chapter 9) that the university system is an organizational setting of the intellectual world historically developed around competing definitions of scientific reward and status. Despite the notion of collegiality sometimes accepted by both academics and outsiders, the university is no different from other organizational settings where political labor and sinecure politics define daily rituals.[9] Moreover, as Flournoy (1982: Chapter 5) suggested, in times of budgetary constraint and the waning of public support college faculties seek to defend their particular interests, which often led to continual interdivisional struggles.

At State College, the politics of integration often brought the sometimes private and invisible world of status competition to the surface. Competing definitions of academic competence including issues of credentialism and teaching versus research emerged in this stage, with the EOD faculty put into a position of defending this status. Because many of the EOD faculty did not hold doctoral degrees and most did not publish, the commitment to teaching and the special labor intensive requirements of compensatory higher education became substitute criteria for academic prestige. However, although these criteria were recognized (although not necessarily supported by non-EOD faculty) within the separate divisional structure, the proposed integration of EOD faculty into boards of study changed the situation. At this point, some State College constituencies rejected the EOD faculty because of both insufficient credentials and a rejection of their teaching competencies in substantive areas. As Basil Bernstein (1971) suggested in a somewhat different context, the classification of knowledge into distinct boundaries often produces conflict between groups who define the classificatory system as their territory.[10] In this realm, as long as the classification boundaries between EOD and other divisions were strong status conflict, while existing, remained beneath the surface. However, as the boundaries began to weaken, status conflict intensified.

Just as the question of status defined a portion of the interorganizational conflict, the defense of organizational autonomy also represented a significant aspect of the opposition to integration. As many organizational theorists (Collins, 1975; Scott, 1981) pointed out, control of decision-making is a central part of the politics of organizational interaction and struggles for control comprise a salient feature of political labor. In this case, as the boundaries between classification systems weakened, the more threatened members within certain divisions became as the degree of organizational autonomy and control began to erode. This was especially significant at a college where the hierarchical divisions of control were sometimes ambiguous; for example, although the State College faculty fully recognized that real control was centralized within the administration, they nonetheless insisted on the proformal existence of participatory democracy and took faculty autonomy over educational issues very seriously. At the academic and curricular level ultimate authority over education rested with the EPC and divisional curriculum committees, and when the various proposals for integration emerged some divisions or boards of study reacted defensively in order to retain autonomy over their own curriculum. In particular, the Humanities Division questioned the right of external forces (either faculty committees or administration) to force integration by fiat. They demanded the right as an autonomous division to accept or reject educational proposals and especially resented the administration's place in these matters. Thus, interdivisional conflicts concerning integration were multifaceted with differences over educational ideology, status definitions, and organizational autonomy and control all contributing to the politics of negotiation.

Another aspect of the politics of integration concerned the negotiated construction of symbolic reality. Collins (1975:Chapter 3) and Karp and Yoels (1979) suggested that everyday life revolves around the negotiation of meanings through the interpretation of symbolic realms of understanding. Drawing upon the cognitive sociology of Cicourel (1973), the symbolic interactionist perspective of Mead (1934) and Blumer (1969) and the ethnomethodology of Garfinkel (1967), Collins suggested that understanding of meanings in everyday discourse is not a given, but rather emerges from the negotiations implicit in situations. Moreover, in rejecting a functionalist conception of social order that states social solidarity presupposed a shared meaning system, he presented a view that organizational reality is sometimes ambiguous and problematic.[11]

In *Conflict Sociology*, Collins proposed the synthesis of Durkheim into an overall approach to organizational struggles.[12] He argued that Durkheim's analysis of ritualistic interaction as the basis for social solidarity holds only within particular social groupings, but not between groups. Thus, the cultural codes and rituals that represent a group's collective conscience and contribute to the affirmation of its social solidarity often form the basis of conflict between groups with different rituals and collective identities. Where Durkheim provided a powerful analysis of intragroup identity and the factors contributing to within-group order, according to Collins, he missed the overall conflictual nature of organizational life. Collins (1975:Chapter 2; 1981:Chapter 1) argued that the integration of a conflict theory between groups completes a comprehensive approach to understanding organizations, with the processes of ritual and meaning systems endemic to one group's solidarity forming the basis for conflict and negotiation between groups.

From this perspective, the political labor engaged in by State College members revolved around the presentation and negotiation of meanings. Since the EOD had its own organizational identity, ideology, and symbolic and meaning systems, the politics of integration often involved its presentations of these ideas. However, where the definitional concepts always had meaning for EOD members, they did not necessarily induce the same connotations for non-EOD members. Therefore, in addition to conflicts over ideology in which both parties understood the concepts, many interdivisional interactions were defined by ambiguity, misunderstanding, and confusion.

Douglas (1972) and Garfinkel (1967) connect the contextual use of language to the problematic nature of meanings. The contextual use of language suggests that language as a symbol system is understood (that is, given meaning) only in the context in which it is used; for example, within a particular culture, group, or situation. Moreover, members understand language in its symbolic and metaphorical context as opposed to its literal translation only if they share the same linguistic and symbolic code.[13] Therefore, drawing upon Garfinkel's indexicality principle (Handel, 1982: 40–42), it appears "that social interactions can be carried out smoothly to the extent that mutually accepted implications do not have to be verbally explicated" (Collins, 1975:153). That is, if members share the same context they can understand the meanings implied by the codes; if they do not, and since conversational interactions often assume the shared possession of linguistic competence, the results are often ambiguous.

In *Being There* (1971), Jerzy Kosinski provided a satirical and cynical critique of linguistic interaction that clearly illustrated both the contextual use of language and the problematic nature of meanings. Chance, the gardener, was an illiterate social incompetent (due to the fact that he has never been "properly" socialized) but managed to pass[14] as a wealthy and intellectual businessman because of the assumptions of members about shared meanings. Because he possessed the correct sign vehicles (Goffman, 1959) that presented an image of status, members assumed he understood the context of their meanings. Throughout the novel, Kosinski concocted a series of exaggerated situations in which Chance, despite his inability to decipher the communication codes and his literal response to a symbolic question, always managed to continue his deception. For example, Kosinski described a conversation with the President of the United States:

> The men began a long conversation. Chance understood almost nothing of what they were saying, even though they often looked in his direction, as if to invite his participation. Chance thought they purposely spoke in another language for reasons of secrecy, when suddenly the President addressed him: 'And you, Mr. Gardiner? What do you think about the bad season on the street?' Chance shrank. He felt that the roots of his thoughts had been suddenly yanked out of their wet earth and thrust, tangled, into the unfriendly air. He stared at the carpet. Finally, he spoke: 'In a garden,' he said, 'growth has its season. There are spring and summer, but there are also fall and winter. And then spring and summer again. As long as the roots are not severed, all is well and all will be well.' He raised

his eyes. Rand was looking at him, nodding. The President seemed quite pleased. 'I must admit, Mr. Gardiner,' the President said, 'that what you've just said is one of the most optimistic statements I've heard in a very, very long time. Like nature, our economic system remains, in the long run, stable and rational... We welcome the inevitable seasons of nature, yet we are upset by the seasons of the economy. I envy Mr. Gardiner his good solid sense. This is what we lack on Capitol Hill' (1971:44–45).

Although Chance replied literally, the President assumed he was responding contextually and rather than discrediting his remarks, he made sense of them; that is, he interpreted them within the context he originally intended. Thus, despite the discrepancy in contexts the interaction appeared to the participants to proceed smoothly; in actuality, the meanings were misunderstood. Therefore, the problematic nature of meaning does not only include misunderstanding where one or more participants request clarification or attempt to discredit the other, but also interactions that appear to have shared meanings, when in fact they do not. In these cases, the meanings are confused but this confusion is not necessarily understood by members.

The problematic nature of meanings defined many of the interdivisional interactions at State College and were an important part of the politics of integration. From this perspective, the members actively negotiated meanings but sometimes did not share the same contexts or give the same meanings to particular ideologies. For example, EOD faculty consistently imputed the "skills-content synthesis" to defend its discipline courses and assumed that others at least understood the meaning of its usage. Likewise, non-EOD faculty defined EOD discipline courses from a different symbolic and ideological context (that is, as remedial) and often the parties talked past one another. At times, it was obvious to members that a misunderstanding had occurred; however, at other times members did not recognize the different contexts and seemed surprised that a consensus could not be reached. The fact that EOD faculty members often talked in code, using the divisional ideology without explicating it, deepened the communication problems. Although this analysis does not suggest that interorganizational conflict was only a matter of definitional ambiguity, it does support the viewpoint that organizational interaction is at times ambiguous and problematic; and that interactional outcomes are the product of on-going situational negotiations.

Another important issue, the question of educational change, is also a central thematic concern. Stage four represented the culmination of fourteen years of evolutionary development and as it ends with the demise of the program, an analysis of the factors leading to this event is essential. In times of crisis, members constructed their own definitions of causality and with the ending of the EOD as a separate division, its members were no different. For example, during the last period of this final stage many students and faculty pointed to *institutional racism, campus elitism, administrative arrogance*, and *conspiracy theories* to account for the merger. Although, in part, all of these explanations have some basis in reality, they all missed the dynamics of educational and organizational change. The demise of the EOD represented the last step in an on-going process of decline whose causes were multidimensional and complex. To understand them is to understand the intricacies of educational and organizational life.

The Decline of the EOD: Student Claims and Stigmatization

Both EOD students and faculty played an intricate role in the decline of their division. During the program's years at State College, it was the students who brought the first claims against divisional separation and who were primarily responsible for the initial loosening of divisional barriers. However, once the boundaries became less structured and the budgetary crises intensified, the concerns of EOD faculty for at first organizational and then individual survival became the central factor in explaining the program's evolution. Within this context, although EOD student needs always were considered, in the last stages they became secondary to organizational and political discussions. Moreover, although EOD students continued to play a role in the last stages, they did become significantly less important. Despite this reduced role, EOD students played a central role; thus, it is important to analyze the factors explaining student involvement.

Chapter 4 discussed the complex set of adjustment problems facing EOD students. Educationally they had difficulty accepting the "under-prepared" label and often become confused and angry about their own abilities. Socially, they often had problems adjusting to campus life and integrating with the non-EOD student population. While the EOD program was structured to help these students successfully adjust, the historical narrative demonstrated that EOD students did not readily accept the divisional label, methods or solutions, but rather often defined the division itself as their central problem.

Throughout its first two years at State College, a sizeable number of EOD students clamored for divisional reforms. Arguing that the college was institutionally racist and that the EOD's separation was a major part of this problem, these students pointed to divisional separation as a barrier to their social and educational development. They tended to reject faculty arguments that the separate EOD was necessary for their educational success and demanded reforms such as increased cross-registration.

Both London (1978) and Willis (1977) pointed out that counter-school cultures, while often developing out of the accurate perceptions of students about school problems, sometimes fail to understand the complexity of the situations. For example, although many of the community college students studied by London dealt with the conflict between their cultural roots and a seemingly antithetical intellectual culture of the liberal arts curriculum and its faculty by developing an anti-intellectual perspective, these perceptions led students voluntarily away from liberal arts education (the BA track) to the vocational track (with a more limited effect on future life chances). Likewise, Willis demonstrated how working class students in England develop an anti-school culture and by choice drop out early to enter factory work. Although Willis suggested that student perceptions are reactions to the conflicts between working class and middle class culture, he also indicated that such working class response was central in reproducing the class system. The perceptions and motivations of EOD students may be understood within a similar class and culture conflict model, as both a reaction to the conflicts perceived by minority students and the effects of the labeling process endemic to a separate educational opportunity program.

The central feature of student claims making activities was its demand for a loosening of the divisional boundaries. Charging that the EOD isolated and stigmatized its students, the claims pointed to the divisional structure as the primary factor in low student performance. On this level, then, it appears that student claims become a primary way of deflecting individual responsibility for success and failure and taking the blame off students and putting it on the institution. Therefore, many EOD students rejected EOD labels of underpreparation and did not accept the division's response that the program was vital for their futures.

It appears that a complex social psychology defined the EOD student reaction to divisional separation and labeling. In *Stigma* (1963), Goffman pointed out that the stigmatized individual may either accept or reject (by passing as normal) an institutional label in order to manage his spoiled identity. Although a primary objective of the EOD faculty was to enable students to accept the underprepared label in a positive light and to embrace the division as their ally in overcoming their weaknesses, a significant number of students chose to reject the label and attack the division. Interviews with students suggested that a primary function of this behavior helped students deflect the emotional pain of the labeling process, as well as the fears associated with overcoming substantial educational difficulties.

Another important feature of student claims making involved the issue of institutional racism. EOD students faced the complex adjustment problems of minority students on a majority campus. Research suggests (Allen, 1992; Fordham and Ogbu, 1986; McMannus Report, 1979; Willie and McCord, 1972) that minority students must struggle to deal with the complex issues of assimilation, culture conflict, and cultural betrayal (that is, viewing assimilation as a loss of one's own culture), and these problems significantly affect minority student performance. EOD students reported feelings of alienation, estrangement, and isolation on a campus where minority students were isolated in an educational division. Moreover, the segregation of EOD students educationally combined with their integration socially in housing arrangements appeared to have intensified the conflicts and confusion. EOD students did not seem to know whether they wanted to remain separate in their safety of a minority subgroup or integrate into the dominant college mainstream. While the EOD provided some sanctuary from what they perceived as campus racism, it also symbolized that racism (as it represented segregation). Thus, EOD students wavered between ambivalence and anger in their response to EOD separation.

The eventual rejection of divisional separation by EOD students and their active claims making for integration is an interesting phenomenon. Willie and McCord (1972), in their study of black students at white colleges in the late 1960s, concluded that separation was often adopted by minority students as a reaction to institutional racism. During a period when black nationalism and separatism were viewed positively by students, minority students sought support and solidarity in a readily identifiable campus subculture of their own formation. That is, the students studied by Willie and McCord voluntarily rejected integration and assimilation as a solution to perceived racism and chose separation as a way of retaining their cultural identities. Like the anti-school subcultures described by Willis (1977) and London (1978) these students rejected dominant culture but, unlike them, did not choose to drop out. However, EOD students faced with a preexisting cohesive structure that forced racial isolation did not use it to form cohesive bonds, but tended to escape from it. The important point was that EOD students were not given the chance to voluntarily retreat into their sub-cultural world, but rather were forced into it with the added burden of institutional labeling. Faced with the negative connotation that minority status, EOD, and underpreparation were synonymous, many EOD students turned their anger against the division.

The EOD student reaction against divisional separation was an extraordinarily complicated one. Although they certainly retained primary friendships with other EOD students, they often tried to pass as "regular" students. The EOD label was not something they were proud of, and they constantly reported that they received differential treatment because of it especially from non-EOD students. However, while the EOD faculty urged them to be proud of their division and to form a cohesive student culture, many EOD students rejected this remedy to their perceptions of stigmatization. What seems to explain this was a complex reaction to minority status and divisional separation. Most EOD students would have apparently formed subcultural bonds without the EOD (like those in the Willie study). However, the preexisting institutional structure that equated minority status with underpreparation made racial segregation and subgroup solidarity a part of the labeling process. To avoid negative labeling, EOD students chose to attack the division and demand integration. Thus, in avoiding stigmatization they also had to assimilate and face feelings of cultural betrayal. At the least, this argument suggests a complex set of factors explaining EOD student claims against a separate EOD.

The student reactions to the division after the rigid boundaries were unfastened suggest a similar analysis. Once EOD students felt that the EOD was not forcing them to remain isolated and once they began to face the problems of mainstreaming into regular division courses, many EOD students became less angry about the EOD. In fact, as forces mitigated against the retention of a separate EOD, the EOD students began to support the program. While there still was little support for total separation, these students strongly supported the need for a developmental and skills program. Students began to talk of the value of the skills program and opposed the complete elimination of the EOD. It appears that EOD students recognized their weaknesses through experiences outside the EOD and only then began to see the utility of certain aspects of the program. Although they did not want the program eliminated, they likewise did not support its return to isolation. Therefore, they wanted the program opened to all students in need of its services. In this way, they felt that minority students would not be stigmatized as they had been in the past.

The reaction of EOD students to the final elimination of the division supports this viewpoint. Upon hearing the college's decision, EOD students immediately charged the college with institutional racism and reacted angrily to the attack on them. It was clear to these students that the college was trying to eliminate the black presence on campus, and they vehemently opposed the move, despite its explicit retention of an integrative educational opportunity program. It was ironic that EOD students who strongly opposed EOD separation now so adamantly opposed its elimination. It appears that these students, in both cases, reacted against institutional decision making, first when it isolated them, and second, when it eliminated a program symbolic of a minority population at State College. Although it may appear that these reactions were inconsistent, the important point was that they were not. Rather, they both represented a symbolic reaction to perceptions of racism (whether or not they were accurate) and pointed to the sensitivity of these issues for EOD students.

This analysis suggests that EOD claims against the division were the result of their reactions against stigmatization. Anti-EOD claims were greatest in times of total segregation and decreased with integration. More importantly, as the EOD loosened its boundaries, students showed greater appreciation of its contribution to their lives. Overall, this leads to the conclusion that while developmental and remedial components may be necessary for underprepared students, the total segregation of minority students results in profound social-psychological consequences.

The EOD curriculum and requirements were another central aspect of student claims against the division. A sizeable number of students claimed that EOD courses were unnecessary, repetitious of high school and kept them back. Students also pointed to the compulsory attendance policy as symbolic of their differential treatment at State College and demanded to be treated like all other non-EOD students. While the EOD faculty responded that student underpreparation mandated this treatment, EOD students pointed to these aspects of the EOD as responsible for their educational problems. What was clear, however, is that EOD students felt *infantalized* by their treatment, and the question of its necessity aside, reacted angrily. To accept the requirements meant to accept the label and EOD students apparently could not readily do this and therefore rejected the program. Moreover, it was apparently psychologically easier to blame the program than to accept the reality of one's educational deficiencies. For example, to fail a course like Math Concepts (basic arithmetic) because of skills deficiencies was far more difficult to accept than to fail it because it was so basic and unchallenging. Thus, by attacking the curriculum, EOD students did not consciously have to deal with the realization that many were indeed underprepared. Therefore, the EOD faced the complex problem of balancing the educational needs of their students, with the negative reactions to the labeling of those needs. It seems that only when the EOD label was diminished with EOD students cross-registering in large numbers, did EOD students begin to accept what the EOD had tried to tell them — that they needed extensive help. The EOD director in his justification for loosening all divisional boundaries had been proven correct; that is, once faced with the reality of regular division coursework, and without the totally separate EOD to blame, EOD students came back to seek assistance. However, once the walls came down, the division could not return to the past (nor would students have supported such a move).

The Decline of EOD: An Analysis of Organizational and Educational Change

As much as the analysis of the Educational Opportunity Division provides an examination of particular themes in compensatory higher education, it also presents a more general view of organizations and educational change. Within this context, a number of conclusions may be drawn.

Scott (1981), in his review of the major theories of organizations suggested that the major differences between rational systems perspectives and conflict theories was the concept of rational goal attainment. Theorists subscribing to a rational system approach viewed organizations as "systems rationally designed to pursue specific goals. Recognizing departures due to internal conflicts or external uncertainties does not alter commitment to this basic model" (W.R. Scott, 1983:158). On the other hand, conflict theorists argued that "organizations are fundamentally mechanisms for controlling people, not tools for achieving goals. What is distinctive about organizations is not that their structures are rational, supporting efficient goal attainment, but that their control systems are legitimated by a rationalist ideology" (W. R. Scott, 1983:158). Moreover, as Heydebrand (1977) and Collins (1975; 1979) pointed out, internal and external contradictions and conflicts contribute to the organization's directions as much or more than the pursuit of its rational goals. Finally, as Collins' distinction between political and productive labor (1979:50–53) suggested, a significant part of all organizational time is spent on the development and presentation of legitimating ideologies to justify the pursuit of seemingly rational goals, but not necessarily on their actual pursuit or attainment.

A central theme in organizational analysis, specifically within the conflict approach, is the discrepancy between organizational goals and practices, between stated and real goals of action, and between normative and behavior structures (Scott, 1981:80). Closely related to these concepts is the view of organizations as self-maintaining and organized for self-preservation. Although the historical narrative did not provide the basis for an evaluation of the division's goal attainment,[15] it did suggest that the processes of organizational life transcended the fulfillment of rationally stated educational goals. That is, the EOD rational goals were all educational and directed to the successful preparation of underprepared students. Likewise, its educational philosophy was presented as a rationalist philosophy of goal attainment. It was clear from the historical narrative that while a significant segment of the division's time was concerned with goal attainment, at least an equal amount was relegated to other organizational processes often having little to do with educational goals, but rather, concerned with political processes. Within this context, the EOD focused on conflict management and resolution, the legitimation of its organizational identity, and finally, organizational survival. Moreover, many of these "nonrational" processes were concerned with the fulfillment of rational goals, as intraorganizational and interdivisional conflicts often revolved around the concern for EOD student needs. Thus, the analysis of the Educational Opportunity Division does not completely reject a rational systems approach, but rather suggests that a significant portion of the organization's processes were directly related to goal attainment. Nonetheless, the identification of the on-going conflictual processes of legitimation and survival, and the variety of claims making and counterclaims making activities rejects such a rational-systems approach as the primary perspective in understanding this program. Rather, a conflict theory of organizations that recognizes goal attainment as one part of the conflictual nature of organizational life is a better theoretical perspective for understanding the EOD's history.

The politics of integration that defined the last two years of the EOD's existence support this conflict approach to organizations. During this period, although the EOD still concerned itself with the fulfillment of its educational goals (as indicated by the preoccupation with matters of student performance even after the plan to merge the division was announced), the majority of organizational processes dealt with survival. Moreover, as the discussion of the problematic nature of meanings suggested, the processes that define organizational life were not always rational, but rather reflected a certain situational ambiguity.

A major component of the conflict approach to organizations is the analysis of ideology as an ongoing foundation of organizational interaction. As Swidler (1979) pointed out in her study of alternative high schools, the use of ideology as a legitimation and coercion device is an important aspect of the educational process, and this is especially true in settings with explicit educational missions and philosophies. This was certainly true of the Educational Opportunity Division, where its special educational mission and its perception of a unique educational philosophy became ideology and constantly emerged to legitimate its existence and define its identity. Throughout its history, the presentation of this ideology, although its specifics changed, defined the politics of interaction, both within and between divisions. The use of the ideology of expertise combined with the special mission and population of the program consistently emerged as the tactic for organizational survival, at first as a separate division, and then as an integrated part of the college.

The imputation of an ideology of expertise suggested a significant theme in organizational analysis concerning the contradictions between goals and attainment. Whatever the complex reasons, it was clear to even the most diehard supporter of the EOD philosophy and methods that its special approach did not produce significantly superior outcomes. Throughout its history as a separate division at State College, the problems of student performance were obvious to members. Although most faculty did not attribute this to programmatic deficiencies but rather to student deprivation or shortcomings, they always acknowledged the reality of the problem. Nonetheless, throughout the politics of defense (defending the separate divisional structure) and integration, the ideology of expertise was used despite the fact that no concrete empirical evidence could support the claims. Although this does not prove that no evidence exists to support any of the division's claims about itself, it does point to the ideological nature of the legitimation process. It does seem clear, however, that if the EOD had been undeniably successful by college standards (low attrition, high graduation) or even significantly superior to other state programs without a separate division, its ability to legitimate its existence would have been strengthened, even in times of budgetary constraint. The fact that divisional claims had to be ideological, since concrete empirical evidence for a defense was lacking, was a significant factor in explaining the division's decline; nevertheless, it was only one of a more complex set of factors.

If the analysis of the EOD provides an interesting look at organizational processes, it also provides an investigation of the dynamics of educational change. First, the emergence, development and decline of an educational opportunity program is important, if only to understand the factors leading to the decline of educational reform; second, the significant changes in the direction of the division (from the defense of separation to the movement toward integration) provide an important tapestry of educational innovation and adaptation, and the opportunity to explain the dynamics of these changes.

Educational Change

The analysis of educational change and reform is a central theme in the sociology of education research. Functionalist, neo-Marxist, and conflict approaches differ in their explanations of educational expansion and the dynamics of change. While the earlier discussions suggested the factors leading to the development of educational reform programs such as the EOD, it did not emphasize the processes leading to the development and decline of such programs. With so many of the reform programs of the

1960s dying by the 1980s it behooves us to provide a framework for understanding the reasons for this trend.

Neo-Marxist theories of educational change emphasized the corresponding relationship between the capitalist relations of production and the relations of schooling in the United States and argued that changes in the economic sphere facilitated corresponding changes in the educational system. Rejecting the liberal-democratic theories of schooling as an agency for social mobility, revisionist historians of education[16] argued that "educational expansion is not a march of progress toward greater equality of opportunity, but a story of betrayal and false promises" (Hurn, 1978:66). Some critics of revisionist approaches (Ravitch,1978) have pointed to the successes of educational reform. Others (Hurn, 1993; Collins, 1979) have criticized their one-dimensional view of change, noting that although economic factors are certainly important, other factors often independently affect the evolution of schools. Citing the relative independence of the educational realm, and the relative autonomy of particular educational programs, these conflict theorists argued that organizational factors are critically important in effecting change. Hurn (1993:87-96) and Collins (1979:73-130) emphasized the processes of status competition and political labor within educational organizations as key factors in their evolution. Although both authors recognized that economic factors contribute to educational change, they argued that the neo-Marxist perspective was often too rational in its explanation by overstating the "perfect fit" between schools and society; and thus missed the multidimensional dynamics of educational change. As Hurn argued:

> ...What is more and more accurate is a picture of schools frustrating the objectives of all who seek to use them to convey particular messages to the young: objectives of progressive educators, capitalist elites, parents and local communities. No longer is any one group able to exercise decisive control over the content of schooling; and equally important decreasingly convey a set of consistent values and ideals to the young (1978:78).

Therefore, while conflict theorists did not necessarily reject the neo-Marxist perspective in whole, they did suggest it was too narrow in its emphasis on economic relations and too mechanical in its emphasis on structure. Thus, neo-Marxist theory, in seeing educational change as the product of economic crises often ignored the effects of actors within the schools. As Joseph Featherstone (1976), in his review of Bowles and Gintis pointed out, their entire history of American education fails to understand the conflictual nature of intraeducational interactions between teachers, administrators and students and their independent effect on educational change. Therefore, it seems the synthesis of neo-Marxist and conflict approaches provides the best framework for understanding educational change. As Chapter 2 explained the development of compensatory higher education as a reform, the following section examines its decline.

Beginning with Persell's (1977:17) model of the relationship between society and education, the dynamics of educational change may be viewed in the context of societal, institutional, and interactional spheres. Neo-Marxist approaches placed the primary emphasis on the societal-institutional levels; conflict theorists placed equal emphasis on the institutional-interactional levels, with schools viewed as sometimes independent from societal influence.

Bowles and Gintis (1976) provided the most sophisticated version of a neo-Marxist theory of educational reform, and although in the final analysis their view is too mechanical, they did attempt to incorporate the complexities of conflict into their model. Stressing the dual and often contradictory functions of capitalist accumulation and reproduction, they argued that educational reforms emanate from legitimation crises. However, although many of the intentions of reformers were well meaning, Bowles and Gintis suggested that the realities of economic production and the requirements of capitalist accumulation made the success of these reforms impossible. Most importantly, if the reforms began to threaten the accumulation process the state responded by eliminating reform programs. This approach to liberal reform was supported by Piven and Cloward's (1971) analysis of welfare reform and by Wolfe's (1977) theoretical examination of the limits of legitimacy. Both saw liberal reform emanating from the contradictions of capitalist reproduction and declining due to their impact on the accumulation process. Wolfe (1977) suggested that the political reforms that developed in response to legitimation crises often led to the fiscal crisis of the state, as in the final analysis the government had pay to solve the social problems of the advanced capitalist economy. Drawing upon O'Connor's (1975) fiscal crisis theory, he suggested that governmental cutbacks were the inevitable response to the development of reforms. From this perspective, then, the decline of educational reform programs was essentially a product of economic factors.

The history of the EOD certainly may be understood within this framework. Just as the educational opportunity program's emergence represented a response to legitimation crisis and the demands for equality of educational opportunity, its decline may be traced, at least in part, to the fiscal crisis of the state. Certainly the external budgetary constraints placed upon the program throughout its life contributed to the processes that resulted in its merger. One might even argue that all institutional and programmatic processes, especially in its last three years, were responses to external societal pressures, and would not have occurred without them. Although the budgetary factors are crucial in understanding the program's decline, they by no means provide the essential factors or the overall picture. The history of this program must be viewed within a more multidimensional perspective, with the conflict theories proposed by Collins and Hurn central to this approach.

Although one cannot argue that the EOD was independent of external forces (that is, outside of the State College realm), the evolution of the program can only be viewed within the context of intradivisional and interorganizational politics. From the transition to the State College campus in 1978, the EOD's development related primarily to the interactions within the division and between itself and other college constituencies. Therefore, the history of EOD was the history of internal and external conflicts over a variety of educational issues. As the historical narrative demonstrated, no unicausal theory is appropriate in analyzing these processes. Rather, the program's evolution involved a variety of interest groups (EOD students, non-EOD students, EOD faculty and non-EOD faculty and administration) as well as a variety of controversial issues (institutional racism, separate versus regular placement, EOD student performance, elite versus egalitarian views of higher education), and through a sometimes rational and often nonrational sequence of interactions, the program's development proceeded.

Some of the conflicts were educational and directly concerned the division's mission to provide equal educational opportunities for under-prepared students; others were mostly political and organizational. That is, they were concerned with issues like organizational autonomy and survival. The attempts of the EOD to survive, first as a separate division and then as an integrated program, defined the EOD's direction as much as the fulfillment of its educational goals. From Collins' perspective, the development of the program depended on both productive and political labor. Although the EOD's members remained passionately concerned with their students' needs even after the division's demise became apparent (and the evidence does not support a view that this concern was totally ideological), these educational concerns are not sufficient in explaining the dynamics of educational change. The final integration of the EOD into the overall State College program, and with it the expansion of many of the EOD's educational ideas, was to a large extent the product of ongoing inter-organizational negotiations, some of which had very little to do with education.

The merger resulted in many quick analyses of its causes. Many students and some EOD faculty immediately charged the college with institutional racism and viewed the dismantling of the EOD as an outrage and insult to minority students. Some EOD faculty viewed it as a victory for State College elitism and a step backward from accessible college education. Many non-EOD faculty viewed it as a return to the "meritocratic" basis of higher education. What is clear from the historical evidence is that although all of these simple explanations have some merit, none alone is sufficient in explaining the final outcome. A careful examination of the evidence suggests that while the budget crises facilitated the decision, the roots of the merger developed early in the State College years.

The continual internal conflicts and claims making over the separate divisonal structure led to forms of integration. Once this integration began, the politics of survival resulted in continual movements away from separation. In the final analysis external budgetary, educational and organizational factors led to the decline, with the decision to merge the final step in a process initiated at least two years earlier. There are no simple causal explanations to educational change, and this case study proves this point. Only a multicausal theory stressing the various interest groups and factors that affect educational institutions is capable of addressing the emergence, development, and decline of the EOD.

Lavin, Alba and Silberstein (1981:308) concluded their study of CUNY Open Admissions by asking which theory of American education its history supported; a liberal-democratic approach that would view CUNY's program as an example of increased educational opportunity for the disadvantaged or a radical-revisionist perspective that would view it as another broken promise. They concluded that, although the program represented a significant step in opening higher educational opportunities, its demise in part represented a broken promise. "In the end," they argued, "it has moved closer to the older view: higher education is a privilege not a right" (1981:308). The discussion so far suggests a similar decline in an educational reform program that viewed college as a right. Although the historical evidence suggested a great deal about the dynamics of organizational and educational change, it does not provide the kind of evidence to make well reasoned conclusions about the overall meaning of the decline of EOD.

The final merger did not eliminate the educational opportunity program at State College, but removed it as a separate division of the college. Many EOD faculty and its director accused the college administration of breaking its commitment to the disadvantaged and suggested that without the separate division educational opportunity students would not be served at State College. Data on the post-merger years, although indicating EOP student performance has to some degree been negatively affected, does not provide conclusive support for the hypothesis that the program should have been retained in its separate form. The conclusion will present a brief discussion of this issue.

In summary, a number of major factors explain the elimination of the EOD as a separate compensatory higher education program. These factors were economic, educational, philosophical and ideological, and organizational:

1.   Economic: the continuing budgetary constraints and the expenses of the program certainly played a large role in the demise. To the extent that economy matters, Marxist approaches to the political economy of higher education and the decline of liberal reform are somewhat supported. Overall, however, the evidence does not support economics as the primary or even major explanatory variable.

2.   Educational: the differing conceptions of higher education and educational organization are central in understanding the program's demise. Within this context, elite versus egalitarian models of higher education and separate versus regular placement of the underprepared student became central thematic questions. In the end, the rejection of the separate model proved victorious, with an integrated approach to mainstreaming special students enacted. Although some of the evidence suggests a victory for elitism and privilege, conclusive evidence to support this view is not available.

3.   Organizational: the evaluation of the program revolved around the conflict between various college divisions over a series of organizational and educational issues and interests. Questions of divisional autonomy and control and lower divisional versus majors were examples of these. Incorporating an analysis of group ritual into a conflict approach to organizational interaction, the evidence suggests that interoraganizational and intradivisional negotiation of conflict and meanings was a significant factor in determining the eventual outcome of the EOD. Within this process, the application of Bernstein (1971) on the classification and framing of educational knowledge is extremely useful. His analysis of educational change as the outcome of the strengthening or loosening of systems of classification aptly describes the EOD's demise as a separate classificatory system.

NOTES

1. See for example the discussion of meritocratic discontent and popular options in Grant and Riesman (1978:Chapter 9).

2. This study focuses on the evolution of the EOD at State College and therefore will not spend a great deal of time on the Coop College years, other than placing them within an analytical framework.

3. Objectivist approaches treat social problems as objective conditions and analyze their possible causes and solutions. Subjectivist approaches treat social problems as the construction of members' definitions. For an excellent discussion of this distinction see Tallman (1976).

4. For a critical discussion of conservative, liberal, and radical approaches to social problems see Gordon (1977). For a discussion of these approaches to education see Sadovnik, Cookson, Jr. and Semel (1994: Chapter 2).

5. See Persell (1977:Chapters 4-8) for a discussion of tracking, teacher expectations, and their effects. The classic statement is presented by Richard Rosenthal and Lenore Jacobsen (1968), although their study has never been replicated and their findings are considered suspect. For discussions of tracking see Oakes (1985) and Sadovnik, Cookson, Jr. and Semel (1994:Chapter 9). Fordham and Ogbu (1986) discuss the social psychological effects of racism on black students. To succeed, many black students feel they have to pass culturally as white.

6. See for example, Allen (1992); Claerbaut (1978b) and Peterson et al. (1978).

7. Although from 1978 to 1980 the idea of external threat was not explicitly discussed, it was always an implicit aspect of divisional politics.

8. Multidimensional refers to a theory that accounts for the social, political, economic, cultural, ideological, interactional, interorganizational, and intradivisional dynamics of change.

9. For a comprehensive discussion of sinecure politics see Collins (1979: 53–58).

10. Bernstein (1977) continues and extends the analysis in a number of important respects.

11. The problematic nature of meanings is also discussed in Karp and Yoels (1979) and Handel (1982: Chapters 1, 3).

12. Collins proposes the integration of Durkheim's *micro-functionalism* and its emphasis of intragroup ritual and solidarity and a rejection of his *macro-functionalism* with its failure to recognize stratification and intergroup conflict, see Collins (1981: Chapters 1, 2).

13. See Bernstein (1973a; 1973b; 1973c; 1977; 1990) for a comprehensive analysis of communication codes with respect to class and cultural differences.

14. For a discussion of *passing* see Garfinkel (1967: Chapter 5) and Goffman (1963).

15. An empirical analysis of some of these goals and the extent they were implemented and attained is presented in Sadovnik (1983).

16. The revisionist historians of education include Bowles and Gintis (1976: Part III); Greer (1973); and Katz (1968; 1971). For a critique of this school of thought see Ravitch (1978).

8

CONCLUSION:
EQUITY AND EXCELLENCE
IN HIGHER EDUCATION

Writing ten years after the decision to eliminate the EOD as a separate compensatory education program, it is now possible to look back and evaluate the charges of institutional racism leveled against the college at the time. Critics of the college's decision stated that the new, integrative EOP program would make State College less accessible for underprepared students and mark a return to State College's elitist roots. Although there is insufficient evidence available to draw reliable conclusions, it is possible, based on available data, to make some general comments.

As the historical narrative suggested EOD student attainment and achievement were consistent problems throughout the division's history. It was not as if the college eliminated a program that was having exceptional successes. Nonetheless, on a campus that had never considered remediation its central role, advocates had reason to be concerned. Student retention data[1] provide some basis for assessing the impact of the elimination of the EOD. Table 8.1 provides data on completion rates for EOP students before and after the program was eliminated (1977-1982 Admissions classes came in under a separate EOD; 1983-1987 Admission classes came in under an integrative EOP). Table 8.1 indicates that there have been some effects of eliminating the EOD. Under a separate division students retention was much higher in the first year, with over 89% of the students from 1977-1980 completing at least one year at State College,[2] as compared to 55% from 1983 to 1987, under an integrative EOP program. Differences in completion rates for two and three years are a little less dramatic however, with 59% of students in EOD completing two years and 44% completing three years, as compared to 38% completing two years and 30% completing three years under the EOP program. Although these data lend some support to the hypothesis that the new EOP program did less well in promoting retention, without comparable admissions data to control for precollege abilities and performance data to analyze the factors leading to attrition, no overall conclusions may be drawn. Moreover, as the graduation rates for 1977--

1980 are much lower than the three-year completion rates, it would be unfair to suggest that the EOD provided a significantly better chance for its students to graduate. Without comparable graduation rates there are insufficient data to draw this conclusion; further, it appears that although a separate divisional structure increased retention during students' stay in the division, their attrition rates began to increase the longer they stayed at State College; that is, once they were mainstreamed into the regular programs. This suggests that one of the main claims of the EOD, that a separate division was necessary to prepare students for the rigors of the regular programs, was not supported by the evidence. Nonetheless, the claim that EOP students would have had more difficulty remaining at State College without the EOD seems to have been the case.

TABLE 8.1 RATES OF COMPLETION AT STATE COLLEGE EOD PROGRAM (EOP STUDENTS): 1977–1988 ADMISSION YEARS

YEAR	Admission (N)	COMP 1 YEAR	COMP 2 YEARS	COMP 3 YEARS
1977	59	.93	.66	.54
1978	88	.92	.63	.42
1979	94	.82	.54	.40
1980	108	.90	.51	.39
1982	37	.43	.16	.16
1983	24	.50	.50	.41
1984	55	.58	.29	.23
1985	41	.51	.34	.31
1986	53	.53	.38	.26
1987	70	.61	.40	.31

The efficacy of separate versus regular placement of underprepared students was a constant source of debate during the EOD's years at State

College. Although there is a wealth of literature on this question concerning precollege special education programs (Bryson and Bentley, 1980; Blankenship and Lilly, 1981; Carlberg and Kavale, 1980; Gartner and Lipsky, 1987) and tracking and ability grouping (Oakes, 1985; Hurn, 1993; Persell, 1977; Sadovnik, Cookson, Jr. and Semel, 1994), there is little scholarship on similar processes at the college level. There are insufficient data available to draw overall conclusions, nevertheless, comparisons of State College with similar EOP programs in the state provide some evidence to provide speculative inferences. Whereas the differences at State College before and after the elimination of EOD could lead to the conclusion that a separate program was necessary, comparisons to other campuses suggest caution in reaching this conclusion. Table 8.2 (below) provides data for students in 12 other EOP programs at four state year colleges most similar in admissions criteria to State College.[3] Table 8.2 indicates that 70% of the EOP students completed at least one year; 49% completed two years; and 39% completed three years. For 1977–1980, the years the EOD was separate, these data indicate 80% completed one year; 56% completed two years; and 46% completed three years. The data show that when comparing the separate EOD to the other integrative programs (1977–1980) there is little difference (+9% EOD in the first year; +3% EOD for two years; -2% EOD for three years). Comparing the years when both State College and the other programs were integrative the data indicate a clear pattern favoring the other programs (-10% EOD for one year; -6% EOD for two years; and -6% EOD for three years). Thus, the data suggest that students in other integrative programs remained in college at relatively similar rates to students in the separate EOD program; but in greater numbers than students in the State College integrative EOP program. When combined with the data in Table 8.1, they suggest that State College may be more of the problem than the type of placement of underprepared students. However, these data cannot be used to argue for the superiority of separate placement, as students in the other programs have persisted in similar or greater numbers. It may suggest, however, that on certain campuses such as State College, with little institutional support for underprepared students that, in the absence of such support, a separate program may have some rationale. Once again, without admissions and achievement data such a conclusion remains speculative.

TABLE 8.2 RATES OF COMPLETION AT STATE EOD PROGRAMS
(EOP STUDENTS): 1977–1988 ADMISSION YEARS (excluding 1981)

YEAR	Admission (N)	COMP 1 YEAR	COMP 2 YEARS	COMP 3 YEARS
1977	1266	.79	.60	.45
1978	1284	.77	.60	.47
1979	1361	.77	.55	.45
1980	1406	.85	.51	.46
1982	767	.59	.39	.30
1983	864	.62	.42	.34
1984	1087	.73	.43	.33
1985	950	.64	.45	.35
1986	997	.62	.45	.38
1987	1122	.66	.46	.38

In order to examine the impact of State College, it is necessary to look at retention data for State College and the other 12 colleges for non-EOP students as well. Tables 8.3 and 8.4 provide this. Tables 8.3 and 8.4 indicate some differences in retention rates between State College and the other colleges for non-EOP students. Completion rates are lower for State College for one year (-5%); two years (-8%); and three years (-10%). Although there are insufficient data to ascertain why this is the case, it appears that EOP student retention reflects overall college retention, lending further support to the hypothesis that State College may have been a high risk institution for high risk students, with the processes negatively impacting all students including EOP students.

TABLE 8.3 RATES OF COMPLETION AT STATE COLLEGE (NON-EOP STUDENTS):
1977–1988 ADMISSION YEARS (excluding 1981)

YEAR	Admission (N)	COMP 1 YEAR	COMP 2 YEARS	COMP 3 YEARS
1977	345	.76	.60	.45
1978	322	.74	.52	.47
1979	334	.75	.55	.42
1980	398	.74	.66	.48
1982	356	.74	.59	.50
1983	368	.75	.57	.54
1984	392	.69	.48	.41
1985	381	.70	.47	.42
1986	383	.67	.49	.44
1987	482	.67	.49	.46

TABLE 8.4 RATES OF COMPLETION AT OTHER STATE PROGRAMS (NON-EOP
STUDENTS): 1977–1988 ADMISSION YEARS (excluding 1981)

YEAR	Admission (N)	COMP 1 YEAR	COMP 2 YEARS	COMP 3 YEARS
1977	8745	.79	.64	.55
1978	8522	.77	.62	.57
1979	8834	.75	.65	.55
1980	8698	.85	.66	.58
1982	8619	.76	.60	.54
1983	7986	.75	.59	.54
1984	9039	.74	.60	.55
1985	9387	.74	.60	.56
1986	9662	.74	.61	.57
1987	11059	.77	.65	.60

Compensatory Higher Education and the Reduction of Educational Inequality

Whether or not the EOD at State College or for that matter the other state EOP programs were successful depends on one's definition of success. This is a political not an empirical question. With graduation rates below 20% during the EOD years, clearly students had difficulty completing their studies at State College. With student grades consistently low and student performance and retention decreasing as mainstreaming began, it was clear that the EOD had a difficult time making up for its students precollege deficiencies. An examination of differences between EOP and non-EOP students at both State College and the other colleges indicates that EOP students have lower completion rates across the board. Given their economic and educational disadvantages upon admission this should not be surprising, nor alarming. That for the admissions years 1977–1988 39% of EOP students across the state completed at least three years of college and that 36% completed three years at State College perhaps should be viewed positively. Assuming that a majority of those completing three years eventually graduated within six years then at least 25-30% of EOP students will have attained college degrees. Given the fact that many or most would not have attended college without such programs provides reason for optimism. Moreover, there is insufficient evidence to conclude that these students were merely pushed along based on lowered standards, as State College data (Sadovnik, 1983) suggest a correlation between low grades and attrition. Even if, as conservatives have argued, standards were lowered in the 1980s, then they were for everyone not just EOP students. This study of the EOD at State College provides a different perspective from the conservative critiques of liberal educational reform.

Chapter 2 examined the rise of compensatory higher education programs and the development of conservative and radical criticisms. This study, although providing evidence to support some of the criticisms of each perspective, should not be used as ammunition in the continued withering of support for these types of reform. Let us begin with the findings supporting particular criticisms of compensatory programs.

The conservative critique concentrated on the lowering of standards and the passing along of unqualified students and charged that these programs destroyed the meritocratic selection and reward system in postsecondary education. This study illustrated some degree of lowered standards, especially at the senior thesis level at State College. Nevertheless, there was no evidence to conclude that this was caused by the EOD, rather it seemed more symptomatic of overall trends at the college. Moreover, the relatively high attrition rate and low graduation rates suggested that weak students did not pass through in large numbers and that academic standards, to some degree, remained central barriers to educational attainment for disadvantaged students.

The radical perspective pointed to the inevitable failure of liberal educational reform and the development of tracking systems at the postsecondary level to reproduce educational inequality. These findings could be used to support this thesis, with less than 30% of the EOD students completing 120 college credits and less than 20% actually graduating from State College. However, an alternative explanation appears to be more appropriate. From 1978–1981 (admission years) the EOD accepted 383 students, who without the program would not have been accepted to State College. Of these, 214 (56%) completed two years at State College; for the 1978–1980 admissions classes, 109 (38%) completed the EOD program; for the 1978 and 1979 classes, 64 (35%) completed four years at State College. Some critics would argue that these figures are low, nevertheless, they are not far below the 40% rate for regular admissions students at State College, and this alone represents a fair degree of success. Additionally, although the evidence suggests that these students perform less well than regular admissions students, this is beside the point. If educational attainment is indeed the more important determinant of future economic success than educational performance (Collins, 1979:1–22) then by this measure the program cannot be considered a failure. With over half of its population completing at least two years of college, and considering their levels of disadvantagement upon entry documented in Chapter 3, the EOD certainly made a difference in the lives of a significant number of students. More-over, although the EOD represented a form of institutional tracking, there is no evidence to support the criticism by radicals that students were placed on class, ethnic or racial lines independent of precollege ability. Whereas the EOD was overwhelmingly racially segregated, this reflected both its mission to provide educational opportunity for minorities, as well as the realities of minority group underpreparation in the recruiting area. Furthermore, there is some evidence to conclude that a different form of placement might have been more problematic for EOP students at State College, as the data above indicate.

This study outlined the various problems facing compensatory higher educators and revealed various conflicts over philosophy, methods, and the very existence of these types of programs at the college level. Moreover, it revealed a portrait of a program with a faculty that agonized, debated and conflicted over the best approaches to the educational redemption of the disadvantaged learner. The evidence suggested that ideological and organizational concerns were at least as important as educational problems. Nevertheless, preoccupation with student needs remained a central theme, even in the worst of times, with budget cuts threatening the division and its faculty. One of the important contributions of this study, then, is the documentation of the everyday processes that defined educational reform programs and the realization that the institutional solutions to educational problems created a complex set of organizational interactions and concerns.

Although some may interpret the historical narrative within a narrow and cynical perspective, agreeing with Randall Collins (1979:49–71) that the driving force in organizations is to maximize political advantage and to ensure ideological domination and organization survival, this was only partly true. Certainly the use of political labor defined major aspects of the program's history. However, the existence of productive labor for rational educational goals was equally important. Overall, the portrait of the EOD must include a picture of a dedicated faculty groping with educational problems with varying degrees of success and failure. If one concludes that the failures outweigh the successes (which does not seem a warranted conclusion) then it happened despite the dedicated and concerned service of its faculty, staff, and administration.

Equity and Excellence in Higher Education

The math required in Bruce Newling's Geography 100 course was stuff most college-bound high school juniors have under their belts, and Newling had, from the first day of class, let his students know in writing that math would be on all tests and quizzes. So when many students failed the first quiz in March 1991, and the grumbling began, the British born professor ignored it and carried on as he had for most of the twenty-five years he had taught the course at the City College of New York. Soon, however, eleven of his seventeen students went over his head and presented a petition to Morris Silver, the chair of the economics department... Silver was more sympathetic to their plight. Couldn't he teach a course without math... Refusing to drop the math, he (Newling) flunked more than half the class. The chairman then canceled Newling's course for the Fall 1992 semester. 'Until I am sure that Geography 100 will be taught in a nonmathematical fashion,' Silver wrote in a terse note to Newling, '[it] will no longer be offered' (McGowan, 1993:1,24).

According to William McGowan, in his article on the conflicts over standards at City University of New York, the above situation must be understood in the context of historical debates over open admissions and the putative decline of academic standards. The controversy over Professor Newlin's class occurred at the same time that CUNY Chancellor Ann Reynolds was preparing to propose a new, more rigorous admissions plan for the system. Under this plan, students who do not have sixteen college prep credits in high school will be required to complete these courses or demonstrate proficiency in them during college.

The new admissons plan is a response to growing criticism that in opening admissions to all high school graduates in 1968, CUNY began the process of dismantling academic standards. The conflict between proponents of Open Admissions, who supported the opening of access to students previously underrepresented in postsecondary institutions, many of whom were black and Latino, and its opponents, who argued that Open Admissions represented lowering of academic standards and the destruction of a merito-cratic system of higher education, has continued in the 25 years since CUNY implemented its open admissions policy.

The debate about academic standards cannot, however, be removed from issues concerning race and higher education, as well as the tensions between equity and excellence at the heart of those liberal educational reforms aimed at increasing minority access to higher education. Further, as many discussions of the decline of CUNY in general, and City College of New York in particular, speak to its glorious past as the "poor people's Harvard," the implication that the shift from an overwhelmingly white student population to a largely black and Latino population was responsible for its decline cannot be ignored. Unfortunately, most discussions of these issues, at CUNY and elsewhere, become reduced to political and ideological polemics in which the battles between conservatives and liberals prevent a clear headed analysis of very difficult and troubling problems. Although the opening of access to higher education in the 1960s and 1970s benefitted white working class, as well as minority students,[4] the implication that the increase in minority enrollments was responsible for the decline of standards must be examined in the context of the complex social, economic, and educational issues that gave rise to liberal educational reforms.

Most would not condone policies that reduce academic standards in the interests of access and opportunity. However, the relationship between liberal educational reforms and the putative decline of standards is more complex than the story about Professor Newlin indicates. Many college faculty believe that the decline in educational preparation has reached epidemic proportions, with a majority of college bound students, both majority and minority, underprepared for the requirements of a traditional college curriculum. This supports a major claim of the EOD in its quest for organizational legitimacy and survival, that colleges need a developmental component to effectively deal with this growing problem. At a time when the backlash against liberal educational reform programs continues to be considerable, this study of the EOD should be used to support their continuation and expansion, not their elimination and demise. Although it does not necessarily support the need for a separate compensatory division, it does indicate the importance of integrating various types of developmental strategies to the entire college.

While educational underpreparation is widespread, the relationship between race, class and academic performance remains a central component of the problem. So long as elementary and secondary schools continue to contribute to the undereducation of minority and working class students (Fine, 1991), and so long as race and social class are barriers to educational attainment, the need for compensatory higher education will continue to exist. Perhaps attempting to solve problems of educational inequality at the college level is unsound, as it addresses the symptoms of larger educational and social problems rather than their causes; however without any evidence of a national commitment to solve these problems, liberal educational reforms at this level are a better alternative than a return to higher education as the right of only the privileged and prepared. Moreover, the study of the EOD suggests that compensatory higher education has the *potential* to reduce inequalities of performance, and that strengthening and improving existing models combined with new innovative approaches should be an important objective of national educational policy.

The potential of these types of educational reforms to ameliorate educational inequalities is evident. However, their effect on social inequality is less certain. At a future date, evidence on the relationship between attendance in the EOD and similar programs and occupational and economic outcomes is essential. Even without such data some speculation is possible. Based on the work of Jencks (1972), Ogbu (1978), Persell (1977), Bowles and Gintis (1976) and others, there is no reason to believe that educational reform alone, without subsequent changes in the social and economic structure will drastically alter the stratification system. With this in mind, compensatory higher education, like all liberal reforms, is extremely limited in affecting major social change. However, as Bowles and Gintis (1976:245--263), certainly not defenders of liberalism suggest, small changes are better than none.

Writing in the 1990s one cannot help but be dismayed at the dismantling of access and opportunity. In the last decade we have witnessed the reaction to the reforms of the 1960s and 1970s. An article in the New

York Times Magazine (Fiske, 1983) pointed to the effects of economic inflation on the ability of students from all socioeconomic backgrounds to attend the colleges of their choice. While the children of the middle and upper middle classes bemoaned their inability to attend selective private colleges such as Bennington and Smith due to spiraling costs and settled for public institutions, the children of working class families were often forced out of college entirely. When combined with the return to more selective admissions procedures and stricter educational standards for retention and financial aid, the gains (albeit small) of the past decades appear to be in trouble, with minority and working class students most adversely affected.

With the election of President Clinton there may be renewed interest in liberal educational reform. This study indicates the need for continued support of developmental college education. Its policy applications are widespread and suggest a number of important points:

1. With the growing number of underprepared students developmental higher education programs should be expanded, not cut, in order to provide services for these students.

2. Since the quality of instructional and support services appears more important than the type of placement, underprepared students should be integrated into regular college classes as soon as possible, with some type of institutional program providing remediation and support services to all needy students.

3. Colleges should avoid the complete separation of underprepared students, but recognize that remedial sections in reading, writing, and quantitative skills are necessary.

4. The educational redemption of the underprepared student is the responsibility of the entire college and should not be left to one division or faculty. All faculty should rotate in the teaching of lower division and developmental offerings, and developmental techniques should be integrated into all courses, where appropriate. Moreover, if colleges elect to open admissions to underprepared students, they have a responsibility to provide services. To provide access without a real chance to translate it into success is *morally* indefensible.

5. Although there is evidence to support a revolving door syndrome in many programs, the EOD data support Roueche and Snow's

(1977:77–111) contention that programming for success is possible, but certainly difficult. Colleges need to continue to explore ways to translate opportunity into academic success, without lowering academic standards.

This study of the EOD may not please either conservative or radical critics of liberal educational reform. Nor does it pretend that these programs are overly successful. What it does address are the complexities of the problems and indicates the limited potential of compensatory higher education in ameliorating the persistent problem of minority and working class underpreparation and attainment. If our society is to remain committed to the ethos of social justice and democracy than these programs remain a necessity. One should not pretend that they will have overwhelming results; the faith in educational reform should not be abandoned, only viewed as one aspect of larger reform efforts.

Randall Collins (1983) in a paper given at the American Sociological Meetings, argued that radical analyses of schooling often lead to the same conclusions as conservative critiques; that is, to eliminate educational reforms as unsuccessful or unworkable and to thus encourage a return to the elitist roots of education. Collins, noting that liberal educational solutions will not solve societal problems, argued further that the elimination of reforms is equally a questionable alternative. Although some may use this study to suggest compensatory higher education programs make too little difference to justify their existence, its conclusions do not support this position. Certainly their ability to reduce inequality is limited; however, in the absence of larger structural reforms their continuation appears warranted. Moreover, as Christopher Hurn has noted, educational reform and innovation should not be eliminated but should be viewed critically with an eye toward improvement. As Hurn suggested:

> Schools cannot transform the wider society, compensate for all prior inequalities of students, or even create jobs that presently do not exist. Nor is it easy to change schools even if we have, as is far from always the case, a very clear blueprint of the kind of institution we desire. At the same time, however, I think we have hardly begun to exhaust the possibilities of schooling. We are beginning to make considerable strides in understanding the barriers to learning among disadvantaged and lower class youth. That accumulating knowledge will, I believe, gradually replace the ideological slogans and rhetoric that have characterized so much of the discussion of the problem in the past.... We

are, in other words, just at the beginning of the difficult
task of equipping everyone with the intellectual tools that
in the past were confined to a small elite. The next step in
this task requires continued faith in the possibilities of
schooling (1978:275–276).

The history of the Educational Opportunity Division suggests just
this: a sobering view of the limitations and faith in the possibilities of
education. Let us hope that this faith reemerges and the possibilities continue
to be explored. Faith, however, does not mean blind commitment and herein
lies the promise of the sociology of education: to provide empirical and
critical analysis of those processes that constrain and those that enhance the
success of educational programs and the foundation for further investigation
and implementation of workable strategies and models.

NOTES

1. Data for Tables 8.1–8.4 are based on data from the New York State Office of Special Programs. Retention data include only seven semesters in college and do not include graduation rates. Achievement data for these years are not available.

2. 1982, although the last year of EOD as a separate division, has been left out of these calculations. It appears, perhaps due to the turmoil that year, that student retention is more characteristic of the new, integrative EOP program. In fact, in 1982–1983, although the EOD existed, it did so only in name only as the process of merger had already begun to take place.

3. These 12 colleges are the four-year university colleges in the state system. The University Centers, those research universities with undergraduate colleges with the highest admission standards in the system, are left out, as well as the community colleges. The colleges under examination have differing racial compositions as they reflect the communities that they draw upon; in terms of educational and economic disadvantage the populations are similar as all EOP students must meet the state's economic and educational guidelines for educationally and economically disadvantaged students.

4. See Lavin, Alba, and Silberstein (1981) for a discussion of the demographics of Open Admissions at CUNY; See Carter and Wilson (1992) for an analysis of enrollment trends in the 1980s.

REFERENCES

Allen, Walter R. 1992. "The Color of Success: African-American Student Outcomes in Predominantly White and Historically Black Public Colleges and Universities." *Harvard Educational Review* 62(1):26--44.

American Council on Education. 1973. *Higher Education for Everybody Issues and Implications*. Washington, D.C.: American Council on Education.

_____. 1988. *One-Third of a Nation*. Washington, D.C.: American Council on Education.

Apple, Michael W. 1976. "Rationality as Ideology." *Educational Theory* 26:121–131.

_____. 1977. "What do Schools Teach?" *Curriculum Inquiry* 6:341–358.

_____. 1978. "Ideology, Reproduction and Educational Reform." *Comparative Education Review* 22(3):367–387.

_____. 1979. *Ideology and Curriculum*. Boston: Routledge and Kegan Paul.

Atkinson, Paul. 1985. *Language, Structure, and Reproduction: An Introduction to the Sociology of Basil Bernstein*. London: Metheun.

Baratz, Stephen and Joan Baratz. 1970. "Early Childhood Intervention: The Social Science Base of Institutional Racism." *Harvard Educational Review* 40(1):29–50.

Bernstein, Basil. 1971. "On the Classification and Framing of Educational Knowledge." Pp. 47–69 in *Knowledge and Control*, edited by Michael F. D. Young. London: Collier-Macmillan.

_____. 1973a. "Social Class, Language and Socialization." Pp. 473–486 in *Power and Ideology in Education*, edited by Jerome Karabel and A. H. Halsey. New York: Oxford University Press, 1977.

_____. 1973b. *Class, Codes and Control*, Volume 1. London: Routledge and Kegan Paul.

_____. 1973c. *Class, Codes and Control*, Volume 2. London: Routledge and Kegan Paul.

_____. 1977. *Class, Codes and Control*, Volume 3. London: Routledge and Kegan Paul.

_____. 1990. *The Structuring of Pedagogic Discourse: Class, Codes and Control*, Volume 4. London: Routledge.

Blankenship. C., and S. Lilly. 1981. *Mainstreaming Students with Learning and Behavior Problems*. New York: Holt, Rinehart and Winston.

Bloom, Benjamin, A. Davis and R. Hess. 1965. *Compensatory Education for Cultural Deprivation*. New York: Holt.

Blumer, Herbert. 1969. *Symbolic Interactionism*. Englewood Cliffs: Prentice Hall.

Bogdan, Robert and Biklen, Sari. 1992. *Qualitative Research for Education: An Introduction to Theory and Methods*. Needham Heights, MA: Allyn & Bacon.

Boguslaw, Robert and George Vickers. 1977. *Prologue to Sociology*. Santa Monica: Goodyear.

Bourdieu, Pierre and Jean Claude Passeron. 1977. *Reproduction in Education, Culture and Society*. New York: Sage.

Bowles, Samuel and Herbert Gintis. 1976. *Schooling in Capitalist America*. New York: Basic Books.

Brint, Steven and Jerome Karabel. 1989. *The Dream Deferred: American Community Colleges, 1945–1980*. New York: Oxford University Press.

Bryson, Joseph and Charles Bentley. 1980. *Ability Grouping of Public School Students*. Charlottesville, VA: The Michie Company.

Carlberg, C., and K. Kavale. 1980. "The Efficacy of Special Versus Regular Placement for Exceptional Children: A Meta Analysis." *Journal of Special Education* 14(3):296–309.

Carter, Deborah and Reginald Wilson. 1992. *Minorities in Higher Education: 1992 Eleventh Annual Status Report.* Washington D.C.: American Council on Education.

Cicourel, Aaron. 1973. *Cognitive Sociology.* Baltimore: Penguin.

Claerbaut, David Paul. 1976. "A Study of Black Student Alienation at Small Private Liberal Arts Colleges." Doctoral Dissertation, Loyola U. of Chicago, Univ. Microfilms Order No. 76-11, 711.

_____. 1978a. "Alienation Among Black Students at Small Liberal Arts Colleges." In "The Urban Minority Experience." *Selected Proceedings of the 4th Annual Conference on Minority Studies*, edited by George Carter and James R. Parker. LaCrosse, WI: Institute of Minority Studies, U. of Wisconsin-LaCrosse.

_____. 1978b. *Black Student Alienation: A Study.* Palo Alto, CA: R & E Research Associates.

Clark, Burton. 1960a. "The Cooling Out Function in Higher Education." *American Journal of Sociology* 65:569-576.

_____. 1960b. *The Open Door College: A Case Study.* New York: McGraw-Hill.

Collins, Randall. 1971. "Functional and Conflict Theories of Educational Stratification." *American Sociological Review* 36:1003-1019.

_____. 1975. *Conflict Sociology.* New York: The Academic Press.

_____. 1979. *The Credential Society.* New York: The Academic Press.

_____. 1981. *Sociological Insight.* New York: Oxford University Press.

_____. 1983. "Policy Positions on Higher Education: Two Liberal Factions and a Radical/Conservative Ambiguity." Paper presented at the Seventy-Eighth Annual Meeting of the American Sociological Association, September 1983.

Cremin, Lawrence A. 1990. *Popular Education and its Discontents.* New York: Harper and Row.

Cross, K. Patricia. 1971. *Beyond the Open Door*. San Francisco: Jossey Bass.

_____. 1976. *Accent on Learning*. San Francisco: Jossey Bass.

Danzig, Arnold. 1992. "Basil Bernstein's Sociology of Language Applied to Education: Deficits, Differences, and Bewitchment." *Journal of Educational Policy* 7:285–300.

Davis, Kingsley and Wilbert Moore. 1945. "Some Principles of Stratification." *American Sociological Review* 10(2):242–249.

Delone, R. 1979. *Small Futures*. New York: The Free Press.

Denzin, Norman. 1970. *The Research Act*. Chicago: Aldine.

Dougherty, Kevin. 1987. The Effects of Community Colleges: Aid or Hindrance to Socioeconomic Attainment? *Sociology of Education* 60:86–103.

_____. 1991. "The Community College at the Crossroads: The Need for Structural Reform." *Harvard Educational Review* 61(3):311–336.

_____. 1992. "Community Colleges and Baccalaureate Attainment." *Journal of Higher Education* 63(2):188–214.

Douglas, Jack. 1972. *Introduction to Sociology: Situations and Structures*. New York: The Free Press.

_____. 1976. *Investigative Social Research*. Beverly Hills, CA: Sage.

D'Souza, Dinesh. 1991. *Illiberal Education: The Politics of Race and Sex on Campus*. New York: The Free Press.

Educational Opportunity Division. 1980. "EOD Faculty Statements on the Grading System." Unpublished document.

Educational Opportunity Division. 1981a. "EOD State Accreditation Report." Unpublished document included in the State College 1981 Self-Study.

Educational Opportunity Division. 1981b. "EOD Director's 1981–82 Budget Statement." Unpublished document.

Educational Opportunity Division. 1981c. "EOD Curriculum Committee Report."

Educational Opportunity Division. 1982a. "EOD Disciplines Coordinator Proposal for the Freshman and Sophomore Years at State College." Unpublished document.

Educational Opportunity Division. 1982b. "EOD Disciplines Coordinator Statement on the Freshman Studies Program." Unpublished document.

Educational Opportunity Division. 1982c. "EOD English Coordinator Statement on the Merger of EOD."

Educational Opportunity Division. 1982d. "EOD Proposal for a College-Wide Lower Division." Unpublished document.

Educational Opportunity Division. 1982e. "EOD Proposal for a College-Wide Writing Program at State College." Unpublished document.

Educational Opportunity Division. 1982f. "EOD Director's 1982–83 Budget Statement." Unpublished document.

Etzkowitz, Henry and Joseph Fashing. 1977. "Ideology and Educational Utopias." Unpublished paper.

Featherstone, Joseph. 1976. "Review of Bowles and Gintis' *Schooling in Capitalist America.*" *The New Republic* 174(22):26-29.

Feinberg, Walter. 1975. *Reason and Rhetoric: The Intellectual Foundations of the 20th Century Liberal Educational Policy.* New York: Wiley.

Fine, Michelle. 1991. *Framing Dropouts: Notes on the Politics of an Urban Public High School.* Albany: State University of New York Press.

Fiske, Edward B. 1983. "Higher Education's New Economics." *New York Times Magazine*:46-58.

Flournoy, Don. 1982. *The Rationing of American Higher Education.* Cambridge: Schenkman Publishers.

Fordham, S. and John Ogbu. 1986. "Black Students' School Success: Coping with the 'Burden' of 'Acting White'." *The Urban Review* 18(3):176–206.

Fuller, Richard and Richard Myers. 1941. "The Natural History of a Social Problem." *American Sociological Review* 6:320–328.

Garfinkel, Harold. 1967. *Studies in Ethnomethodology.* Englewood Cliffs: Prentice Hall.

Gartner, Alan and Deborah Lipsky. 1987. "Beyond Special Education." *Harvard Educational Review* 57(4):367–395.

Giddens, Anthony. 1981. *Sociology: A Brief But Critical Introduction.* New York: Harcourt Brace Jovanovich.

Goffman, Erving. 1959. *The Presentation of Self in Everyday Life.* New York: Anchor.

_____. 1963. *Stigma.* New York: Spectrum.

Gordon, David. 1977. *Problems in Political Economy: An Urban Perspective* 2nd Ed. Boston: D.C. Heath.

Gorelick, Sherry. 1978. "Open Admissions: Design for Failure." *Politics and Education* Summer:8–13.

_____. 1981. *City College and the Jewish Poor: Education in New York, 1880–1924.* New Brunswick, NJ: Rutgers University Press.

Grant, Gerald and David Riesman. 1978. *The Perpetual Dream: Reform and Experiment in the American College.* Chicago: University of Chicago Press.

Greer, Colin. 1973. *The Great School Legend.* New York: Basic Books.

Gross, Theodore. 1978. "How to Kill a College: The Private Papers of a College Dean." *Saturday Review.* (February).

Handel, Warren. 1982. *Ethnomethodology*. Englewood Cliffs: Prentice Hall.

Hanushek, Eric. 1972. *Education and Race*. Lexington, MA: D.C. Heath.

Heller, Louis. 1973. *The Death of the American University: With Special Reference to the Collapse of the City College of New York*. New Rochelle: Arlington House.

Heydebrand, Wolf. 1977. "Organizational Contradictions in Public Service Bureaucracies." In *Organizational Analysis: Critique and Innovation*, edited by Kenneth Benson. Newbury Park, CA: Sage.

Hirsch, E.D. 1987. *Cultural Literacy*. Boston: Houghton Mifflin.

Hurn, Christopher. 1978. *The Limits and Possibilities of Schooling*. Boston: Allyn and Bacon.

____. 1993. *The Limits and Possibilities of Schooling* 3rd ed. Boston: Allyn and Bacon. Third Edition.

Institute for the Study of Educational Policy. 1976. *Equal Educational Opportunity for Blacks in U.S. Higher Education*. Washington: Howard University Press.

Jencks, Christopher. 1992. *Rethinking Social Policy*. New York: Harper-Collins.

Jencks, Christopher, et al. 1972. *Inequality*. New York: Basic Books.

Karabel, Jerome. 1972a. November. "Community Colleges and Social Stratification." *Harvard Educational Review* 42:521–562.

____. 1972b. Winter. "Perspectives on Open Admissions." *Educational Record*:30–44. Also pp. 265–288 in *Universal Higher Education*, by Wilson and Mills.

____, and A. H. Halsey. 1977. *Power and Ideology in Education*. New York: Oxford University Press.

Karp, David and William Yoels. 1979. *Symbols, Selves and Society*. New York: Harper & Row.

Katz, Michael. 1968. *The Irony of Early School Reform*. Cambridge: Harvard University Press.

_____. 1971. *Class, Bureaucracy and Schools: The Illusion of Educational Change in America*. New York: Praeger.

Kimball, Roger. 1990. *Tenured Radicals: How Politics Has Corrupted Higher Education*. New York: Harper & Row.

Kosinski, Jerzy. 1971. *Being There*. New York: Bantam.

Kübler-Ross, Elizabeth. 1979. *On Death and Dying*. New York: Harper.

Lareau, Annette. 1989. *Home Advantage* London: Falmer Press.

Lasch, Christopher. 1979. *The Culture of Narcissism*. New York: Norton.

Lavin, D., Alba, R., and R. Silberstein. 1981. *Right Versus Privilege: The Open Admissions Experiment at the City University of New York*. New York: The Free Press.

Lemann, Nicholas. 1991. *The Promised Land*. New York: Knopf.

Lemert, Edwin. 1951. "Is There a Natural History of Social Problems?" *American Sociological Review* 16:217-233.

London, Howard. 1978. *The Culture of a Community College*. New York: Praeger.

Marshak, Robert E. and Gladys Wurtemburg. 1982. "Open Access, Open Admissions, Open Warfare, Part I." *Change* 13(8):12-19, 51-53.

_____. 1981. "Open Access, Open Admissions, Open Warfare, Part II." *Change* 14(1):30-42.

Mayer, Martin. 1973. "Higher Education for All?: The Case for Open Admissions." *Commentary* 55(2):37-47.

McGowan, William. 1993. "The Battle for City University." *Lingua Franca* January/February:1-9; 23-25.

McMannus and Associates. 1979. *Report on Educational Opportunity Programs in the State University of New York*. Albany: SUNY Press.

Mead, George Herbert. 1934. *Mind, Self and Society*. Chicago: University of Chicago Press.

Meyer, John and Brian Rowen. 1977. "Institutionalized Organization: Formal Structure as Myth and Ceremony." *American Journal of Sociology* 83:340-363.

Milner, Murray. 1972. *The Illusion of Equality*. San Francisco: Jossey Bass.

Moynihan, Daniel P. 1965. *The Negro Family*. Washington, D.C.: U.S. Department of Labor.

National Commision on Excellence in Education. 1983. *A Nation at Risk*. Washington D.C.: Government Printing Office.

Oakes, Jeannie. 1985. *Keeping Track: How Schools Structure Inequality*. New Haven: Yale University Press.

O'Connor, James. 1973. *The Fiscal Crisis of the State*. New York, New York: St. Martin's Press.

Office of Special Programs, State University of New York. 1977-1981. *Educational Opportunity Programs of the State University of New York Annual Report*.

Ogbu, John. 1978. *Minority Education and Caste*. New York: Academic Press.

Orfield, Gary. 1992. "Money, Equity and College Access," *Harvard Educational Review* 62 (3):337-372

_____, and Carole Ashkinaze. 1991. *The Closing Door: Conservative Policy and Black Opportunity*. Chicago: University of Chicago Press.

Persell, Caroline H. 1977. *Education and Inequality*. New York: The Free Press.

Peterson, Marvin, et al. 1978. *Black Students on White Campuses: The Impact of Increased Enrollments*. Ann Arbor: Institute of Social Research.

Pincus, Fred. 1980. "The False Promises of Community Colleges: Class Conflict and Vocational Education." *Harvard Educational Review* 50(3):332–361.

_____. 1983. "Open Admissions at the City University of New York: Review of Lavin, Alba and Silberstein's *Right vs. Privilege*." *Contemporary Sociology* 12(2):136-138.

Piven, Frances and Richard Cloward. 1971. *Regulating the Poor: The Functions of Public Relief.* New York, New York: Random House.

Prillman, D. 1975. "An Analysis of Placement Factors in Special Education Classes." *Exceptional Children* 42:107–108.

Ravitch, Diane. 1978. *The Revisionists Revised: A Critique of the Radical Attack on the Schools*. New York: Basic Books.

_____. 1983. *The Troubled Crusade*. New York: Basic Books.

_____, and Chester Finn. 1987. *What Do Our Seventeen Year Olds Know?* New York: Basic Books.

Riessman, Frank. 1962. *The Culturally Deprived Child*. New York: Harper & Row.

Rist, Ray. 1970. "Social Class and Teacher Expectations: The Self Fulfilling Prophecy in Ghetto Education." *Harvard Educational Review* 40:411–451.

_____. 1977. "On Understanding the Processes of Schooling: The Contributions of Labeling Theory." Pp. 292–306 in Karabel and Halsey (1977).

Rose, Mike. 1989. *Lives on the Boundary: The Struggles and Achievements of America's Underprepared*. New York: The Free Press.

Rosen, David, Seth Bruner and Steve Fowler. 1973. *Open Admissions: The*

Promise and Lie of Open Access to American Higher Education. Lincoln: University of Nebraska Press.

Rosenthal, Richard and Lenore Jacobsen. 1968. *Pygmalion in the Classroom.* New York: Holt, Rinehart and Winston.

Rossman, Jack E., Helen S. Astin, Alexander Astin, and Elaine El-Khawas. 1975. *Open Admissions at CUNY: An Analysis of the First Year.* Englewood Cliffs: Prentice Hall.

Roueche, John E. 1968. *Salvage, Redirection or Custody: Remedial Education in the Community College.* Washington, D.C.: American Association of Community Colleges.

_____, and R. U. Kirk. 1973. *Catching Up: Remedial Education.* San Francisco, CA: Jossey-Bass.

_____, and J. C. Pittman. 1972. *A Modest Proposal: Students Can Learn.* San Francisco, CA: Jossey-Bass.

_____, and Jerry J. Snow. 1977. *Overcoming Learning Problems.* San Francisco, CA: Jossey-Bass.

Sadovnik, Alan R. 1983. *The Decline of a Liberal Educational Reform: A Sociological Analysis of a Higher Education Opportunity Program.* Unpublished Ph.D. Dissertation, New York University.

_____. 1991. "Basil Bernstein's Theory of Pedagogic Practice: A Structuralist Approach." *Sociology of Education* 64(1):48–63.

_____. 1994. *Knowledge and Pedagogy: The Sociology of Basil Bernstein.* Norwood, NJ: Ablex Publishing Corporation.

_____, Peter W. Cookson, Jr. and Susan F. Semel. 1994. *Exploring Education: An Introduction to the Foundations of Education.* Boston: Allyn and Bacon.

Scott, Barbara. 1983. *Crisis Management in American Higher Education.* New York: Praeger.

Scott, W. Richard. 1981. *Organizations: Rational, Natural and Open*

Systems. Englewood Cliffs: Prentice Hall.

_____. 1983. "Design for Whom: Power for What" *Contemporary Sociology* 12(2):153–155.

Semel, Susan F. 1992. *The Dalton School: The Transformation of a Progressive School*. New York : Peter Lang Publishing.

Shaughnessy, Mina P. 1977. *Errors and Expectations*. New York: Oxford University Press.

Spector, Malcolm and John Kitsuse. 1977. *Constructing Social Problems*. Menlo Park: Cummings Publishing.

State College Student Newspaper. 1983. Interview with the College President. April, 6–7.

Swidler, Ann. 1979. *Organizations Without Authority*. Cambridge: Harvard University Press.

Tallman, Irving. 1976. *Passion, Action and Politics*. San Francisco: Freeman.

Thomas, Gail E. 1992. "Participation and Degree Attainment of African-American and Latino Students in Graduate Education Relative to Other Racial and Ethnic Groups: An Update from Office of Civil Rights Data. *Harvard Educational Review* 62(1):45–65.

Trimberger, Ellen Kay. 1973. "Open Admissions: A New Form of Tracking." *Insurgent Sociologist* Fall:29–43.

Trow, Martin (ed.). 1975. *Teachers and Students: Aspects of American Higher Education*. New York: McGraw-Hill.

Trow, Martin. 1970. "Reflections on the Transition from Mass to Universal Higher Education." *Daedalus* 99(1):1–42.

Wagner, Geoffrey. 1976. *The End of Education: The Experience of CUNY with Open Enrollment and the Threat to Higher Education in America*. Cranberry: Barnes.

Wexler, Philip. 1976. *The Sociology of Education: Beyond Equality.* Indianapolis: Bobbs Merrill.

Wilcox, Kathleen. 1982. "Ethnography as a Methodology and Its Applications to the Study of Schooling: A Review." Pp. 457–479 in *Doing the Ethnography of Schooling,* edited by George Spindler. New York: Holt, Rinehart and Winston.

Williamson, John B., Karp, David A., and John R. Dalphin. 1977. *The Research Craft.* Boston: Little Brown and Company.

Willie, Charles and Arline McCord. 1972. *Black Students at White Colleges.* New York: Praeger.

Willis, Paul. 1977. *Learning to Labor.* London: Saxon House.

Wilson, William Julius. 1987. *The Truly Disadvantaged: The Inner City, The Under Class and Public Policy.* Chicago: University of Chicago Press.

Wolfe, Alan. 1977. *The Limits of Legitimacy.* New York: The Free Press.

Youdelman, Jeffrey. 1978. "Limiting Students: Remedial Writing and the Birth of Open Admissions." *College English* 39(5):562–572.

Zwerman, Gilda. 1981. "The Organization of Industry and the Organization of Academe: A Study of Managerial Ideology in the American University, 1880–1980." Unpublished Doctoral Dissertation, New York University.

INDEX